D0903410

Physical Chemistry on a Microcomputer

D
55.3
E4
64
985

Physical Chemistry on a Microcomputer

Joseph H. Noggle
University of Delaware

WITHDRAWN

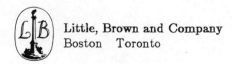 Little, Brown and Company
Boston   Toronto

Tennessee Tech. Library
Cookeville. Tenn.

357268

Library of Congress Cataloging in Publication Data

Noggle, Joseph H., 1936-
Physical chemistry on a microcomputer.

Bibliography: p.
Includes indexes.
1. Chemistry, Physical and theoretical- - Data
processing. 2. Microcomputers- - Programming. 3. Basic
(Computer program language) I. Title.
QD455.3.E4N64 1985 541.3'028'54 85- 106
ISBN 0- 316- 61140- 9

Copyright © 1985 by Joseph H. Noggle, Ph.D, Inc.

All rights reserved. No part of this book may be reproduced
in any form or by any electronic or mechanical means including
information storage and retrieval systems without permission
in writing from the publisher, except by a reviewer who may
quote brief passages in a review.

Library of Congress Catalog Card No. 85- 106

ISBN 0-316-61140-9

9 8 7 6 5 4 3 2

MV

Published simultaneously in Canada
by Little, Brown & Company (Canada) Limited

Printed in the United States of America

PREFACE

Scope and Intent of this Book

This book has three themes: It is a book about intermediate-level programming using microcomputer BASIC. It also introduces some methods of numerical analysis that are of general use in chemistry and related subjects. Primarily, it is an introduction to the use of a computer for applications characteristic of physical chemistry. As such, the envisioned use is as a companion text for the standard chemistry-major physical chemistry course. All of the illustrations and applications involve material that is usually taught in a first course in physical chemistry. Of course, like physical chemistry itself, it will have a far broader utility in other fields of chemistry and in closely related fields such as the other physical sciences and engineering. It is hoped that it will also be useful for graduate students and practicing chemists; it should be particularly useful for those who have had no previous experience in computer programming or numerical analysis.

Although this book contains a number of useful programs, its intent goes beyond a simple listing of applications programs. The intent is to teach the reader not only how to program but how to approach problem solving with a computer. A compendium of a dozen (or a hundred) programs will help you solve a dozen (or a hundred) types of problems. But if you learn how to program and how to solve problems, you will be equipped for a far larger variety of challenges. In keeping with this philosophy, most of the programs of this book will require some modification by you in order to solve the problems presented — they are not very "user friendly." This in turn will require that you study them and learn from them. This will, in the long run, be more valuable than simply using a program as a "black box."

Which Computer?

Microcomputers are notorious for their lack of standardization and general incompatibility. Fortunately, as it affects programs written in the BASIC language, there is some degree of standardization. Still, even in BASIC there are a number of "dialects." All programs in this book are written in Microsoft© BASIC. This is a very common dialect that seems to be becoming the industry standard. It is used by IBM, Radio Shack, and many other computers. Notable exceptions include Apple computers (which use a proprietorial version called Applesoft© BASIC) and Commodore computers. (Microsoft© BASIC is available for Apple computers from Microsoft Corporation, 10700 Northup Way, Bellevue, Washington, 98004.)

The programs of this book were developed and tested on a TRS80 Model III. They have also been tested on an IBM PC, where they ran with only minor modifications (these are noted as they occur). Versions of the major programs that have been adapted for and tested on an Apple II and a Commodore 64 are given in the appendix.

What You Need

Most obviously, you need a computer, either your own or one to which you have ready access. This book contains many examples, illustrations and "miniprograms" that illustrate the concepts being explained. The best, and perhaps only, way to learn this is by sitting at a computer and trying it. Your computer doesn't need much memory. The programs of this book will not challenge an 8 K RAM, although you may be happier in the long run with a larger memory.

Since this book deals with intermediate-level BASIC programming, you must learn the elementary part yourself. In most computer stores, and many book stores, you will find a number of books with title such as "Beginning BASIC" or "Getting Started with BASIC." There will probably be one specifically for your computer. Buy one of these, and work your way through it — then you will be ready.

Once you get started, it will probably be useful to have, or have available, the reference manual for your computer. This will permit you to look up unfamiliar commands and to find out how your computer handles various situations. By their nature, reference manuals do not make very good reading — they are intended for looking up things — but they are usually the only source that will tell you everything (more often, nearly everything) you need to know about your computer.

Finally, since this is a book about physical chemistry, you will need a physical chemistry text. This book discusses physical chemical applications, but provides relatively little background on the theory or derivation of the equations used; for these you will need a good general physical chemistry text. If you are using this book in conjunction with a class in physical chemistry, the text you are using will probably be adequate. Otherwise it is recommended that you use *Physical Chemistry* by Joseph H. Noggle (Reference 1; all references are listed at the end of this book) since, when specific references are made, they are to this particular text.

Acknowledgements

The programs of this book were tested on and adapted for other computers by Cecil Dybowski (IBM PC), Doug Claffey (Apple II) and Karl Blom (Commodore 64). Gary Bertrand of the University of Missouri — Rolla, and Cecil Dybowski and Harvey Gold of the University of Delaware read early versions of the manuscript and made many valuable suggestions. The manuscript was cast in its final form with invaluable help from Dean Giblin.

CONTENTS

xi

Physical Chemistry on a Microcomputer

CHAPTER 1: INTRODUCTION

The Best Way to Compute

Suppose you have a problem, a question that needs to be answered, and finding the answer requires computation. Which is the best method to find the answer? The choices are manual computation (count on fingers, figure with pencil and paper or in your head, use an abacus), or the use of an electronic calculator, a programmable electronic calculator, a microcomputer, or a mainframe computer. The answer, contrary to what some experts will tell you, is that there is no answer; it depends on the type of computation you want to do and how often you want to do it. It also depends on factors extrinsic to the mathematical nature of the problem, such as ease of access, convenience, and so forth. Subtracting a check amount from your bank balance might be best done with a calculator, unless the calculator is at home and you are at the grocery store; a computer is unlikely to be the best method, unless it is part of a general accounting program that is doing many other things.

Next, we shall discuss the various methods of computations (excepting the manual methods), their advantages, disadvantages and limitations.

Calculators

The major advantage of calculators is their ready access, low cost, and ease of use. Problems such as an ideal gas law calculation or balancing your checkbook will always be more conveniently done on a calculator than on a computer. Also, scientific calculators carry a lot of significant figures, 10 to 14 compared to as few as 7 on some microcomputers, and permit the size of a number to be as large as 1×10^{99} (on a typical micro, numbers are limited to 1×10^{38}). A more complex problem, for example, a van der Waals gas law calculation, will still be more conveniently done on a calculator if it is to be done only once. However, when repeated calculations involving the same mathematical steps are required, a programmable device becomes advantageous. This repetition may occur in several ways; to use the van der Waals gas law calculation as an example, you may wish to do a calculation for a number of different gases or you may want to do a series of calculations (an isotherm, for example) for one gas. For such problems, a programmable calculator will do nicely, but (assuming they are equally accessible) a computer will do as well. On the other hand, if the van der Waals calculation is part of a larger problem, such as calculating the thermodynamic properties of a gas, a problem in which there are a number of steps and a number of intermediate results that must be saved and reused, you are ready for a computer.

Computers

The major advantages of a computer *vis-à-vis* a calculator (programmable or not) are its large capacity for data storage and its flexibility. But even here there are choices as to programming language and type of computer (micro vs. mainframe). Once again, the best choice depends heavily on the nature of the problem and extrinsic factors. The question on language is the more fundamental, so we shall discuss it first.

Languages

The only symbols a computer recognizes are 1 and 0 — that is, binary codes. It can only carry out relatively simple operations on these symbols, for example, binary addition ($1 + 1 = 0$ carry 1) and logical comparisons (1 AND $0 = 0$); anything else it does has been programmed by someone. To instruct the computer, therefore, the instructions must be in binary code; this is called machine language. It is rare to write machine language code directly; rather a simple mnemonic *assembly language* is used to translate instructions into machine language. Assembly language is difficult to use, but it produces programs that are very efficient in use of memory and execution speed. Major applications software such as word processing, spreadsheet, and accounting programs are usually written in this way. A hundred programmer-hours of effort may be worthwhile for a program that will be used by thousands of users a hundred times each, but for the type of material to be covered in this book, it would be a waste of time.

BASIC (Beginners All-purpose Symbolic Instruction Code) is an example of a high-level language; one instruction in BASIC may represent dozens of machine language instructions, but the symbols to implement this instruction are written in a kind of pseudo-English that is highly mnemonic. BASIC is implemented on nearly all microcomputers. It is also implemented on some mainframe computers, but mainframe BASIC is substantially different from microcomputer BASIC, and nobody takes it seriously: Rule-of-thumb #1 — if you need a mainframe computer to do the job, you probably don't want to use BASIC. BASIC is easy to use but relatively slow compared to other languages. However, it is not necessarily slow in total time. The time required to do a computation with a computer includes time for programming and debugging, as well as for execution. The first two are done only once, so, if a program is to be used many times without change, the effort required for more efficient programming may be worthwhile. BASIC is an interpreter language — that is, each instruction is interpreted into machine language as it is encountered and executed. The machine code thus produced is not saved, so each time it is executed, the commands must be interpreted again. It is this feature that is responsible for the slowness of BASIC. There are compiler BASICs available that translate the entire program into machine language before execution, and these provide substantial enhancements in execution speed.

FORTRAN (FORmula TRANslation) was one of the first high-level languages to be developed for computers and is specifically suited for mathematical applications (that is, it is good with numbers but poor with words). Despite numerous updated versions, it still retains an air of punched cards and lilac. Compared to BASIC, FORTRAN is more difficult to write and debug, and the writing of such programs requires more advance thought. (However, advance thought never hurt any program.) Also, it is a compiler language, so you cannot test and debug the program until it has been compiled. However, the final compiled program is very fast and efficient. This may be, as many say, an obsolete language, but there is a large amount of scientific and engineering software written in this language, so it is unlikely to go away very soon. FORTRAN compilers are available for some microcomputers, but these may be, in some sense, the worst of both worlds: Rule-of-thumb #2 — if your problem is such that you need FORTRAN, you are probably better off using a mainframe computer. This is not to say that there are not good FORTRAN compilers available for micros — but mainframe computers offer many other amenities that become advantageous when the program becomes large and complex enough to make FORTRAN desirable. The recent appearance of faster and more powerful microcomputers may alter this conclusion drastically.

Pascal is widely touted by computer experts as the successor to FORTRAN; however, the fact that many Pascals do not implement the exponentiation operation (y^x) and usually lack double-precision makes one wonder whether it is a serious scientific language. It is similar to FORTRAN in difficulty of programming and is even more structured — that is, it requires more advance planning before you begin to write a program. It also is a compiler language.

There are many other languages, for example, ALGOL, COBOL, ADA, FORTH. Applications programs such as dBase© and VisiCalc© are so extensive and general that they are virtually in the class of computer languages.

Mainframe *vs.* Micro

Compared to micros, mainframe computers have much more extensive memories and faster execution times. They are certainly the only choice for serious number crunching (for example, an *ab initio* calculation of the wave function of water). However in many applications, the speed advantage may be negated by other factors. For example, you may spend considerable time in simply getting access to the computer; then, since you are sharing its use with many others, you may spend most of your time waiting for the computer to get to your problem. Nonetheless, if your problem involves operations such as diagonalizing a 50×50 matrix, the mainframe is likely to be a lot faster. On the other hand, your micro is likely to be there, immediately, for your personal use. The fact that a computation takes 12 hours may not matter — you paid for the computer, so you do not pay for the time as you would with a mainframe.

One of the major advantages of mainframe computers is that they usually have available an extensive library of mathematical functions and routines. Your micro will surely have logarithms, sines, exponentials, and a few others, but the mainframe may have Bessel functions, error functions and many more. Also, if your problem involves solving simultaneous linear equations, this may require hours of programming with a micro; the mainframe is likely to have this in its library, and a much better method to boot. (Some effort is being made to provide such libraries for micros.)

With technological advances, as mainframes become more friendly and micros more powerful, these distinctions may disappear. It is likely that most of the statements made in this chapter will become dated and wrong, perhaps before they are even in print.

Why BASIC?

This book uses BASIC exclusively, and perhaps this deserves some explanation. BASIC has an odious reputation among computer experts, often because they are familiar only with mainframe BASIC; partly it is pure snobbery. Microcomputer BASIC has many fine features and is, in some respects, superior to the "better" languages. It is a powerful language for scientific computations and could be more so if provided with a library of mathematical routines and a compiler. (However, the most enduring problem of BASIC is the lack of "local" variables and true "subroutines" or "procedures"; at least one microcomputer, the Acorn, manufactured by the British Broadcasting Company, has remedied this defect to some extent. It can be fervently hoped that other manufacturers will follow suit, for, with such improvements, microcomputer BASIC would be a truly powerful and easy-to-learn language.)

Most important, BASIC is easy to learn and, like training wheels on a bicycle, can make your entry into the world of computer programming easier.

In questions such as mainframe vs. micro or BASIC vs. Pascal, it is important to keep in mind that the "experts" may have a different agenda from yours. Professional programmers are rightfully concerned with efficiency, speed, and elegance; but the only appropriate question for the user is, "what is the fastest and most accurate method to solve the problem?" As mentioned several times, this question is closely connected with how often you wish to solve the problem without change and, thus, there is no single answer for all occasions. There is also an inverse snobbery; you can do very involved calculations with a programmable calculator and do "mainframe"-type jobs on a micro. You can also build a house without nails but it is questionable whether it is worth the effort. It is best to eschew all types of snobbery and choose the tool best suited to the job.

Operating Systems

The operating system of a computer is the part that makes the computer go; it acts as a director in accepting commands (whether from you via the keyboard or from a program resident in memory) and tells the "machinery" what to do. It is this feature that largely determines whether two computers are "compatible" — that is, whether they can use each other's programs. (Disk compatibility is another problem that is not automatically solved by using the same operating system.) If a computer has a disk, the disk operating system (DOS) handles communications between the computer memory and the disk.

The closest thing to a standard operating system, until recently at least, has been CP/M. This system was adopted by many of the smaller computer companies so they could compensate for their smallness by being compatible with each other. The large companies went their own way; Apple with APPLEDOS and Radio Shack with TRSDOS. MS-DOS was developed by Microsoft Corporation for the IBM PC, and it is becoming fairly standard as computer companies seek "IBM compatibility."

The question is still open about whether there will ever be a standard operating system or which it will be. MS-DOS seems to be favored, but others cannot be counted out. One new possibility is that the UNIX system, developed by AT&T for mainframe computers, will be adopted for the next generation of micros. For the types of applications we shall be discussing, the operating system is of marginal relevance. Its primary impact concerns machine-language applications programs and disk interchangeability. The differences among BASIC languages for various microcomputers was discussed in the Preface.

Bits, Bytes, and Variable Types

In this section, we shall discuss briefly how computer memory is organized, how data are stored, and the types of data BASIC recognizes. The fundamental unit of computer memory is the binary digit, or bit. The binary digit may have only two values, 1 or 0, and functions, logically, like an on/off switch. More complex data, for example a number or a letter, can be coded using a series of bits; N bits can code up to 2^N symbols, this being the number of off/on combinations of N binary switches. For example, three binary switches may have eight off (0)/on(1) combinations: 000, 001, 010, 011, 100, 101, 110, and 111.

The minimum addressable unit of a microcomputer's memory is a set of bits, called a byte. On a typical (8-bit) microcomputer, a byte can code $2^8 = 256$ symbols. For BASIC to be able to interpret the code contained in a byte, it must know what type of data it is. For example, the binary sequence

$$01011010$$

could represent a binary number (90 decimal), a letter ["Z" if the standard (ASCII) coding is being used], or a program instruction.

In BASIC, a datum stored in the computer's memory is accessed and manipulated via a name. For most microcomputers, this name is either one or two characters long, and the first character must be a letter. Examples of legal variable names are: A, B, AB, A5. This name will be associated by the BASIC interpreter with the contents of some byte or group of bytes in the memory. Often more than two letters can be used for a variable name, but the interpreter may look at only the first two. This means that variables named MAX, MAN, or MASS will be all interpreted as MA and will refer to the identical datum. For that reason, use of variable names longer than two characters is not recommended unless your computer recognizes the whole name. (Some of the newer versions of BASIC do recognize longer variable names.)

Next we shall discuss the types of variables permitted by BASIC. There are four types of such variables: string, integer, real and double precision.

String Variables

A string variable contains the ASCII (American Standard Code for Information Interchange) code for a symbol; this requires one byte for each symbol, one byte to store the address of the string, and one byte to store the length of the string (*i.e.*, the number of characters in the string). For example, the number "1" is represented by code 49 (decimal), a space by code 32, a period by code 46, the capital letter "A" by code 65, and the small letter "a" by code 97. A computer does not generally recognize lowercase letters as being related to the uppercase equivalent — that is, "B" and "b" are not the same. However, in some applications it may consider them to be the same, so it is inadvisable to use lowercase letters for naming BASIC variables. A variable name followed by a dollar sign ($) is assumed to be a string variable by the computer. Also, the DEFSTR statement can be used to create string variables:

50 DEFSTR S

will mean that any variable in the following parts of the program that begin with the letter "S" will be string variables— for example, S, SA, S2. The variables S and S$ will be different variables *unless* a DEFSTR S statement is used.

A string assignment statement must put the data in quotes so that the computer will know that it is to be treated as a string. An assignment statement, A = 10, will store the binary representation of the number 10 in the location named "A." On the other hand, the statement, A$ = "10", will store the ASCII representation of the number ten in the location named "A$." Arithmetic can be preformed only on numbers stored in binary. The statement

420 A$ = "Physical Chemistry"

would require 18 bytes for storage, one byte for each character (including spaces), plus two bytes to tell the computer where the data are stored (a pointer) and the length of the string.

Integer Variables

Numbers are stored by the computer as a binary code. As the name implies, integer variables may only have integer values (positive or negative) and are generally used for counting things. Variables that represent real numbers (called floating point numbers) are treated differently — this will be discussed next. In FORTRAN, all integer variables must have names that begin with the letters I, J, K, L, M, or N. While this is not required in BASIC, it is a good programming practice to use these letters exclusively for integer variables; this practice will be followed in this book. The statement

40 DEFINT I-N

at the beginning of the program will force all variables beginning with letters I through N to be integer variables. Such variables must be used carefully in computations; for example the assignment statement

568 I=3/2

will result in a value of 1 for the variable I.

Integer variables usually use two bytes for storage; 16 bits can store 2^{16} codes, which are used to represent numbers from -32767 to $+32767$; an attempt to assign a larger number to an integer variable will result in an ERROR condition. Integer variables may also be defined with a percent symbol — the variable X% will be an integer regardless of any preceding DEF assignments. In the absence of DEFINT declarations or special symbols (such as %), BASIC treats all numerical variables as integer variables as long as it can; if the value assigned becomes larger than that allowed for an integer variable, or if a fractional value is assigned, it is automatically converted to a real variable. The variable I% will be identical to the variable I if I has been previously defined as an integer. If your computer does not have the DEFINT statement, it is best to use % on all integer variables.

Real Variables

Real variables are stored in a computer in scientific notation — that is, a mantissa and an exponent. This permits numbers of larger magnitude (1×10^{38} is the typical maximum) and the representation of fractions. Real variables may require 4 or more bytes for storage, depending on the number of significant figures saved; a TRS-80 Model III uses 4 bytes and keeps 7 significant figures. Names for real variables are usually, by default, any not used for another purpose; however a DEFREAL statement or an exclamation point (!) may be used to force a variable to be real. (The variable I! is real, even if there is a DEFINT I-N statement preceding.) Why use integer variables at all? The principal reason is that integer arithmetic is exact, there is no round-off error. Integer arithmetic is also faster, and storage of integer data requires less memory. Assignment statements or inputs for real variables may use "E" to denote a power of 10; for example, the value 123,000 can be entered as 1.23E5.

Double Precision

In many applications, real arithmetic (especially if there are only 7 significant figures) produces unacceptable round-off errors in the result. In such situations, double precision variables, which use more storage and save more significant figures, must be used. Not all dialects of BASIC include this feature. For example, Applesoft BASIC carries 9 significant figures but does not permit double precision. Variable names ending with # are automatically double precision (for example, X#, I#, X2#). The statement DEFDBL can be used to create double precision variables without the special symbol. The number of significant figures is not, as the name implies, necessarily double the number for a real variable; on the TRS-80 Model III, 8 bytes are used for storage of a double precision number and 17 significant figures are saved. (Unfortunately, the maximum magnitude of double precision numbers is usually the same as for single precision; obviously these machines were not designed by or for scientists.) Assignment of values to double precision numbers should use "D" in place of "E" to denote a power of ten; for example, the number 123,456,789 can be entered as 1.23456789D8. Why not use double precision all of the time? The principal reason is that double precision arithmetic is slower, and more memory is required.

Program Organization

As you probably know, BASIC programs require statement numbers that define the order of execution. There are no restrictions on what numbers may be used, but it is a good practice to follow some sort of conventional system for all programs. Doing this requires some experience, so I offer below the system I use as a suggestion of one way to do it. This system is generally followed in this book.

Statement numbers 1-99 are used for initial housekeeping at the beginning of the program. DEFINT, DEFDBL, DEFSTR, DIM, ON ERROR, and DEFFN type statements should be placed in this section. This section can also be used for assigning initial values to variables, defining constants (R = 0.08206), and so forth. This part of the program should be passed through only once, when the program is started. If disk files are used, they could be OPENed and FORMATted in this section.

Statement numbers 100-199 are used to display the main menu and to give the user a choice of action. All other program segments will, upon completion, transfer control back to statement 100; *i.e.*, they should end with a GOTO 100 command. The following "miniprogram" illustrates this idea. (Throughout this book, miniprograms will be used to illustrate new concepts; it is recommended that you try these programs, and variations of them, on your computer. Do not type them in and run them mindlessly; most contain a lesson, so study them and try to see the purpose for each step — try modifications!)

Miniprogram 1.1

```
100 CLS' This is the Command Center
110 PRINT TAB(20)"MAIN MENU"
120 PRINT TAB(10)" (1) INPUT DATA"
122 PRINT TAB(10)" (2) DO CALCULATION"
```

```
124 PRINT TAB(10)" (3) PLOT RESULTS"
126 PRINT TAB(10)" (4) STOP"
130 PRINT "X=";X,"Y=";Y
150 INPUT"COMMAND";K
160 ON K GOTO 200,1000,300,990
199 GOTO 100
200 REM THIS SEGMENT CONTAINS DATA INPUT STATEMENT
210 INPUT"X=";X
220 GOTO 100
300 REM THIS SEGMENT PLOTS THE DATA
310 CLS: PRINT "SECTION 300"
320 FOR I=1 TO 500: NEXT: GOTO 100
990 END
1000 CLS: Y=2*X+23: PRINT"Y(";X;")=";Y
1010 FOR I=1 TO 500: NEXT: GOTO 100
```

In statement 100, CLS is the Microsoft BASIC command to clear the screen; on the APPLE the equivalent command is HOME — check your manual. (Note that statements 320 and 1010 are simply pauses to give you a chance to read the screen; we shall discuss a better method for doing this later.) The ON . . . GOTO statement (160) is a multiple branch statement that will transfer program control to different places depending on the value of the argument (K, in this case). Try this program with values for K of 1, 2, 3, and 4, and observe the results. Also, explore the effect of "illegal" inputs (other than 1, 2, 3, or 4) on its operation; try 0, 5, 1.234, −8, XYZ. The "menu" section can also be used to display program parameters (statement 130).

Segments beginning with statement numbers 200, 300 . . . 800 can be used for short utility routines — data input, data output, plotting etc. — and general purpose short subroutines.

Statement numbers 900-999 can be used for error-handling routines and program-ending statements. [In the simple example above, the need for a special segment to END the program will not be obvious; in more complicated programs there may be housekeeping details (CLOSE files, for example) that need to be done before ending the program.]

Statement number segments beginning 1000, 2000, . . . , 9000 can contain the main computational segments of the program.

Statement number segments beginning 10000, 20000, . . . should be reserved for major subroutines that may be useful in more than one program — for example, the subroutine given in the Chapter 4 for solving simultaneous linear equations (SLE).

It is a good idea to use some such organizational convention even for small programs; like mighty oaks from little acorns, big programs can grow out of small ones, and this is made easier by keeping different types of code in specific "places" — that is, with statement numbers in particular ranges. However, it is not appropriate for all types of programs. It is recommended that you follow, generally, the statement numbering used in this book for the programs given here because, in some cases, these may be used later as part of another program. That is, a segment numbered 200-299 should be numbered (in your program) in the same range; however it will not usually be necessary to use the exact numbers as in this book.

CHAPTER 2: SIMPLE COMPUTATIONS

In this chapter we shall discuss how to do mathematical computations on a microcomputer and some of the hazards and common errors you are likely to encounter. Methods for writing efficient and easily used programs will also be discussed. Arrays, sums, products and recursive calculations will be introduced.

Hierarchy of Operations

The fundamental operations of arithmetic are addition (+), subtraction (−), multiplication (symbolized by * on nearly all computers), division (/) and exponentiation. The last operation is generally denoted with an up-arrow (↑) or caret (^) in microcomputer BASIC; on TRS-80 computers, this operation is typed using the up arrow key, but it is printed as a left bracket ([); in this book it will be denoted as a caret (^) unless the text is a direct print-out of a computer program, in which case it will be denoted as "["; consult your manual to see how this should be done on your computer; making the required changes should be trivial.

In a mathematical expression, the computer first carries out all exponentiation operations; it will then do all multiplications and divisions, working from left to right; next it will do all additions and subtractions, from left to right. This order of evaluation may vary somewhat from computer to computer, so you should consult your manual (particularly if you do not get the same results as given for the examples that follow). This hierarchy of operations is very important in determining whether a particular code gives the correct answer; however, parentheses can be used to any extent desired to alter the order of evaluation and make an expression totally unambiguous; all parenthetical expressions are evaluated first (inner to outer) following the order given above. Now, let's look at some simple examples to illustrate the rules given above.

In the van der Waals equation, there is a term (a/V^2); if this is coded as

A/V*V

the result will probably be equal to A. (Try calculating 5/2*2 on your computer — is the answer 5?) The reason for this result is that, working from left to right, the computer first divides A by V and then multiplies the result by V, giving A as the answer. On the other hand, in the code

A/V^2

the computer first squares V and then divides A by the result, giving the desired answer. Parentheses can make the first form correct; the code

A/(V*V)

will multiply the V times V before dividing, thus giving the desired result.

Consider the computation of the quotient:

$$y = \frac{a + x}{b + x} \tag{2.1}$$

The code

Y=A+X/B+X

will not give a correct answer; the computer will first divide X by B, and then add the result to A and X. In this case, parentheses are required:

Y=(A+X)/(B+X)

will give the correct result. Try these two statements on your computer, and compare the results to your hand computation for various values of A, B, and X. (As mentioned above, there may be minor variations among computers so you should check your manual; *when in doubt, use parentheses!*)

Suppose you wish to evaluate the expression:

$$y = A \, B^{x^2} \tag{2.2a}$$

The code Y=A*B^X*X will give the result

$$y = A \, B^x x \tag{2.2b}$$

because the exponentiation operation will be done before the multiplication; once again, parentheses are required, and the correct code is:

Y=A ∗ B^(X ∗ X)

Another care that must be observed involves variable type. For example, the ideal gas law calculation may be coded as

P=N∗R∗T/V

and this will work *unless* you have previously used a DEFINT I-N statement (as recommended in Chapter 1). In such a case, the number of moles will be truncated to an integer: N = 1.999 will give N = 1, and N = 0.925 will give N = 0. Admittedly, this is an artifact of using the DEFINT statement, but the advantages of maintaining strict separation between integer and real variables is so great that it will be better to alter your notation in such a case. If the number of moles is denoted as XN, with

P=XN∗R∗T/V

the problem is avoided. (You could also use N!, which will be distinguished from N if DEFINT N has been used earlier.)

Another point: the computer doesn't know what "R" means unless you tell it, so a statement such as

R=0.082057

(depending on the units you are using) should appear at the beginning of the program (statement numbers 1—99, using the system outlined in Chapter 1). Likewise, it never heard of "e" (2.71828) or "pi" (3.14159) so, if you use them, you will have to define these constants early in the program.

Some Gas Law Examples

The critical pressure (P_c) and temperature (T_c) of a gas are readily measured and can be found in reference books even when other characteristics of the gas are not given. These constants can be used to calculate the van der Waals constants:

$$a = \frac{27R^2T_c^2}{64P_c} \qquad b = \frac{RT_c}{8P_c} \qquad (2.3)$$

The van der Waals equation of state is

$$P = \frac{RT}{V_m - b} - \frac{a}{V_m^2} \qquad (2.4)$$

where V_m is the molar volume.

Another equation of state, which sometimes works better than the van der Waals equation, is the Dieterici equation:

$$P = \frac{RT}{V_m - b}e^{-a/RTV_m} \qquad (2.5)$$

where a and b are constants whose qualitative meaning is the same as the van der Waals a and b, but whose numerical values are different. The Dieterici constants can also be calculated from the critical constants:

$$a = \frac{4R^2T_c^2}{e^2P_c} \qquad b = \frac{RT_c}{e^2P_c} \qquad (2.6)$$

where $e = 2.71828$ is the base of natural logarithms.

At moderate pressures, the behavior of a gas can also be approximated using the second virial coefficient, B(T); for example:

$$P = \frac{RT}{V_m} + \frac{RTB}{V_m^2} \qquad (2.7)$$

(Reference 1, Eq. (1.11).) The second virial coefficient can be estimated from the critical constants using Berthelot's equation:

$$B = \frac{9RT_c}{128P_c}\left[1 - \frac{6T_c^2}{T^2}\right] \qquad (2.8)$$

Assignment 2.1: Write a program (named "GAS") that will do the following:

1. Define the constants e and R. (Use statement numbers 1-99.)
2. Permit input of the critical constants (call them TC and PC). (200-299)
3. Calculate and print the van der Waals constants (denoted as

AV and BV respectively) and the Dieterici constants (AD and BD). (300-399)

4. Permit input of a temperature, and calculate and print the second virial coefficient (B, Eq. 2.8). (400-499)
5. Permit input of a molar volume (V); then calculate and print the pressure as calculated by Eqs. 2.4, 2.5, and 2.7 (label the output appropriately). (1000-1999)

The following BASIC statements can be used to code Eqs. 2.3 through 2.8:

```
AV=(27*R*R*TC*TC)/(64*PC)
BV=R*TC/(8*PC)
P1=R*T/(V−BV) − AV/(V*V)
P2=R*T*EXP(−AD/(R*T*V))/(V−BD)
AD=(4*R*R*TC*TC)/(E*E*PC)
BD=R*TC/(E*E*PC)
P3=R*T/V−R*T*B/(V*V)
B=9*R*TC*(1−(6*TC*TC/(T*T)))/(128*PC)
```

Clearly, this is not the order they would appear in the program. The following data can be used to test your program (more can be found in Reference 1, Chapter 1):

Carbon Monoxide:			TC=134 K		PC=35 atm
van der Waals constants:			AV=1.49		BV=0.0399
Dieterici constants:			AD=1.87		BD=0.0425

T	V	B	P1	P2	P3
200	1.0	−.0374	15.625	15.254	17.025
200	10.0	−.0374	1.633	1.629	1.647
500	1.0	0.1257	41.248	40.941	40.513
500	10.0	0.1257	4.104	4.012	4.098

[All temperatures in kelvins, pressures in atmospheres, and volumes in cubic decimeters (liters).]

The following code can be used to permit optional input of temperature in kelvins (K) or degrees Celsius:

```
430 INPUT"TEMPERATURE INPUT: TYPE
     <K> FOR KELVIN,
     <C> FOR CELSIUS";A$
440 IF A$="K"
     THEN INPUT T
     ELSE IF A$="C"
         THEN INPUT C: T=C+273.15
         ELSE GOTO 430
```

(If it is not clear to you what this code does, use it and try various inputs.)

Recursive Calculations

There are many examples of problems that cannot be solved in closed form, but which can be solved by successive approximations. A good example is calculating the volume of a gas as a function of T and P using Eq. 2.4 or 2.5.

The volume of a gas can be easily calculated using the ideal gas law— $V = RT/P$ (here, as above, V denotes the molar volume; if you need to know the volume of 5.265 moles of gas, this can be easily calculated by multiplying the molar volume by 5.265). A somewhat better approximation can be made using the second virial coefficient:

$$V = \frac{RT}{P} + B \tag{2.9}$$

(Reference 1, Eq. 1.13). However, for higher pressures, the van der Waals or Dieterici equations (or some such) must be used.

The van der Waals equation can be solved by successive approximations in the following form:

$$V = \frac{RT}{P + \dfrac{a}{V^2}} + b \qquad (2.10)$$

provided the a/V^2 term on the right-hand side is small compared to P. The procedure is to estimate a value for V — the ideal gas law can be used to do this — and then use this V on the right-hand side of Eq. 2.10 to calculate a more accurate value. This new value is then used on the right-hand side to calculate a better value. This process is continued until it converges — that is, until successive values of V are equal within some tolerance. This process may not converge at all, especially in the vicinity of the critical point; for that reason, it is a good idea to include in the computational loop a counter that will terminate the calculation if it continues too long. The following code will do this for the van der Waals equation (the van der Waals constants, a and b, are denoted AV and BV respectively).

```
810 V1=R*T/P: K=0
820 V=R*T/(P+AV/(V1*V1))+BV
830 PRINT V; : IF ABS(V−V1)<1E−6
        THEN GOTO 100
840 V1=V: K=K+1
842 IF K>100
        THEN GOTO 890
        ELSE GOTO 820
890 PRINT"NOT CONVERGED": STOP: GOTO 100
```

In this example, you must supply code to input the constants and values for T and P; it is assumed that this is done at statement 100, where the value of V must also be printed. For example:

```
100 CLS: PRINT"V=";V, "P=";P,"T=";T
110 INPUT"A,B"; A,B
130 PRINT"TYPE <ENTER> TO CONTINUE"
```

```
140 INPUT A$: GOTO 800
800 INPUT"T,P";T,P
```

In the code above, K is a counter (the 100 in statement 840 can be set as desired) and V1 is a temporary volume used to test for convergence. The test for convergence is set for 1×10^{-6} (which you can reset as you wish). The STOP in statement 890 is followed by a GOTO so that you can resume the program by typing CONT. The input variable A$ in statement 140 is a dummy; the program will wait until you do something before proceeding. Here, and elsewhere in this book, the brackets < and > are used to enclose the name of a key to be typed; on some computers, the ENTER key may be called RETURN or something else; it is the key you must use to terminate an input.

Assignment 2.2: Using the program you wrote for the previous assignment as a base, write a program that will calculate the molar volume of a gas by either (1) van der Waals, (2) Dieterici or (3) Eq. 2.10 using the virial coefficient of Eq. 2.8. Instead of doing all three (as we did earlier), write it so the user has a choice of methods. The following code will do this (R and E must be defined in statements 1−99):

```
100 CLS: PRINT"TC=";TC, "PC=";PC
110 PRINT"VDW:",AV, BV
120 PRINT"DIETERICI:",AD,BD
130 PRINT"P=";P,"V=";V,"T=";T, "B=";B
140 PRINT" <1> ENTER CONSTANTS
              <2> USE VIRIAL EQUATION
              <3> USE DIETERICI
              <4> USE VAN DER WAALS"
150 INPUT J
160 ON J GOTO 200, 400, 600, 800
199 GOTO 100
```

At statement 200, the critical constants are input, and the gas constants (a,b) are calculated. At statement 400, the temperature and pressure are input, and the virial coefficient and approximate volume are calculated. The Dieterici calculation begins at statement 600, and the van der Waals at statement 800 (the code given earlier can be used).

Sums and Products

The manner in which a computer is used to calculate sums is very informative in understanding how computers do arithmetic. For example, the equation

$$S = S + X$$

makes no sense algebraically (unless $X = 0$), but makes perfect sense to a computer; it says "take the value stored as S, add X to it, and store the result as S." The following code will permit you to enter a series of numbers, and calculate the sum of those numbers:

Miniprogram 2.1

```
200 INPUT"HOW MANY NUMBERS";N : S=0
210 FOR I=1 TO N
220 INPUT X
230 S=S+X
240 NEXT
250 PRINT"THE SUM IS=";S
```

Note that the summation variable (S) must be initialized to zero (statement 200). The mathematical equation for the operation above is:

$$S = \sum_{i=1}^{N} x_i \tag{2.11}$$

Another operation frequently encountered is the product:

$$P = \prod_{i=1}^{N} x_i \qquad (2.12)$$

This can be coded as follows:

Miniprogram 2.2

```
300 INPUT"HOW MANY NUMBERS";N : P=1
310 FOR I=1 TO N
320 INPUT X
330 P=P*X
340 NEXT
350 PRINT"THE PRODUCT IS=";P
```

Note that in this case, the variable (P) must be initialized to one. (Why?)

Assignment 2.3: Calculation of factorials and the sum of the first N integers. The following equations are to be evaluated for a positive integer N:

$$SN = \sum_{M=1}^{N} M \qquad (2.13a)$$

$$FA = \prod_{M=1}^{N} M = N! \qquad (2.13b)$$

The second case is, of course, the factorial. You should trap for illegal input; for example:

```
200 INPUT N
210 IF N<=0
     THEN PRINT"POSITIVE INTEGER ONLY": GOTO 200
```

(The factorial of zero is defined, but this must be treated as a special case.) Sample data: $N = 12$, $SN = 78$, $FA = 4.790016 \times 10^8$. What is the largest value of N your computer can use in this program without overflow?

Calculation of Binomial Coefficients: Subroutines

If there is a portion of code in your program that is used several times, it may be advisable to make it a subroutine. The statement GOSUB #, will transfer program control to the statement indicated (#); the subroutine is terminated by the statement RETURN, which returns program control to the statement following the GOSUB statement. The following code should be tried to illustrate the use of subroutines:

Miniprogram 2.3

```
200 PRINT"STATEMENT 200"
210 GOSUB 300
220 PRINT"STATEMENT 220"
230 GOSUB 300
240 PRINT"STATEMENT 240"
250 END
300 'SUBROUTINE STARTS HERE
310 PRINT"STATEMENT 310"
320 RETURN
```

Why is statement 250 needed? END statements in BASIC are sometimes optional, but it is needed in this case. Try running this program without statement 250.

A good application of a subroutine is found in the evaluation of the binomial probability factor:

$$W(p,q) = \left(\frac{1}{2}\right)^N \frac{N!}{p!\,q!} \qquad (2.14a)$$

$$(N = p + q)$$

The logarithm of this equation will be used:

$$\ln W = \ln N! - \ln p! - \ln q! - N \ln 2 \qquad (2.14b)$$

This represents, among other things, the probability of getting p heads and q tails in N flips of a coin ($N = p + q$); other applications are illustrated in Reference 1, Chapters 5, 9, and 15. One problem, illustrated by the last assignment, is that factorials grow very fast and overflow may result. In the program to follow (FAC), NX (which must be supplied by you) represents the largest value of a number whose factorial will not cause an overflow error. If the number is greater than NX, Stirling's approximation for $\ln(N!)$ must be used:

$$\ln N! \approx \frac{1}{2}\ln(2\pi) + \left(N + \frac{1}{2}\right)\ln N - N + \frac{1}{12N} + \cdots \qquad (2.15)$$

This approximation is accurate for large N; for that reason, program FAC will do the exact calculation for numbers smaller than NX.

The following program is complete except for introductory statements that must define NX and PI. (You will also want to add some prompting statements to make it more "user friendly.") This program is worth careful thought; note that M and FL are temporary variables whose meanings change through the program.

PROGRAM FAC

```
200 INPUT P,Q
210 N=P+Q: WL=−N*LOG(2)
220 M=N: GOSUB 1000: WL=WL+FL
240 M=Q: GOSUB 1000: WL=WL−FL
250 M=P: GOSUB 1000: WL=WL−FL
260 W=EXP(WL): PRINT"PROBABILITY="; W
270 END
1000 'SUBROUTINE TO CALCULATE LOG FACTORIAL
     (FL) OF M
1005 IF M<0
     THEN PRINT"ILLEGAL INPUT": GOTO 200
```

1010 IF M=0

       THEN FL=0: RETURN 'ZERO FACTORIAL=1

1020 IF M<NX

       THEN 1100

1030 FL=0.5*LOG(2*PI)+(M+0.5)*LOG(M)−M+1/(12*M)

1040 RETURN

1100 PR=1

1110 FOR I=1 TO M: PR=PR*I: NEXT

1120 FL=LOG(PR): RETURN

The following test data were calculated on an 11 digit calculator; your computer may be less accurate.

$$P = 4 \qquad Q = 5 \qquad W = 0.24609375$$
$$P = 7 \qquad Q = 60 \qquad W = 5.8929654 \times 10^{-12}$$

Polynomial Evaluation: Arrays

An array is a group of variables that are referred to by the same variable name, which is followed by an index variable in parentheses. For example, the array variable A(I) for I = 1, 2, and 3, denotes three variables: A(1), A(2), and A(3). The advantage of this method is that the index (I in this case) can be computed within the program. If an array has more than 10 elements, if must be declared in advance by a DIM statement; for example

50 DIM A(100)

sets aside 101 memory locations (numbered 0 to 100) for the array A(I). It is possible in BASIC to allow input of the array size, for example:

50 INPUT N

52 DIM A(N)

but, unless memory is limited, it is usually better to dimension the arrays larger than the likely maximum.

This concept can be illustrated by the evaluation of a polynomial:

$$P(x) = \sum_{i=0}^{N} a_i x^i \qquad (2.16)$$

The coefficients (a_i) can be stored in an array (A). The following code would evaluate a polynomial (P) with coefficients A(I) and I = 0 to N:

```
330 P=A(0)
340 FOR J=1 TO N
350 P=P+A(J)*X^J
360 NEXT
370 ...
```

Of course, to use this you must provide statements to input the coefficients and values for X; for example:

```
200 INPUT"ORDER OF POLYNOMIAL";N
210 FOR I=0 TO N: INPUT A(I): NEXT
220 ...
```
and
```
300 INPUT"X=";X
```

There is a much more efficient method for evaluating polynomials. A fourth-order polynomial can be written as:

```
Y = A(0) + A(1)*X + A(2)*X*X + A(3)*X*X*X + A(4)*X*X*X*X
```

To evaluate Y in this form requires 10 multiplications. On the hand, if written in the following way:

```
Y = A(0) + X*(A(1)+X*(A(2)+X*(A(3)+X*A(4))))
```

it can be calculated with only four multiplications. The following code implements this faster (and sometimes more accurate) method for evaluating a polynomial:

```
400 INPUT X
430 P=A(N) 'N IS THE POLYNOMIAL ORDER, INPUT EARLIER
440 FOR I=N-1 TO 0 STEP -1
450 P=A(I)+P*X
460 NEXT
470 ...
```

It will probably require a lot of careful thought to see exactly what this code is doing; a good method of analysis is to play "dumb computer" and write out each step (algebraically) as the computer would execute the code; this could be done for some low order case such as N = 3.

Assignment 2.4: Write a program (named POLYEV) which will evaluate a polynomial by both of the methods given above. If there are no errors, both should give the same results but the second method will be faster. It is not easy to judge the speed of a computer — it is very fast — unless there are numerous repetitions. Try putting the calculations into a loop; for example:

```
300 FOR X=1 TO 100        400 FOR X=1 TO 100
.....                     .....
370 PRINT"/";             470 PRINT"#";
380 NEXT X                480 NEXT X
```

With N = 5 or 6, the speed difference should be dramatic. (The PRINT statements, 370 and 470, are just to let you see how fast things are going.)

Mean and Standard Deviation: DATA Statements

The average (mean) of a set of numbers x_i, $\bar{x}$, is given by the formula:

$$\bar{x} = \frac{1}{N} \sum_{i=1}^{N} x_i \tag{2.17}$$

The standard deviation of this set is defined as:

$$\sigma = \left[\frac{1}{N-1} \sum_{i=1}^{N} (x_i - \bar{x})^2 \right]^{1/2} \tag{2.18}$$

There is an alternative form for the standard deviation that is often used because it is faster and easier to calculate:

$$\sigma = \left[\frac{1}{N-1} \left\{ \sum x_i^2 - \frac{(\sum x_i)^2}{N} \right\} \right]^{1/2} \tag{2.19}$$

(All sums from $i = 1$ to N.)

Equation 2.19 can be shown to be mathematically identical to Eq. 2.18, but mathematical proofs implicitly assume infinite precision for computation. With finite mathematics (that is, computation with a limited number of digits, as on a computer), these two forms for calculating σ are not identical in all cases. Nonetheless, the second form is a great deal faster, so we shall prefer to use it when possible. (The reason it is faster is that, usually, the sums are calculated anyway.) The problem with Eq. 2.19 comes in the computation of the sum of squares; because of round-off error, the argument of the square root could be negative in some cases and an attempt to take the square root of a negative number will give an error condition. For that reason, we must first calculate the variance (σ^2) to be certain it is positive before attempting to take the square root.

The data to be averaged will be stored in an array X(I). One way to input data, and sum the values and their squares is illustrated below:

```
200 INPUT"NUMBER OF VALUES=";N
210 FOR I=1 TO N: INPUT X(I): NEXT
220 S=0
230 FOR I=1 TO N: S=S+X(I): NEXT
240 AV=S/N: SS=0
250 FOR I=1 TO N: SS=SS+X(I)*X(I): NEXT
260 . . . .
```

This is a very inefficient method both in terms of memory required and time of execution. There are two methods to speed it up: (1) combine the three FOR . . . NEXT loops into one (this is called loop packing); (2)

minimize the number of array references (which are very time consuming) by using a temporary variable. These changes give the following code:

```
200 INPUT"NUMBER OF VALUES=";N
210 S=0: SS=0
220 FOR I=1 TO N
222 INPUT X
224 X(I)=X
230 S=S+X
232 SS=SS+X*X
234 NEXT
240 AV= S/N
244 VA=(SS- S*S/N)/(N-1)
250 IF VA<0
      THEN 300
260 SD=SQR(VA)
270 PRINT"AVERAGE=";AV,"STANDARD DEVIATION=";SD
280 ...
```

In statement 240, VA (for variance) is the square of the standard deviation. In statement 250, control is transferred to 300 if VA is negative; this indicates a computational problem and the code at 300 should print an appropriate message and then calculate the standard deviation (σ) using Eq. 2.18.

Assignment 2.5: Write a program (named "AVE") to calculate the mean and standard deviation of a set of numbers. For demonstration purposes you may wish to calculate σ by both methods — they are likely to differ significantly if the deviation of the data points is small compared to their size. Try the following data sets (N = 3 for all): (a) 2.1, 2.2, 2.3 (b) 2.001, 2.002, 2.003 (c) 2.00001, 2.00002, 2.00003. The first set is unlikely to cause a problem, but the last probably will. Try it again, adding a DEFDBL X,S statement at the beginning of the program. (For additional test data, make up a set of numbers and compare your results on the computer to those calculated with a calculator. This will make you appreciate, if you don't already, the efficiency of a computer!) Another useful addition you could make to program AVE would be a routine to calculate and print the deviations of each point.

Data Statements

When doing procedures such as calculating the mean and standard deviation, it is often useful to be able to recalculate with certain points omitted. One method would be to rerun the program, but this would require typing all of the data again. You could also incorporate code for eliminating or correcting data after it has been input; this is rather complicated. The simplest method is to use the READ . . . DATA method of data input. To do this, you must replace the INPUT statement with a READ statement, and then put the data to be read in a DATA statement. For example:

300 READ N

310 FOR I=1 TO N: READ X(I): NEXT

390 DATA 4, 2.12, 2.43, 2.55, 2.09

DATA statements may be placed anywhere in the program, and (if there are more than one such statements) will be read sequentially until there are no more data to be read. (An attempt to READ past the last datum will usually result in an error.) With this method, the editing feature of your computer can be used to eliminate or change data points. Another advantage is that typographical errors are more easily spotted and corrected. If you are using several data sets, additional DATA statements can be incorporated; the statement

392 DATA 6, 5.46, 4.98, 5.34, 5.11, 5.21, 4.95

could be added to the code above for the second pass.

Assignment 2.6: Modify your AVE program to use READ . . . DATA input. Include DATA statements to do several runs without stopping the program.

Plotting

In many situations, it is more useful and informative to present the result of a computation graphically rather than as a list of numbers. This gets us into the area of "computer graphics." As this term is ordinarily used, it refers to a graphical representation on the screen of a computer. This type of presentation is informative but insufficient for scientific purposes where a permanent record is likely to be required. The permanent record ("hard copy") can be obtained using a plotter or (less satisfactorily) a printer. We shall divide our discussion into two parts: screen graphics and plotter graphics. More than any other area, graphics is very device-dependent. Screen graphics differs substantially from computer to computer and you will need to read your manual carefully; the discussion to follow will be very general. Plotter graphics depends on the device to be used for plotting, and (if you have such a device) its manual will have to be studied carefully. Our comments regarding plotter graphics will be even more general.

Screen Graphics

For purposes of graphics, the CRT (cathode ray tube) screen of your computer is divided into cells, called pixels. Each of these pixels is addressed by two integers giving the horizontal and vertical displacements (we shall call these IX for the horizontal axis and IY for the vertical axis). Each of these pixels can be turned on or off independently. The BASIC statements to do this vary from computer to computer; we shall assume that the statement SET(IX,IY) turns on the pixel and RESET(IX,IY) turns it off; consult your manual to find the appropriate command for your computer. (It is PSET on an IBM PC, PLOT or HPLOT on an Apple.) The number of pixels also varies widely; for purposes of illustration we shall assume a pixel matrix of 256 (vertical) by 512 (horizontal). Since each pixel requires one byte of RAM (Random Access Memory), a 256 × 512 screen will require 256*512/8 = 16 K (bytes) RAM. (In computer talk, 1 K = 1024, that is, 2^{10}.) The RAM for video display is usually separate from the RAM used for data and programs and is called VIDRAM.

With our presumed size (which will almost surely be different from that of your computer) the horizontal pixel axis (IX) will be numbered from 0 to 511, left to right. The vertical axis (IY) will be numbered from 0 to 255 but, perversely, on most computers the numbering is from top to bottom. By most people's standards (with the possible exception of computer engineers) this numbering system would produce a graph that is upside-down. This is easily remedied; if you use the statement SET(IX,255−IY), the origin (IX = 0, IY = 0) will be at the lower left-hand corner. Figure 2.1 illustrates this numbering system.

We are still not ready to plot. In the first place, we may not want the origin of the plot to be at the lower left corner; also, our variables will probably not be conveniently represented by the pixel numbers. In order to scale the plots properly we define four constants to "frame" our graph. The independent variable (X) will have limits called X1 and X2, with X1 < X < X2; the dependent variable (Y) will have limits called Y1 and Y2,

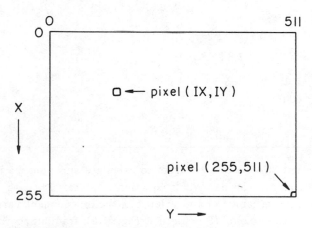

Figure 2.1: Pixel numbers for a typical microcomputer screen. The actual number of pixels will vary from computer to computer.

with $Y1 < Y < Y2$. Thus, the lower left corner will be the point $(X1,Y1)$ and the upper right corner will be $(X2,Y2)$. The following code illustrates a subroutine that will turn on a pixel for a point (X,Y) with proper scaling:

```
600 'SUBROUTINE FOR SCREEN PLOTTING X,Y
610 IX=LX*(X−X1)/(X2−X1)
620 IY=LY*(Y−Y1)/(Y2−Y1)
630 IF IX<0 OR IX>LX
      THEN RETURN
640 IF IY<0 OR IY>LY
      THEN RETURN
650 SET(IX,LY−IY)
660 RETURN
```

In this program, LX and LY are the number of pixels on the X and Y axes respectively (for our example, $LX = 511$, $LY = 255$); these should be defined at the beginning of the programs as is appropriate for your computer. The following code could act as a "driver" program for testing the above subroutine:

```
50 LX=511: LY=255
200 X1=0: X2=1: Y1=0: Y2=0.30
210 FOR X=X1 TO X2 STEP 0.01
220 Y=X*(1−X)
230 GOSUB 600
240 NEXT
```

Assignment 2.7: Write a program to calculate and plot the isotherms of a gas obeying the van der Waals equation of state. Treat the pressure as the dependent variable (Y) and volume as the independent variable (X); for a gas such as ammonia (Reference 1, Fig. 1.8), framing coordinates of $X1 = 0$, $X2 = 0.4$, $Y1 = 0$ and $Y2 = 400$ will be suitable. Try a variety of temperatures above, at, and below the critical temperature. For ammonia, $a = 4.17$, $b = 0.0371$ and $T_c = 405.5$ K.

Be careful! If you set up the FOR . . . NEXT loop for volume (X) as:

FOR X=0 TO X2 STEP 0.004

you are likely to run into trouble. In the van der Waals equation, Eq. 2.4, there is a division by $(V - b)$; in your loop, this is negative when $V < b$ and, should you happen to hit $V = b$, you will be dividing by zero. If you do this, your computer may respond rudely! A little thought about what the van der Waals "b" correction means may convince you that this is silly; the "b" correction is an excluded-volume correction and "b" represents the portion of the volume of the container that is actually occupied by molecules. Thus, there is no physical significance to any volume less than b. Therefore the loop should be set up as:

FOR X=B+XS TO X2+XS/2 STEP XS

where XS is the step size (0.004 in the earlier example) that must be defined or input in an earlier part of the program. (A more sophisticated way to do this would be to use the method discussed earlier to calculate the volume of the gas at the highest pressure desired, Y2. Since this is the smallest volume of interest, the volume loop can begin with this value.) The end of the loop is set for X2 + SX/2 to be certain that the last point is calculated; because of roundoff error, a loop to X2 could omit the last calculation if the last X is even slightly greater than X2.

Plotter Graphics

As mentioned earlier, the manner of plotting varies greatly with the device being used, and only the plotter instruction manual can tell you how to do it. However, for purposes of illustration, a general discussion of plotting using the Radio Shack CPG-115 Color Graphic Printer will be given. This plotter costs less than $200 and will work with any computer that has a standard parallel or serial printer interface.

Instructions are sent to the printer/plotter from the computer using the BASIC LPRINT command. (Computers that do not implement the LPRINT command or some equivalent may not be able to use such devices.) The printer/plotter has two modes of operation: printing and graphics (that makes sense, doesn't it?). The command LPRINT CHR$(18) places it in graphics mode; the command LPRINT "A" returns it to printer mode. (As a printer, the CPG-115 is rather slow and limited, but it does work.) The following commands control pen movement:

LPRINT "M";IX;",";IY 'PEN UP MOVEMENT TO IX,IY

LPRINT "D";IX;",";IY

    'DRAW LINE FROM CURRENT POSITION TO IX,IY

LPRINT "H" 'PEN TO ORIGIN

There are a number of other commands, but these will suffice to give you the idea. If the X axis is across the paper, then the number of steps are $0 < IX < 400$; along the Y axis, $0 < IY < 999$. The scaling of the real variables X,Y to the step numbers can be done as illustrated earlier for screen plotting. The steps for plotting calculated values (X,Y) are as follows: (1) Calculate the first point, Y(X1), and move the pen (pen up) to that position. (2) Calculate successive values of Y(X), moving the pen (pen down) from point to point. (3) After the last point, move the pen back to the origin. Note that you are plotting point-to-point; this is quite different from pixel plotting, which can be done in any order. However, for sequential calculations (such as an isotherm), this is of little consequence.

Scaling of Arrays

Often it is a good idea to calculate the points and put them into arrays [for example, AX(I) for the X points, and AY(I) for the corresponding Y points] before plotting. In this case, you may wish to find out what the maximum and minimum values of Y are, so the vertical scale can be set appropriately. The following code will find the largest (Y2) and smallest (Y1) elements of the array AY, print them out, and permit you to enter the desired values (which may not be exactly the largest and smallest. It is assumed that none of the numbers are greater than 1E36 or less than −1E36):

```
1500 Y1=1E36: Y2=-1E36
1510 FOR I=1 TO MX 'MX IS THE ARRAY DIMENSION
1520 IF AY(I)>Y2
     THEN Y2=AY(I)
1530 IF AY(I)<Y1
     THEN Y1=AY(I)
1540 NEXT
1550 PRINT"MAX";Y2,"MIN";Y1
1560 INPUT"Y2,Y1";Y2,Y1
```

General Comments

If you are looking for a plotter, there are two characteristics you should check. The first is the step size (0.3 mm on the CPG-115); too large a step size and your graphs will not be smooth. Another is the ability of the pen to go both up and down (actually, it is usually the paper that moves while the pen remains stationary, but that depends on your frame of reference). Some dot matrix printers can do "graphics" but cannot reverse the paper; without it you will be unable to plot circles or other multiple-valued functions. With respect to screen graphics, computer companies seem to be in a contest to see which will have the highest resolution (most pixels); the thing to remember about high-resolution graphics is that you have to calculate all those points; this can make programs very slow. Since, for scientific purposes, it is the hard copy that is important, the screen resolution may be a minor concern. (However, some computers do hard copy plots by dumping the screen to a printer, in which case the screen resolution will determine the hard-copy plot resolution.)

Advanced Programming Techniques: van der Waals Again

A computation such as the van der Waals gas law is an example of a multiple-branch program. You may wish to do a number of things such as enter or calculate P, V, or T, or enter parameters. As mentioned earlier, the "command center" menu method is best for such purposes. In this section we shall discuss two new BASIC functions, INKEY$ and INSTR, and show how they can be used to create "user friendly" and flexible programs.

The INKEY$ function returns a character corresponding to the last key struck on the keyboard, no matter how long ago it was struck. The following will illustrate its use.

Miniprogram 2.4

```
200 CLS
210 PRINT"HIT ANY KEY",
220 A$=INKEY$: IF A$=""
        THEN GOTO 220
230 IF ASC(A$)<32
        THEN STOP
240 IF ASC(A$)=32
        THEN PRINT"SPACEBAR": GOTO 210
250 PRINT"YOU HIT KEY ";A$
260 GOTO 210
```

In line 220, there is no space between the quotes; this command compares A$ to a empty string ("") to see if the keyboard has been struck. The ASC function in statements 230 and 240 returns the numerical ASCII code for the character. ASCII codes less than 32 are generally used for control codes and are usually nonprinting; in this program, any such key will stop the program. ASCII 32 is usually the code for a space (note the distinction between a "space" and an "empty string").

Another use for the INKEY$ function is to put pauses into your program; you may want to do this to allow you to do something (inspect the screen output, turn on the printer, think the situation over, and so on) before letting the program proceed. The following code will cause the computer to wait until any key is struck before branching to 100:

```
299 A$=INKEY$: IF A$=""
        THEN GOTO 299
        ELSE GOTO 100
```

The INKEY$ function is also useful for menu commands, since it permits the use of letters rather than numbers for commands; this can make it easier to remember the commands of a complex menu (for example, hit the key <P> rather than <3> to calculate pressure). Also, the ENTER/RETURN key is not needed after the command, so the program is faster. If commands are letters, they must be changed to a number so that the ON . . . GOTO command can be used. This can be accomplished using the INSTR function. The function INSTR(B$,A$) will return an integer value corresponding to the position of the string A$ in the string B$. For example

J=INSTR("ABCD",A$)

will give J = 1 if A$ = "A", J = 2 if A$ = "B", J = 3 if A$ = "C", J = 4 if A$ = "D" and zero for any other (including lowercase "a", "b", etc.). The following illustrates the use of a menu with these functions:

Miniprogram 2.5

```
100 PRINT"THIS IS THE COMMAND CENTER: ENTER COMMAND"
120 PRINT"<I> INPUT DATA"
122 PRINT"<C> CALCULATE"
124 PRINT"<P> PLOT"
126 PRINT"<Q> QUIT"
130 A$=INKEY$: IF A$=""
        THEN GOTO 130
140 J=INSTR("ICPQ",A$): IF J=0
        THEN GOTO 130
150 ON J GOTO 200, 300, 400, 900
199 GOTO 100
```

```
200 PRINT"STATEMENT 200": GOTO 100
300 PRINT"STATEMENT 300": GOTO 100
400 PRINT"STATEMENT 400": GOTO 100
900 END
```

This code will branch to 200 if "I" is typed, 300 if "C" is typed, 400 if "P" is typed, 900 if "Q" is typed (this ENDs the program), and ignore all others.

If your computer does not have the INSTR function, a fall-through filter of IF . . . THEN tests must be written. For the example above, statements 140-150 would be replaced by:

```
140 IF A$="I" THEN GOTO 200
145 IF A$="C" THEN GOTO 300
150 IF A$="P" THEN GOTO 400
155 IF A$="Q" THEN GOTO 900
```

The program below (VDW) shows how this method could be used for the van der Waals calculation. Note that the commands are dual-purpose; <P> is the command to enter a value for pressure, but if a value of zero is entered it will calculate the pressure. There are also two strings, G$ and F$. G$ is just the name of the gas — a nice touch but hardly necessary. F$ addresses another problem: It is possible with this program to enter arbitrary values of P, V, and T, but they do not necessarily "go together" — that is, the pressure displayed is not necessarily the correct one for the temperature and volume displayed. This is taken care of with the string F$, that will be "NO" if they do not go together and "OK" if they do. (It will be equal to "NOT CONV" in the event you try a volume calculation that does not converge.)

PROGRAM VDW

```
1 'PROGRAM VDW, VANDERWAALS GAS LAW CALCULATIONS
10 DEFINT I-N
```

```
20 R=0.082057: G$="NITROGEN": F$="NO"
30 A=1.39: B=0.0391
100 CLS
110 PRINT"G=";G$,"A=";A,"B=";B,F$
120 IF T<>0
      THEN Z=P*V/(R*T) ' COMPRESSIBILITY FACTOR
130 PRINT"P=";P,"T=";T,"V=";V,"Z=";Z
140 PRINT"TYPE VARIABLE NAME TO CHANGE-
      ENTER 0 TO CALCULATE"
145 PRINT"(TYPE <C> FOR CELSIUS, <Q> TO QUIT)"
150 A$=INKEY$: IF A$=""
      THEN GOTO 150
160 J=INSTR("GABPVTCQ",A$): IF J=0
      THEN GOTO 150
170 ON J GOTO 200,300,400,500,600,700,750,900
199 GOTO 100
200 INPUT"NAME OF GAS, A,B";G$,A,B: GOTO 100
300 INPUT"A=";A: GOTO 100
400 INPUT"B=";B: GOTO 100
500 INPUT"P=";P: IF P<>0
      THEN F$="NO": GOTO 100
510 P=R*T/(V-B)-A/(V*V)
520 F$="OK": GOTO 100
600 INPUT"V=";V: IF V<>0
      THEN F$="NO": GOTO 100
610 V1=R*T/P: K=0
620 V=R*T/(P+A/(V1*V1))+B
630 IF ABS(V-V1)<1E-6
      THEN F$="OK": GOTO 100
640 K=K+1: V1=V: IF K<100
```

```
      THEN GOTO 620
650 F$="NOT CONV": GOTO 100
700 INPUT"T=";T: IF T<>0
      THEN F$="NO" GOTO 100
710 T=((P+A/(V*V))*(V−B))/R
720 F$="OK": GOTO 100
750 INPUT"DEGREES CELSIUS=";C
760 T=C+273.15: F$="NO"
770 GOTO 100
900 END
```

Error Handling

When a BASIC program encounters an error, it stops program execution. You can, of course, restart the program by typing RUN, but then all of your calculations are lost. Since not all errors are truly fatal (that is, of the type which would prohibit continuation of the program), this can be annoying and time consuming. The way around this is the ON ERROR statement. The following statements added to any program will accomplish this:

```
90 ON ERROR GOTO 990
990 PRINT"ERROR MESSAGE, CONSULT YOUR MANUAL"
999 STOP: RESUME 100
```

The specific form of statement 990 must be determined by reading your manual; it should be possible to print an error number and the line number in which the error occurred. After the STOP in statement 999, you can continue execution (unless you have altered the program, or the error is truly fatal) by typing CONT; the RESUME statement cancels the error condition and transfers control to statement 100. (This demonstrates another advantage of the "command center" program structure; no matter where in the program the error occurs, you can recover control by branching back to statement 100.)

CHAPTER 3: ROOTS OF EQUATIONS

Whys and Wherefores

If some physical quantity (y) is expressed as an implicit function of some variable (x), $y = F(x)$, the root of that function is the value of x for which $F(x) = 0$. The need to find roots arises frequently in chemistry. For example, the calculation of the pH of a weak acid in water involves solving the cubic equation:

$$[\text{H}^+]^3 + K_a [\text{H}^+]^2 - (K_w + K_a C_a)[\text{H}^+] - K_a K_w = 0 \qquad (3.1)$$

where K_a is the acid dissociation constant, $K_w = 1 \times 10^{-14}$ is the ion-product constant of water, and C_a is the concentration of the weak acid. Closed-form solutions to cubic equations have been published, but they are complicated and difficult to use. We shall see shortly that a simple numerical method can not only solve cubic equations such as this one but can be applied to other problems as well.

Another example of a problem that can involve cubic equations arises in the calculation of the properties of a gas using the Beattie-Bridgeman equation of state (Reference 1, Eq. 1.7). The second virial coefficient of such a gas is:

$$B(T) = B_0 - \frac{A_0}{RT} - \frac{c}{T^3} \qquad (3.2)$$

and the Joule-Thomson coefficient (μ) at low pressure is given by:

$$\mu = \frac{1}{C_{pm}} \left[-B_0 + \frac{2A_0}{RT} + \frac{4c}{T^3} \right] \qquad (3.3)$$

where A_0, B_0 and c are constants characteristic of the gas and C_{pm} is the molar heat capacity ($R = 0.08206$ and volume must be in liters, temperature in K, and pressure in atm). Given values for the constants, you would probably have little difficulty in calculating values for $B(T)$ or μ

for a given temperature; however the opposite problem involves solving for the roots of a cubic equation. The Boyle temperature is defined as the temperature at which $B(T) = 0$ and the Joule-Thomson inversion temperature is the temperature at which $\mu = 0$. The last is an important property of the gas since, above the inversion temperature, the gas will warm rather than cool during a Joule-Thomson expansion. (Such expansions are used in refrigeration and for liquefying gases, so the usual intent is that the gas should cool on expansion.) The three problems mentioned can be solved by the same BASIC program, changing no more than a few statements.

An example of a root problem that does not involve a polynomial can arise in dealing with vapor pressures. One form of equation for calculating the vapor (P) as a function of T is (Reference 1, Chapter 4):

$$\ln P = A + \frac{B}{T} + C \ln T \tag{3.4}$$

Once again, calculating P given T is no problem, but finding the boiling temperature of the liquid at some pressure P is more difficult; Eq. 3.4 can be rearranged as a function of T:

$$f(T) = (A - \ln P) + \frac{B}{T} + C \ln T = 0 \tag{3.5}$$

whose root, $f(T) = 0$, will give the boiling temperature for a given pressure.

Root problems arise frequently in equilibrium problems. For example, the reaction:

$$A + 2B \rightleftarrows C + D \tag{3.6}$$

with initial concentrations A_0 and B_0, gives the following equation for the concentration equilibrium constant:

$$K_c = \frac{x^2}{(A_0 - x)(B_0 - 2x)^2} \tag{3.7a}$$

where x is the concentration of C or D at equilibrium. This can be arranged into a root problem as follows:

$$f(x) = K_c(A_0 - x)(B_0 - 2x)^2 - x^2 = 0 \tag{3.7b}$$

The value of x for which $f(x) = 0$ will give the concentrations of all species at equilibrium. (Reference 1, Chapter 6, gives more details on such problems.) Such problems are polynomial type problems, but simplifying equations such as 3.7b to a polynomial is subject to mistakes, so a method that can solve such equations without simplification has some advantage.

Newton's Method: Function Statements

The Newton method for finding real roots of a function is illustrated in Figure 3.1. This involves the calculation of the value of the function, $f(x)$, and the derivative of the function $f'(x) = df/dx$. Given an approximate value for the root, x_n, the next approximation is calculated as:

$$x_{n+1} = x_n - \frac{f(x_n)}{f'(x_n)} \qquad (3.8)$$

To start this iterative procedure, an initial guess must be provided for the value of the root. This value is usually suggested by the physical situation. For example, in the equilibrium problem of Eq. 3.7, since the concentrations cannot be negative, you know that $x>0$ and $x<A_0$ or $x<(B_0/2)$ (whichever is smaller). Similarly in the pH problem, Eq. 3.1, an initial guess of $[H^+] = C_a/10$ would be appropriate.

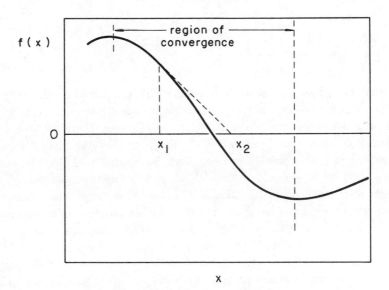

Figure 3.1: Newton's method for finding roots.

Newton's method converges very rapidly if the function is smooth and well-behaved and the initial guess is on the "near" side of any maximum or minimum of the function; like most iterative methods, it has problems with roots that are near a maximum, minimum, or an inflection point (for example, the volume of a gas near the critical point) and with multiple or closely spaced roots. Compared to other methods, the Newton method converges rapidly but is rather unstable — that is, it may fail in some circumstances, especially if the initial guess is very poor.

A very useful BASIC function for doing root problems, and in many other situations, which is found in most microcomputer BASICs, is the DEF FN statement. The following miniprogram illustrates the use of this statement; the DEF FN statement, like DIM and DEFINT, should be placed at the beginning of the program.

Miniprogram 3.1

```
10 DEF FNA(Z)= A*Z+1
20 DEF FNB(Z)= SQR(Z)*(1+6*Z*Z)
100 INPUT X
110 Z=1: A=2
120 PRINT FNA(2), FNA(X), FNB(X), FNA(2*X+4)
130 GOTO 100
```

Function names consist of three letters with the first two being "FN"; thus you could have as many as 26 functions in one program. The third letter will determine the function type; for example, if a DEFINT I-N statement is used, the functions FNI, FNJ, and so forth, will return integer values. The default symbols can be used; thus, FNA% is an integer-, FNA# is a double-, and FNA$ is a string-type function. The variable in parentheses in the DEF FN statement is called the argument; it need not be the same letter as that used in the program. For example, the function calls in statement 120 will calculate the functions for $Z = 2$ and $Z = X$. Statement 110, which defines Z, has no effect unless FNA(Z) is used explicitly. On the other hand, function statements may use other variables or constants of the program that are not listed as arguments (for example, "A" of statement 110). Some computers permit more than one argument. For example:

DEF FNZ(X,Y) = X*X+Y*Y+7

Consult your manual to see what your computer permits. (If your computer does not implement the DEF FN statement, you will have to use subroutines in place of functions in the subsequent programs.)

The following program illustrates the use of Newton's method for solving a general cubic equation, $f(x)= a + bx + cx^2 + dx^3$:

PROGRAM NEWTON

```
10 DEFINT I-N
20 DEF FNY(X) = A + X*(B+X*(C+D*X))' FUNCTION
30 DEF FND(X) = B + X*(2*C+3*D*X) 'DERIVATIVE FUNCTION
40 T=1E-6
      'CONVERGENCE CRITERION, CHANGE TO SUIT
100 INPUT"CONSTANTS,A,B,C,D";A,B,C,D
110 INPUT"INITIAL X";X
200 'NEWTON ITERATION
210 K=0
220 X1=X
230 X=X1-FNY(X1)/FND(X1)
240 K=K+1
250 IF ABS((X-X1)/(X+X1))<T
      THEN GOTO 300
260 IF K<100
      THEN 220
270 PRINT"TRIED 100 ITERATIONS W/O FINISHING"
280 PRINT"LAST TWO VALUES";X,X1
290 PRINT"PERHAPS...";
```

300 PRINT"THE ROOT IS ";X

310 END

Comments on NEWTON

Statements 200-300 constitute a "shell program," which, by adding other code as desired, could be used for solving many different problems. The relative convergence criterion (statement 250) may not be suitable for all cases; especially if a root near zero is possible. If the root has a known magnitude (for example, $0.1 < X < 10$), an absolute convergence test such as:

250 IF ABS(X−X1)<T THEN 300

may be more appropriate. Test data for program NEWTON with DEF FN as above: Coefficients 1, 1, 1, −1, initial guess 2, converges to root = 1.8399 in 4 iterations. Coefficients 1, 0, 1, 0 and any initial guess, will not converge (the roots are complex).

Assignment 3.1: Modify program NEWTON to calculate the Joule-Thomson inversion temperature using Eq. 3.3. Test data for CO_2: $A_0 = 5.0065$, $B_0 = 0.10476$, $C = 66 \times 10^4$. Calculated inversion T: 1183 K.

Assignment 3.2: Modify program NEWTON to calculate the pH of a weak acid. Test data: $KA = 1 \times 10^{-5}$, $CA = 0.15$, $pH = 2.91373$. Rather than entering an initial guess, let the computer calculate it from the acid concentration (for example, $X = CA/10$). The program should use the hydrogen ion concentration as the variable (X) but calculate the pH at the end. Note that most microcomputers do not implement log base 10, so you must use:

$$pH = -LOG(X)/LOG(10)$$

(The approximation for LOG(10), 2.303, found in most books is not sufficiently accurate in many situations; if you don't want to calculate this quantity each time, at least use 2.30258. Also, don't use KA as the name for the dissociation constant if DEFINT I-N is used.)

Numerical Derivatives: The Secant Method

One of the annoyances of Newton's method is the need to program a statement for the derivative as well as the function. This is a particularly tedious and error-prone procedure for equilibrium problems (Eq. 3.7, for example). One alternative is to use a numerical approximation for the derivative; the simplest of these is:

$$f' = \frac{f(x + h) - f(x - h)}{2h} \tag{3.9}$$

This equation is exact in the limit $h \to 0$ (in which case it is the definition of the derivative); but, of course, a computer will balk at dividing zero by zero, even if the limit is finite. However, for some suitably small value of h, the approximation of Eq. 3.9 will be good enough. Because of the limited precision of a computer (or any computational device for that matter), the accuracy of Eq. 3.9 will not increase indefinitely as h decreases. For a computer with 7 significant figures, h should be about 1×10^{-3} times x; with more significant figures, a smaller value can be used. The following miniprogram should be tried with various values for the parameter S (S = H/X) to explore the accuracy of this method.

Miniprogram 3.2

```
50 DEF FNF(Z) = COS(Z)+3*Z*Z+6*Z−4
100 INPUT"X,S";X,S
110 IF ABS(X)<ABS(S)
       THEN H=S
       ELSE H=S*X
115 X1=X−H: X2=X+H
120 DX=(FNF(X2)−FNF(X1))/(2*H) 'APPROXIMATE DERIVATIVE
130 DT=−SIN(X)+6*X+6 'ACTUAL DERIVATIVE
```

140 PRINT"DERIVATIVES: APPROX=";DX,"ACTUAL=";DT
150 GOTO 100

Statement 110 chooses one of two methods for generating the increment H, depending on the magnitude of X. Try this program with various values for X and S. Note that, for use in Newton's method, the accuracy of the derivative is not crucial because the correction term of Eq. 3.8 disappears as the root is approached.

Assignment 3.3: Modify NEWTON to utilize numerical derivatives and to calculate the boiling point of carbonyl sulfide for a given pressure using Eq. 3.10, below. The vapor pressure of carbonyl sulfide (OCS) is given by:

$$\log_{10}(P/\text{torr}) = 10.15309 - \frac{1318.260}{T}$$
$$- (1.4778 \times 10^{-2})T + (1.8838 \times 10^{-5})T^2 \qquad (3.10)$$

Calculate the boiling temperature of this liquid for P= 760 torr, 750 torr and 100 torr. (Answers: 287.88 K, 287.40 K, 228.89 K).

Given any two values for x, x_n, and x_0 (which need not be close to each other), an approximate derivative can be calculated by:

$$f' \approx \frac{f(x_n) - f(x_0)}{x_n - x_0} \qquad (3.11)$$

Substituting Eq. 3.11 into Newton's formula, Eq. 3.8, gives (after some algebra which the reader should supply):

$$x_{n+1} = \frac{x_n f(x_0) - x_0 f(x_n)}{f(x_0) - f(x_n)} \qquad (3.12)$$

This formula is the basis of both the secant and the *regula falsi* method. The secant method can use any two values for x, whereas the *regula falsi* method requires values of x_n and x_0 on opposite sides of the root.

The *Regula Falsi* Method: The SGN Function

The *regula falsi* method is similar to the secant method, but uses points on opposite sides of the root in Eq. 3.12. One point, called the pivot, is kept fixed while the other is moved; Fig. 3.2 illustrates this method. The advantage of the pivot method is that only one function evaluation is required for each iterative use of Eq. 3.12. However, the speed of convergence depends on proper choice of pivot; the pivot cannot be too close to the root, for then $f(x_1)$ approaches $f(x_0)$ as the root is approached and the evaluation of the denominator of Eq. 3.12 will be subject to excessive round-off errors. On the other hand, if the pivot is too far from the root, convergence will be slow. Compared to Newton's method, *regula falsi* method is slower but more stable. Also, it does not

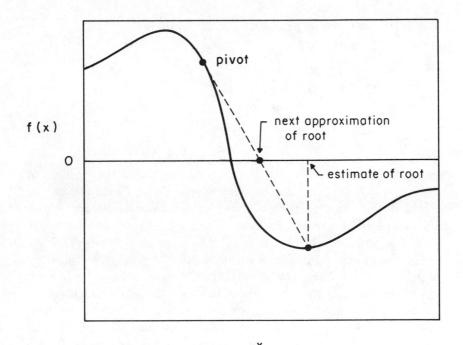

Figure 3.2: The *regula falsi* method for finding roots.

require a program statement for the derivative and is thus easier to program; this is especially advantageous for complex expressions such as those that often occur when doing equilibrium problems.

Programming the *regula falsi* method requires a way to tell when two points (X0 and X1) are on opposite sides of a root; this will be signified when the function values, Y0 = f(X0) and Y1 = f(X1), have opposite signs. This test is conveniently made using the SGN function: the function SGN(X) has a value of +1 when X>0, −1 when X < 0 and 0 when X = 0. The following miniprogram will illustrate the use of this function; you should try this program with various values for the inputs.

Miniprogram 3.3

```
10 INPUT"TWO NUMBERS";X,Y
20 PRINT SGN(X),SGN(Y),SGN(X−Y)
30 PRINT"THE SIGNS ARE ";
40 IF SGN(X)=SGN(Y)
        THEN PRINT "THE SAME"
        ELSE PRINT "DIFFERENT"
50 GOTO 10
```

Program ROOTS, below, shows one way to implement the *regula falsi* algorithm; the DEF FN statement (20) defines the problem and can be changed to suit. This program permits two kinds of searches for preliminary estimates of the roots. The manual search allows the user to type in values of X and prints out values Y = f(X). The auto search should be used when the approximate location of the root is established (in many problems, you may know this in advance); it permits input of a lower limit, upper limit and step size for search. Once the root is bracketed (as indicated by functional values of opposite sign) it proceeds with the iteration (the pivot is X2 , Y2 in this program). If the iteration does not converge after 10 trials (statement 150), it gives the user a choice: (1) continue the iteration, (2) switch pivots and continue the iteration (this can speed up convergence if the initial guess was poor), and (3) choose new limits for the search (you may, by that time, have a better idea where the root is).

PROGRAM ROOTS

```
1 CLS:'                    PROGRAM ROOTS
10 T=1E−6
12 PRINT"ROOTS BY REGULA FALSI- TOL=";T
15 PRINT"FUNCTION DEFINED AT STATEMENT 20"
20 DEF FNY(X)=X^3 +913*X^2 −1023
22 INPUT"Type <M> for manual search, <A> for auto";A$
24 IF A$="M"
      THEN GOTO 600
      ELSE IF A$<>"A"
            THEN GOTO 22
30 PRINT"LOWER LIMIT FOR SEARCH";
32 INPUT X1: Y1=FNY(X1):X=X1
40 PRINT TAB(30)CHR$(27)"UPPER";:INPUT XB
45 REM CHR$(27) SHOULD BE CHR$(30) ON IBM PC
50 PRINT TAB(45)CHR$(27)"STEP";:INPUT XS
70 X=X+XS: IF X>XB+XS/2
      THEN PRINT "NO ROOT IN THIS RANGE": GOTO 30
80 Y=FNY(X):IF SGN(Y)=SGN(Y1)
      THEN X1=X:Y1=Y: GOTO 70
      ELSE X2=X:Y2=Y:GOTO 100
100 PRINT X1;"<ROOT<";X2;:GOSUB 500  'CALC NEW X,Y
110 IF Y=0
      THEN PRINT"ROOT=";Y:STOP:GOTO 10
120 IF SGN(Y)=SGN(Y2)
      THEN X2=X:Y2=Y
      ELSE X1=X2:Y1=Y2:X2=X:Y2=Y
```

```
130 IT=0
140 GOSUB 500: IF ABS(X1−X)<T
      THEN 200
150 X1=X:Y1=Y:IT=IT+1:IF IT<10
      THEN 140
160 PRINT"CHOOSE:Switch pivot,Restart,Continue":INPUT A$
180 IF A$="C"
      THEN GOTO 130
      ELSE IF A$="R"
            THEN GOTO 30
            ELSE IF A$<>"S"
                  THEN GOTO 160
190 X=X2:Y=Y2:X2=X1:Y2=Y1:X1=X:Y1=Y:GOTO 130
200 PRINT"THE ROOT IS "X"(TOL="T")" :END
500 X=(X1*Y2−X2*Y1)/(Y2−Y1):Y=FNY(X):PRINT
510 PRINT"Y("X")="Y;:RETURN
600 INPUT"VALUE OF X";X
602 PRINT CHR$(27)"Y("X")="FNY(X),
610 PRINT"MORE?(Y/N)";:INPUT A$: IF A$="Y"
      THEN GOTO 600
      ELSE GOTO 30
```

Comments on ROOTS

The CHR$(27) in statements 40, 50, and 602 is a cursor control character; it returns the cursor to the previous line and, thereby, permits multiple inputs on the same line of the screen. This is purely cosmetic. If your computer does not support this feature, simply eliminating CHR$(27) from these lines will produce a working program with no more harm than a less attractive display. It is possible that the code is different; for an IBM PC, for example, it is CHR$(30). Check your manual to see how such things are handled by your computer. Similarly, the PRINT TAB statements should be modified to suit your screen width (the ones in this program are suitable for 64-character screens). This program contains several interesting programming tricks and is worthy of careful study. However, it is by no means an optimal program, so you should be able to improve it without difficulty.

Assignment 3.4: Test the program above (with statement 20 as it stands) using the following inputs:

Lower = 0	Upper = 10	Step = 1	Find Root = 1.05792
Lower = −10	Upper = 0	Step = 1	Find Root = −1.05914
Lower = 0	Upper = 500	Step = 500	Converges slowly.
Lower = −920	Upper = −910	Step = 1	Error may result.

The reason for the problem with the last set of inputs is that there is another root of this cubic equation at approximately X = −913. However, the program may not be able to find it because the function is so steep at that point; this problem is related to the precision of the computer's arithmetic and will vary somewhat from computer to computer. (Also, it can be improved by using double precision arithmetic). Use the "manual" part of ROOTS to see how steep the function is around X = −913.

Assignment 3.5: Use ROOTS to solve one or more of the problems you solved earlier using Newton's method.

Multiple Roots: Synthetic Division

Equations may have more than one root, and sometimes it is necessary to find all of them. A polynomial equation of degree n:

$$P_n(x) = \sum_{i=0}^{n} a_i x^i \qquad (3.13)$$

will have n roots; some may be complex. The cubic equation used as a demonstration for program ROOTS had three real roots. Your experience in finding those roots may have convinced you that, while it is possible to find the roots one by one, this procedure can have its problems. A better method is, after finding the first root, to reduce the order of the polynomial by factoring out the known root by synthetic division. If r is a root of the polynomial $P_n(x)$, then:

$$P_n(x) = (x - r) \sum_{i=1}^{N} b_i x^{i-1} + R_0 \qquad (3.14)$$

where R_0 is the remainder. If r is an exact root, the remainder will be zero; this is the basis for another method for finding roots called iterated synthetic division. Below are equations for calculating the coefficients (b_i) of Eq. 3.14 by synthetic division of Eq. 3.13; the element b_0 of this result is the remainder (R_0) of Eq. 3.14. A second synthetic division is used to produce the set of coefficients, c_i.

$$
\begin{aligned}
b_n &= a_n & c_n &= b_n \\
b_i &= r b_{(i+1)} + a_i & &(for\ i = n - 1\ to\ 0) \qquad (3.15) \\
c_i &= r c_{(i+1)} + b_i & &(for\ i = n - 1\ to\ 1)
\end{aligned}
$$

Connoisseurs of synthetic division will recognize that the remainder, b_0, is the value of the polynomial at $x = r$, while c_1 is the value of the derivative at that point. Hence, Newton's formula, Eq. 3.8, becomes:

$$r_{k+1} = r_k - \frac{b_0(r_k)}{c_1(r_k)} \qquad (3.16)$$

When the iteration is complete, as indicated by a remainder less than some tolerance, the coefficients b_i become the coefficients (a_i) of the reduced polynomial. The following program implements this procedure:

PROGRAM SYNDIV

```
1 CLS:'            PROGRAM SYNDIV
2 ' REAL ROOTS OF A POLYNOMIAL BY
        SYNTHETIC DIVISION
8 T=1E-6 'TOLERANCE, TEST FOR CONVERGENCE
10 INPUT"ORDER OF POLYNOMIAL";N
```

```
20 PRINT"ENTER COEFFICIENTS A(I)"
30 FOR I=0 TO N
40 PRINT I;
42 INPUT A(I)
44 NEXT
50 B(N)=A(N): C(N)=B(N)
55 K=0:INPUT"INITIAL GUESS FOR R";R
60 FOR I= N-1 TO 0 STEP -1
70 B(I)=B(I+1)*R + A(I)
80 C(I)=C(I+1)*R + B(I)
90 NEXT
95 IF C(1)=0
      THEN DR=1: GOTO 110
100 DR=-B(0)/C(1)
105 IF ABS(DR)<T
      THEN GOTO 200
110 R=R+DR: K=K+1
114 IF K>100
      THEN PRINT"ITER=";K: GOTO 250
120 PRINT R; : GOTO 60
200 PRINT: PRINT"THE ROOT IS";R
210 FOR I=1 TO N: A(I-1)=B(I): NEXT
220 N=N-1
230 PRINT"COEFFICIENTS OF
      REDUCED POLYNOMIAL"
240 FOR I=0 TO N
242 PRINT"A(";I;")=";A(I)
244 NEXT
250 PRINT: INPUT"TYPE <C> TO CONTINUE";A$
260 IF A$="C"
```

THEN GOTO 50

ELSE STOP

(Reference 2, page 198)

Assignment 3.6: Test the program above using the following data: N = 4, coefficients = 624, −412, 78, −16, and 1. If the initial guess is zero, the first root will probably be 2 and the reduced polynomial coefficients will be −312, 50, −14, and 1. The next root is 12 with reduced polynomial coefficients 26, −2, and 1. This quadratic equation $(x^2 - 2x + 26)$ has no real roots (solve it using the quadratic formula to prove this statement), so if the program is continued, it will go into an infinite loop (try it). (The cure for infinite loops is the <BREAK> key; more elegantly, you could put in a loop counter, as we did previously, to stop the iteration after perhaps 100 tries.) If your first root is other than 2, the reduced polynomial will, of course, be different. For example a first root of 12 gives reduced polynomial coefficients: −52, 30, −4, 1.

The Lin-Bairstow Method

The methods discussed to this point can find only real roots of a polynomial equation; from time to time it is necessary to find all roots, real and imaginary, for a polynomial equation. The Lin-Bairstow method takes advantage of the fact that roots occur in conjugate pairs, and it looks for quadratic factors, $x^2 - ux - v$:

$$P_N(x) = (x^2 - ux - v) \sum_{i=2}^{N} b_i x^{i-2} + b_1 x + b_0 \qquad (3.17)$$

(See Reference 2, page 198.) It is otherwise similar to the iterative synthetic division method discussed above. The following program will accomplish this:

PROGRAM LINBAR

1 CLS:'   PROGRAM LINBAR

```
2 ' ROOTS OF POLYNOMIAL BY LIN-BAIRSTOW METHOD
20 DEFINT I-N
30 T=1E-8' TOLERANCE, CRITERION FOR CONVERGENCE
100 INPUT"N=";N
110 PRINT"ENTER COEFFICIENTS, A(0)...A(";N;")"
120 FOR I=0 TO N: INPUT A(I): NEXT
122 IF A(N)=0
        THEN N=N-1: PRINT"ZERO ROOT": GOTO 122
124 IF N<3
        THEN GOTO 280
130 B(N)=A(N): C(N)=A(N): K=0
140 K=K+1: IF K>20
        THEN K=0: T=T*10: PRINT"CONV???";T;EP
150 B(N-1)=A(N-1)+U*B(N)
152 C(N-1)=B(N-1)+U*C(N)
154 IF N=2
        THEN GOTO 210
160 FOR I=N-2 TO 0 STEP -1
170 B(I)=A(I)+U*B(I+1)+V*B(I+2)
200 C(I)=B(I)+U*C(I+1)+V*C(I+2): NEXT
210 F=C(2)*C(2)-C(1)*C(3)
212 IF F=0
        THEN PRINT"#";:DU=DU+1:DV=DV+1:GOTO 235
220 DU=(B(0)*C(3)-B(1)*C(2))/F
230 DV=(C(1)*B(1)-C(2)*B(0))/F
235 U=U+DU: V=V+DV
240 EP=SQR(DU*DU+DV*DV)
245 IF EP>T
        THEN GOTO 140
250 D=U*U+4*V: IF D<0
        THEN GOTO 300
```

```
      ELSE GOTO 400
260 N=N-2
270 FOR I=0 TO N
272 A(I)=B(I+2)
274 NEXT
276 A(0)=A(0)+B(0)
278 A(1)=A(1)+B(1)
280 IF N>2
      THEN GOTO 130
      ELSE IF N<2
          THEN GOTO 500
          ELSE U=-A(1)/A(2): V=-A(0)/A(2): GOTO 250
300 'COMPLEX ROOTS
310 RE=U/2: W=SQR(-D)/2
320 PRINT"ROOTS: REAL,";RE;"   IMAG,";W
330 GOTO 260
400 'REAL ROOTS
410 R1=U/2+SQR(D)/2: R2=U/2-SQR(D)/2
420 PRINT"REAL ROOTS:";R1;R2
430 GOTO 260
500 IF N=1
      THEN PRINT"LAST ROOT";-A(0)/A(1)
510 PRINT"TOL=";T,"END OF ROOTS"
520 END
```

Assignment 3.7: Use the program above with the following data: N = 5, coefficients 600, −512, 321, 21, 3, and 1. The roots are (0.784571) ± i(1.03702), (1.43104) ± i(6.76015), real root −7.43124. Also solve the polynomial used as an example for the iterated synthetic division method, above.

CHAPTER 4: REGRESSION ANALYSIS

Regression analysis is a method for showing relationships between one or more dependent (or response) variables and one or more independent variables. For example, in an industrial process one may seek correlations between response variables such as product purity, color, and tensile strength and factors such as processing temperature, ambient temperature, humidity, feed rate, and so forth. This type of application, factor analysis, is a common application of regression analysis, but it is not directly the subject of this chapter; however, much of this chapter is applicable to such problems. (Reference 5 provides extensive coverage of such regression analysis.) The principal thrust of this chapter is showing relationships between a dependent variable and an independent variable where there is no question of a causal relationship — for example, the dependence of heat capacity on temperature. Such analysis is perhaps more appropriately called "curve fitting."

Curve Fitting

The problem can be stated as follows: Given a set of data points (measured values of some quantity Y *vs.* an independent variable X) and a mathematical model containing several unknown parameters (that is, an equation giving Y as a function of X), find values for the unknown parameters that best fit the data. This type of problem can be generally divided into two classes. In some cases the motivation may be to obtain a mathematical relationship for purposes of interpolation, differentiation, or integration. For example, heat capacity *vs.* temperature data are often fit to an equation of the form:

$$C_{pm} = A + BT + C/T^2 \qquad (4.1)$$

where T is the temperature in kelvins and A, B, and C are constants to be determined. Such a formula can be used for interpolation — that is, to calculate the heat capacity at temperatures other than those for which it was measured — or for integration. Integration of heat capacities is used to calculate enthalpies (Reference 2, Chapter 2), entropies (Reference 2, Chapter 3), and other thermodynamic properties. This form of curve fitting is closely related to the subjects of later chapters in this book, in particular, Chapters 6 and 8. For this type of curve fitting, polynomial functions are very popular.

A slightly different type of curve fitting arises in the case when there is a theoretical model that provides the equation for the data; the principal distinction between this and the type discussed above is that, in this case, the constants in the model have a distinct physical significance. For example, vapor pressure data (P) *vs.* T can be fit to an equation of the type:

$$\ln P = A + \frac{B}{T} + C \ln T \tag{4.2}$$

where the constant B is related to the heat of vaporization and the constant C is related to the heat capacity difference of the vapor and liquid (Reference 1, Chapter 4).

The velocity (v) of an enzyme catalyzed reaction as a function of substrate [S] concentration is given for the Michaelis-Menton Mechanism as:

$$v = \frac{k_2 E_0[\text{S}]}{K_m + [\text{S}]} \tag{4.3}$$

where E_0 is the enzyme concentration, K_m is the Michaelis constant, and k_2 is the rate constant for the decomposition of the enzyme-substrate complex (Reference 1, Section 10.10). This equation is quite different from the previous two; Eqs. 4.1 and 4.2, while distinctly nonlinear in the independent variable (T), were linear in the undetermined parameters $(A,$ $B,$ and $C)$. Equation 4.3, on the other hand, is nonlinear in the constants to be determined, and the methods to be discussed in this chapter will not apply; we shall return to the question in Chapter 8.

To fit a model having K undetermined parameters (for example, $A,$ $B,$ and C of Eq. 4.1 or 4.2) requires a minimum of K data points. If you have exactly K data points, determining the parameters is a straightforward problem in solving simultaneous linear equations. If there is a possibility of some experimental error in the data, it is preferable to have more data points than required and to find a set of parameters that best fit the data. Defining M as the number of data points, and K as the number of parameters to be fit, the problem is said to have DF degrees of freedom with:

$$DF = M - K \tag{4.4}$$

The usual criterion for "best fit" is that the sum of the squares of the deviations of the experimental points from the calculated curve is a minimum; this is called the least squares best fit. Given data points x_i and y_i, and a model $y = f(x)$, the sum of the squares of the residuals is:

$$R = \sum_{i=1}^{M} \left[y_i - f(x_i) \right]^2 \tag{4.5a}$$

The standard deviation of the points is:

$$\sigma(P) = \left[\frac{R}{M - K} \right]^{1/2} \tag{4.5b}$$

These quantities measure the vertical deviation of the points from the regression line, as shown in Fig. 4.1.

The problem is to find the function $f(x)$ that minimizes R. (This criterion assumes that the error is entirely in the independent variable, y;

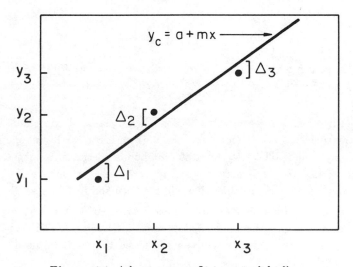

Figure 4.1: A least-squares fit to a straight line.

such is often, but not invariably, the case; all discussions in this chapter will assume that this is true.)

Linear Regression

The fitting of data to a straight line:

$$y = A + Bx \tag{4.6}$$

is the easiest and most common form of regression analysis. Its ease and simplicity are undoubtedly the reason for its wide usage and, no doubt, there are many situations where it is used inappropriately; in this computer age, we should certainly look further than straight-line models.

Many physical problems can be put into linear form by transformation of variables and/or by use of suitable approximations. For example, vapor pressure data are often analyzed as $y = \ln(P)$ *vs.* $x = 1/T$; this is just Eq. 4.2, neglecting the C term. Equation 4.3 for enzyme catalysis can be linearized as $y = 1/v$ and $x = 1/[S]$. Data for rate constants (k) as a function of temperature can be fit to the Arrhenius equation:

$$k = Ae^{-E_a/RT} \tag{4.7a}$$

which can be linearized with $y = \ln(k)$ and $x = 1/T$:

$$\ln k = \ln A - \left(\frac{E_a}{R}\right)\frac{1}{T} \tag{4.7b}$$

In kinetics, concentration (C) *vs.* time (t) data are linear for $y = \ln(C)$, $x = t$ for first-order kinetics, $y = 1/C$, $x = t$ for second-order kinetics, and so forth.

Linearizing data is not always a good idea, because it can result in an uneven treatment of errors (for example, a given error in the independent variable may weigh differently for different points so the unweighted least squares criterion, Eq. 4.5, may not be appropriate). In such cases, nonlinear analysis may be advisable; this will be discussed in Chapter 8.

The equations for linear regression are derived in Reference 1, Appendix I; Reference 4, Chapter 15; and Reference 5, Chapter 1. The following sums must be made (the names given are those that will be used in the program to follow):

$$SX = \sum x_i \qquad\qquad SY = \sum y_i$$
$$PX = \sum x_i^2 \qquad\qquad PY = \sum y_i^2 \qquad\qquad (4.8)$$
$$PC = \sum x_i\, y_i \qquad\qquad (all\ sums,\ i = 1\ to\ M)$$

After these sums are calculated, the intercept (A) and slope (B) are calculated using:

$$A = \left[\sum y_i \sum x_i^2 - \sum(x_i y_i)\sum x_i \right]/D \qquad (4.9a)$$

$$B = \left[M \sum x_i y_i - \left(\sum x_i\right)\left(\sum y_i\right) \right]/D \qquad (4.9b)$$

with

$$D = M \sum x_i^2 - \left(\sum x_i\right)^2 \qquad (4.9c)$$

The variance (σ_x^2), the square of the standard deviation, σ_x, for the x points is:

$$\sigma_x^2 = \frac{1}{M-1}\left[\left(x_i - \bar{x}\right)^2\right]$$
$$= \frac{1}{M-1}\left[\sum x_i^2 - \frac{\left(\sum x_i\right)^2}{M}\right] \qquad (4.10a)$$

where $\bar{x}$ is the average value of x. Similarly, for the y points:

$$\sigma_y^2 = \frac{1}{M-1}\left[\left(y_i - \bar{y}\right)^2\right]$$
$$= \frac{1}{M-1}\left[\sum y_i^2 - \frac{\left(\sum y_i\right)^2}{M}\right] \qquad (4.10b)$$

Note that these standard deviations have nothing to do with errors. They simply reflect the distributions of the data points; even if the data were perfectly linear, σ_x and σ_y would not be zero. However, they are used to calculate two quantities that are related to goodness-of-fit: the correlation factor (r) and the error parameter (E):

$$r = B\left(\frac{\sigma_x}{\sigma_y}\right) \qquad (4.11a)$$

$$E = \frac{1}{|r|}\left[\frac{1-r^2}{M-2}\right]^{1/2} \qquad (4.11b)$$

The correlation factor, r, will be either $+1$ or -1 for perfectly linear data. This is somewhat deceptive since $r = 0.9997$, although it seems to be appropriately close to $+1$, may in fact mean a poor fit. The parameter E is a more appropriate criterion for goodness of fit; it corresponds roughly to the "error" of the fit (that is, $E = 0.02$ corresponds to "2% error" in a loose sort of way). The standard deviations of the slope, $\sigma(B)$, and intercept, $\sigma(A)$, are given by:

$$\sigma(B) = E\,B \tag{4.12a}$$

$$\sigma(A) = \sigma(B)\left[\frac{\sum x_i^2}{M}\right]^{1/2} \tag{4.12b}$$

To get a confidence range for the likely value of the intercept or slope, these standard deviations must be multiplied by a "critical t factor"; References 1 and 4 provide tables. Roughly, for 90% confidence and more than 3 or 4 data points, a confidence interval of twice σ can be used. That is, if $\sigma = 1.2$, an error estimate of ± 2.4 would be reasonable.

The program that follows demonstrates how these formulas can be calculated.

PROGRAM LINREG

```
10 CLS'PROGRAM LINREG: LINEAR REGRESSION
20 DEFDBL S,P
30 DEFINT I-N
40 DIM DX(20),DY(20)
50 READ M
60 FOR I=1 TO M: READ X#,Y#
70 DX(I)=X#: DY(I)=Y#
80 SX=SX+X#: SY=SY+Y#
82 PX=PX+X#*X#: PY=PY+Y#*Y#
84 PC=PC+X#*Y#
90 NEXT
100 D#=M*PX−SX*SX
110 A=(SY*PX−PC*SX)/D#
```

```
120 B=(M*PC−SX*SY)/D#
130 VX#=(PX−SX*SX/M)/(M−1)
140 VY#=(PY−SY*SY/M)/(M−1)
150 RR#=B*B*VX#/VY#
152 R=SQR(RR#)
154 E=SQR((1−RR#)/(M−2))/R
160 RE=(M−1)*VY#*(1−RR#) 'APPROX RESIDUAL
170 GB=ABS(E*B) 'STANDARD DEVIATION OF SLOPE
180 GA=GB*SQR(PX/M) 'STANDARD DEVIATION OF INTERCEPT
190 GP=SQR(RE/(M−1)) 'STD DEV OF POINTS
200 PRINT"INTCPT=";A,"(STD DEV=";GA;")"
210 PRINT"SLOPE =";B,"(STD DEV=";GB;")"
220 PRINT"R=";R,"E=";E,"STD DEV PTS=";GP
230 PRINT"SUM OF SQUARES";RE
240 PRINT"THE INDIVIDUAL RESIDUALS ARE:"
242 RA=0
250 FOR I=1 TO M
252 D=DY(I)−A−B*DX(I)
254 RA=RA+D*D: PRINT D,
256 NEXT
260 PRINT"SUM OF SQUARES";RA
270 DATA 8,1,1.01,2,2.02,3,3.0,4,4.01,5,5.0,6,6.02,7,7.01,8,8.01
```

Comments on LINREG

The sums are made double precision by statement 20; this is very important so that precision is not lost in the differences calculated in statements 120 and 130. Note that this requires that the data be input as double precision numbers (X# and Y#); since data with more than 7 significant figures are rare, these are stored in single precision (in the arrays DX and DY). The residual (denoted RE; in the program R denotes the correlation factor) is calculated using the following formula:

$$RE = (M - 1)\sigma_y^2(1 - r^2) \tag{4.13}$$

At the end of LINREG, this quantity is calculated using Eq. 4.5 for purposes of comparison. In principle, Eqs. 4.5 and 4.13 should give the same answer but, in practice, round-off error may cause them to differ. The factor r^2 is kept as is (as the variable RR#) to avoid errors in calculating (1 − r^2); one result of this is that the variable R in the program is actually ABS(r); the sign of the correlation factor is rarely a concern. Some improvement in precision can be obtained by replacing statement 20 with:

20 DEFDBL A-Z

Note that statement 30 DEFINT I-N, overrides this so the variables I through N are integer, not double. However, there is a limit to the accuracy achievable because the SQR function (and most other BASIC functions) is, on most microcomputers, only done to single precision.

The test data in the program (statement 270) should give the following:

A = 0.01	$\sigma(A)$ = 6.36209E−3
B = 1.00	$\sigma(B)$ = 1.25988E−3
R = .999995	E = 1.25988E−3

$\sigma(P)$ = 7.55929E−3, Sum of squares of deviations = 4E−4. Try the program with and without the DEFDBL statement.

Assignment 4.1: Modify program LINREG to permit input of pressures in torr with $y = \log(P/\text{torr})$, and temperature in degrees Celsius with $x = 1/T$. This should require changes in only two statements. Fit the following data for the vapor pressure of CCl_4 to Eq. 4.2 (without the C term):

$t(\degree C)$	$P(\text{torr})$
30	142.3
50	314.4
70	621.1
100	1463

From this, calculate the enthalpy of vaporization and its standard deviation. Answers: $A = 17.389$, $B = -3765$, $r = -.999896$, $\sigma(A) = 0.115$, $\sigma(B) = 38.4$, $\sigma(P) = 0.01429$, $E = 0.0102$. $\Delta H_v = 31.30$ kJ/mol (std. dev. $= 0.32$ kJ/mol).

Note that linear regression cannot distinguish between random errors (for example, errors in measuring the vapor pressure, above) and model-dependent errors (for example, those caused by the fact that Eq. 4.2 without the C term is not an exact representation of the temperature dependence of vapor pressure, because its derivation assumes an enthalpy of vaporization independent of temperature).

Simultaneous Linear Equations

In order to improve on linear regression, we shall shortly discuss multiple regression and polynomial regression; but this will quickly get us into solving sets of simultaneous linear equations, so it is necessary to discuss that topic first. (Actually, even linear regression required solving two simultaneous equations [Reference 1, Appendix I], but that is easily done; the solution of three or more equations is more involved.)

A general set of N equations in N unknowns can be written as follows:

$$\sum_{j=1}^{N} A_{ij} X_j = C_i \qquad (for\ i = 1\ to\ N) \qquad (4.14)$$

The coefficients, A_{ij} form an array (or matrix) of numbers that, in BASIC, would be denoted A(I,J). Reference 2, Chapter 5, has a discussion of the various methods for solving systems of equations such as Eq. 4.14. The subroutine (SLE) that follows is based on a program in Reference 2 (pp. 286-296); an explanation of its use follows.

SUBROUTINE SLE

10000 'SUBROUTINE SLE
      SIMULTANEOUS LINEAR EQUATIONS

10010 'N is the number of equations, QA(N,N+1) is the matrix
        of coefficients
10020 'Set Flag FL%: −1 matrix inv only, +1 SLE only,
        FL%=0 for SLE with inverse in place.
10050 'Solutions returned as BB(N) (not dbl),determinant as DT
10055 'DIMENSION STMT REQUIRED FOR QA(N,N+1), BB(N),
        JC(N), IR(N), JO(N), VY(N);
        DEFINT I-N RECOMMENDED
        DEFDBL Q MAKES IT DOUBLE PRECISION
10060 DT=1:MZ%=N:IF FL%>=0
        THEN MZ%=N+1
10070 EP= 1E−12' SMALLEST PERMITTED VALUE OF
        DETERMINANT
10080 FOR K=1 TO N
10090 PV#=0
10100 FOR I=1 TO N
10110 FOR J=1 TO N
10120 IF K=1
        THEN 10180
10130 FOR IS=1 TO K−1
10140 FOR JS=1 TO K−1
10150 IF I=IR(IS)
        THEN 10200
10160 IF J=JC(JS)
        THEN 10200
10170 NEXT JS,IS
10180 IF ABS(QA(I,J))<=ABS(PV#)
        THEN 10200
10190 PV#=QA(I,J):IR(K)=I:JC(K)=J
10200 NEXT J,I

```
10210 IF ABS(PV#)<EP
      THEN DT=0: PRINT"DETERMINANT ZERO":RETURN
10220 DT=DT*PV#
10230 FOR J=1 TO MZ% :QA(IR(K),J)=QA(IR(K),J)/PV#:
      NEXT J
10240 QA(IR(K),JC(K))=1/PV#
10250 FOR I=1 TO N
10260 QA=QA(I,JC(K))
10270 IF I=IR(K)
      THEN 10320
10280 QA(I,JC(K))=-QA/PV#
10290 FOR J=1 TO MZ%
10300 IF J<>JC(K)
      THEN QA(I,J)=QA(I,J)-QA*QA(IR(K),J)
10310 NEXT J
10320 NEXT I,K
10330 FOR I=1 TO N:JO(IR(I))=JC(I)
10340 IF FL%=>0
      THEN BB(JC(I))=QA(IR(I),MZ%)
10350 NEXT I
10360 IN=0
10370 FOR I=1 TO N-1
10380 FOR J=I+1 TO N
10390 IF JO(J)>=JO(I)
      THEN 10410
10400 JT=JO(J):JO(J)=JO(I):JO(I)=JT:IN=IN+1
10410 NEXT J,I
10420 IF 2*INT(IN/2)<>IN
      THEN DT=-DT
10430 IF FL%>0
```

THEN RETURN

10440 FOR J=1 TO N

10450 FOR I=1 TO N

10460 VY(JC(I))=QA(IR(I),J)

10470 NEXT I

10480 FOR I=1 TO N

10490 QA(I,J)=VY(I):NEXT I

10500 NEXT J

10510 FOR I=1 TO N

10520 FOR J=1 TO N

10530 VY(IR(J))=QA(I,JC(J)):NEXT J

10540 FOR J=1 TO N

10550 QA(I,J)=VY(J):NEXT J

10560 NEXT I

10570 RETURN

Comments on Subroutine SLE

The coefficients for the set of equations whose dimension is N are in a matrix QA with dimension QA(N, N + 1); the coefficients A_{ij} of Eq. 4.14 are in the first N columns with QA(I, J) = A(I, J) and I = 1 to N, J = 1 to N. The coefficients on the right-hand side of Eq. 4.14, C_i, are in the N + 1 column of QA, with QA(I, N + 1) = C(I). The solutions, x_i of Eq. 4.14, are returned in the vector BB(I). The inverse of the coefficient matrix (A_{ij}^{-1}) is calculated and returned in the first N columns of QA; after the subroutine is used, QA(I, J) is equal to the I, J element of the inverse matrix. The comments at the beginning of the subroutine tell you what DIM statements are needed and explain the options available using the "flag" variable, FL% (which must be set by the program using this subroutine).

Subroutine SLE will be used in a number of programs in this book. You should read your manual to learn to MERGE it with other programs. If this is not possible, or if you don't want to bother, simply LOAD SLE before typing in the code for the program that uses it. (Keep extra copies.) It is recommended that the numbering system used by this book be used generally — that is, the numbers usually need not be exactly the same, but they should be in the same range.

The following program, used together with subroutine SLE, can be used for testing and, generally, for solving any system of simultaneous equations by providing appropriate DATA statements.

PROGRAM SIMLINEQ

```
1 ' DRIVER PROGRAM FOR SLE: PROGRAM SIMLINEQ
10 DEFINT I-N
50 DIM QA(9,10), BB(9),JC(9),IR(9), JO(9), VY(9)
200 READ N 'NUMBER OF EQUATIONS
210 FOR I=1 TO N
220 FOR J= 1 TO N+1
230 READ QA(I,J)
240 A(I,J)=QA(I,J)
250 NEXT
260 NEXT
280 FL%=0: GOSUB 10000
290 PRINT"SOLUTIONS:";
300 FOR I=1 TO N: PRINT BB(I);: NEXT
310 PRINT
320 PRINT"INVERTED MATRIX"
330 FOR I=1 TO N
340 FOR J=1 TO N: PRINT QA(I,J),:NEXT
350 PRINT:NEXT
360 PRINT"DETERMINANT=";DT
400 PRINT "UNIT MATRIX CHECK"
410 FOR I = 1 TO N
```

```
420 FOR J = 1 TO N
430 U = 0.0
440 FOR K = 1 TO N
450 U = U + A(I,K)*QA(K,J)
460 NEXT K
470 PRINT U;
480 NEXT J
490 PRINT
500 NEXT I
700 DATA 3,   0,−7, 4, 1,   1, 9, −6, 1,   −3, 8, 5, 6
800 DATA 3,   2, −7, 4, 9,   1, 9, −6, 1,   −3, 8, 5, 6
900 DATA 3,   −3, 8, 5, 6,   2, −7, 4, 9,   1, 9, −6, 1
990 A$=INKEY$: IF A$<>""
        THEN GOTO 200
        ELSE GOTO 990
10000 'SIMULTANEOUS LINEAR EQUATIONS
```

Comments on SIMLINEQ

Test data for SIMLINEQ: The first DATA statement (700) is for the set of three equations (calling the variables x, y, z):

$$0x - 7y + 4z = 1$$
$$1x + 9y - 6z = 1$$
$$-3x + 8y + 5z = 6$$

The solution for this (and the other two sets as well) is $x = 4$, $y = 1$, and $z = 2$. (Substitute these values into the original equations, above, to prove that these are indeed the correct solutions.)

One of the pitfalls in solving linear equations is that one or more of the equations could be linearly dependent (or almost so); such a system of equations is called "ill-conditioned" and cannot be solved accurately. A simple example is:

$$2x + 4y = 8$$
$$x + 2y = 4$$

This set of equations has no unique solution.

A good diagnostic for such situations is the determinant of the coefficients, which will be zero if any of the equations are linearly dependent. (For the DATA statements in SIMLINEQ, above, the determinants [DT in SLE] are 49, 235, and 235 respectively.) The determinant need not be exactly zero for the problem to be ill-conditioned. In a case such as:

$$2.00001x + 4.00001y = 8$$
$$x + 2y = 4$$

the problem is solvable (the solution is $x = -4.4$, $y = 4.2$), but the solutions are extremely sensitive to small changes in the coefficients that could be caused by round-off error. (Try it on your computer. Do you get the same answer?) If the first coefficient is changed to 2.00002, the solutions change to -1.44262 and 2.72131. The determinants for these cases are on the order of 1×10^{-5}. (Actually, the magnitude of the determinant also depends on the order of magnitude of the coefficients and solutions; it is a good idea to keep these of magnitude 1; see comments about scaling, below.)

Multiple Regression

Suppose we have some quantity y that is a function of x, and that is not adequately fit by a straight line. An equation of the following form can be used:

$$y = a + b_1 f_1(x) + b_2 f_2(x) + b_3 f_3(x) + \cdots \qquad (4.15)$$

For example, for polynomial regression we could use $f_1(x) = x$, $f_2(x) = x^2$, and so forth. For determining the coefficients of Eq. 4.1, $y = C_{pm}$, $f_1 = T$, and $f_2 = 1/T^2$. For Eq. 4.2, $y = \ln(P)$, $f_1(x) = 1/T$, and $f_2(x) = \ln(T)$. The program that follows, MULTIREG, uses a method described by Reference 2 (p. 573) and the subroutine SLE discussed above. As it is currently set up, it will fit data to a cubic polynomial: $Y = A + B(1)*X + B(2)*X*X + B(3)*X*X*X$. [Note: the slope array is BB(I) in the program, but is called B(I) for the output.]

PROGRAM MULTIREG

```
1 CLS' PROGRAM MULTIREG
5 'DEFDBL A-Z
10 DEFINT I-N
20 DIM QA(4,5),BB(4),JC(4),IR(4),JO(4),VY(4) 'FOR SLE
30 DIM SX(4),SY(4),VA(4), DX(30), DY(30)
40 DEF FNF(K,X)=-(K=1)*X-(K=2)*X^2-(K=3)*X^3
50 N=2 'NUMBER OF TERMS TO USE IN FNF(STMT 40)
100 CLS: 'COMMAND CENTER
105 IF M>0
     THEN GOSUB 2900: PRINT
110 PRINT TAB(10)" COMMANDS:
     <R> FOR DATA INPUT AND REGRESSION"
120 PRINT TAB(10)"<I> TO INTERPOLATE"
130 PRINT TAB(10)"<Q> TO QUIT"
150 A$=INKEY$: IF A$=""
     THEN 150
     ELSE J=INSTR("RIQ",A$)
160 ON J GOTO 2000,3000,900
190 GOTO 100
900 END: GOTO 100
2000 CLS:READ M: PRINT " X"," Y", M;" POINTS"
2010 FOR I=1 TO M: READ X,Y
2012 DX(I)=X: DY(I)=Y
2014 PRINT X,Y
2020 SY=SY+Y: SX=SX+X: YY=YY+Y*Y
2030 FOR K=1 TO N
2040 SX(K)=SX(K)+FNF(K,X)
2050 SY(K)=SY(K)+Y*FNF(K,X)
```

```
2060 FOR L=K TO N
2070 QA(K,L)=QA(K,L)+FNF(K,X)*FNF(L,X)
2080 NEXT L,K,I
2100 FOR K=1 TO N
2105 FOR L=K TO N
2110 QA(K,L)=QA(K,L)-SX(K)*SX(L)/M
2120 QA(L,K)=QA(K,L)
2130 NEXT L
2140 QA(K,N+1)=SY(K)-SY*SX(K)/M
2150 NEXT K
2160 FL%=0: GOSUB 10000: A=SY/M
2170 FOR I=1 TO N: A=A-BB(I)*SX(I)/M: NEXT
2172 SS=0: PRINT"DEV OF PTS",
2174 FOR I=1 TO M: X=DX(I): GOSUB 9500: D=DY(I)-Y
2176 PRINT D,: SS=SS+D*D: NEXT
2178 SS=SS/(M-N-1):PRINT
2180 FOR I=1 TO N: VA(I)=QA(I,I)*SS
2200 FOR J=1 TO N: SA=SA+SX(I)*SX(J)*QA(I,J)/M
2210 NEXT J,I
2218 SA=SA*SS/M
2230 GOSUB 2900
2300 PRINT"HIT ANY KEY TO RETURN"
2310 A$=INKEY$: IF A$=""
     THEN 2310
     ELSE 100
2500 DATA 6, 1,6, 2,11.01, 3,17.99, 4,27.01, 5,37.99, 6,51.01
2900 PRINT"INTERCEPT";A;"(STD DEV";SQR(SA);")"
2910 FOR I=1 TO N:
     PRINT"B(";I;")=";BB(I);"(";SQR(VA(I));")"
2920 NEXT: PRINT"STD DEV OF PTS";SQR(SS): RETURN
```

3000 'INTERPOLATION

3010 INPUT"VALUE OF X";X: GOSUB 9500

3020 PRINT"Y(";X;")=";Y

3030 PRINT"<R> to return, else to continue"

3040 A$=INKEY$: IF A$=""

    THEN 3040

3050 IF A$="R"

    THEN GOTO 100

    ELSE GOTO 3010

3900 GOTO 100

9500 Y=A 'SUBROUTINE FOR CALCULATING Y=F(X)

9510 FOR K=1 TO N: Y=Y+FNF(K,X)*BB(K): NEXT

9520 RETURN

10000 'SLE ...

Comments on MULTIREG

The DEFDBL statement (5) currently has a single quote in front, making it a REMark; remove the single quote to improve accuracy. Subroutine SLE must be in memory (Statements 10000–). Statement 50 means that only the first two terms of FNF (40) will be used; change it to N = 3 for a cubic equation. The data in statement 2500 should fit a quadratic polynomial (N = 2) with (standard deviations in parentheses):

$$\text{Intercept A} = 3.00903 \ (.0219688)$$
$$\text{Slope B(1)} = 1.99401 \ (.0143726)$$
$$\text{Slope B(2)} = 1.0009 \ (.00201)$$

(These data were generated by adding small errors to the equation: $y = 3 + 2x + x^2$) The "STD OF PTS" is as defined by Eq. 4.5b with degrees of freedom $(M - N - 1)$ where N is defined in statement 50 and M is the number of data points. Try fitting these data to a cubic polynomial (*i.e.* set N = 3 in statement 50). What is the cubic coefficient? Does the fit (as judged by the STD OF PTS) improve? Try the program in double precision.

The DEFFN statement (40) illustrates an interesting use of logical expressions. A logical statement is the type that is usually used in IF . . . THEN statements. For example, in

$$IF\ K = 1\ THEN\ .\ .\ .$$

the logical expression is (K = 1) and the action will be taken if this expression is true (that is, K is equal to one); if the expression is false (K is not equal to one) then the ELSE clause (if any) or the next statement (in the absence of an ELSE clause) is executed. These logical expressions have numerical values, namely, -1 if *true* and 0 if *false*, and can be used as such in statements other than IF . . . THEN statements. This convention may be different on your computer; for example, on an Apple II, the value is $+1$ for *true*. The following miniprogram should be tried to illustrate this idea and to determine the logical values used by your computer.

Miniprogram 4.1

```
10 INPUT"THREE NUMBERS";A,B,C
20 PRINT A,B,C
30 PRINT (A=B),(A=C),(A<>B),(A<>C)
40 X=123*(A=B)+456*(A=C)+789*(A<>C)
50 PRINT X
60 GOTO 10
```

Now think about statement 40 in MULTIREG; what does it do each time it is used? If your computer does not permit multiple arguments in DEFFN statements, the K could be eliminated from the argument list, so long as it is set correctly in the program before FNF is used; be careful about using K as a variable for other purposes in such cases. Also, if your *true* value is $+1$, the negative signs in statement 40 should be eliminated.

Assignment 4.2: Modify program MULTIREG to fit data to Eq. 4.2. Use your program to fit the following data for the vapor pressure of cadmium:

T (kelvins)	P(torr)	T (kelvins)	P(torr)
600	0.124	850	57.24
650	0.627	900	127.9
700	2.492	950	261.6
750	8.187	1000	496.5
800	23.06		

The answers should be (standard deviation in parenthesis): $A = 28.72$ (0.13), $B = -13447$ (13), $C = -1.31$ (0.02). The standard deviation of points is 6.3E$-$4.

Assignment 4.3: Fit the heat capacity data below, for NH_3, to Eq. 4.1.

T	C_{pm}	T	C_{pm}
300	35.56	700	47.00
400	38.82	800	49.59
500	41.68	900	52.15
600	44.38	1000	54.70

Answers: $A = 29.736$ (0.006), $B = 0.02512$ (0.000007), $C = -1.54 \times 10^5$ (5×10^2), $\sigma(P) = 2.06 \times 10^{-3}$. Interpolate: C_{pm} (550) = 43.04, C_{pm} (750) = 48.30. (Note: These data were generated from an equation like Eq. 4.1 — this is the reason the fit is so good.)

Data Scaling

As mentioned earlier, microcomputers are usually rather limited in terms of the magnitudes of numbers they can handle; the largest number is usually 1E38 and the smallest meaningful number is usually 1E$-$38. Consider polynomial regression with a variable (such as the Kelvin temperature) with order of magnitude 1E3. Fourth-order regression requires making sums of powers of X up to 4; the determinant will be of order of magnitude X to the power $4^2 = 16$. If X = 1E3, then the determinant could be as large as 1E48. In other words, overflow is quite likely. Also, if X<<1 the size of some of the terms could become too small to be meaningful. As mentioned earlier, a near-zero determinant could be an indication of an ill-conditioned problem, but it can also be a result of using variables with very small magnitude. (Generally, microcomputers do not give an error indication for "underflow" — the number is simply set to zero.)

Once you realize what is happening, the problem with overflow or underflow is easy to rectify. For example, if your variable is temperature (in kelvins), simply use X = T/100 instead of X = T. Similarly, 1000/T can be used in place of 1/T. This is another reason for keeping an eye on the size of the determinant (DT) and using the error-handling procedures outlined at the end of Chapter 2. Even so, regression with polynomials of order greater than 6 is likely to cause problems; in program POLYREG (below), a maximum order of 6 will be assumed. (Your program MULTIREG should be modified to print DT, and the ON ERROR and RESUME statements should be added as described at the end of Chapter 2.)

Assignment 4.4: Use your program for vapor pressure of cadmium with X = T/100; explain how the coefficients of this calculation are related to those calculated earlier.

Polynomial Regression

Of the various types of multiple regression, polynomial regression is, by far, the most widely used and generally applicable. It is used for data smoothing, interpolation, and extrapolation. Those who have never used it tend to overestimate its power and generality. In principle, it can fit any and all functions; in practice, the limitations of finite mathematics (limited precision and magnitude numbers) severely limit its scope. Polynomial extrapolation is a dangerous procedure when carried out in ignorance. It is legitimate to use polynomial extrapolation, for example, to extrapolate certain types of results to infinite dilution (that is, concentration → 0) if it is certain, theoretically, that the function is well-behaved in this limit. On the other hand, heat capacity data between 300 and 1000 K, fit to a polynomial or even an equation like Eq. 4.1, should not be extrapolated outside of this range. Clearly, program MULTIREG can handle polynomials, but polynomials have special features that make it possible to write a better program that is, however, strictly limited to polynomial regression. In polynomial regression, you will want to vary the degree (N) until the sum of squares (or standard deviation of the points) is a minimum, so a program that permits this coefficient to be input and changed is desirable.

The following subroutine will calculate the best-fit polynomial (degree N) for M data points in arrays DX(I) and DY(I). The intercept is denoted AA, and the slopes as BB(J). It is assumed that this program segment (it is not, strictly, a subroutine) is accessed from a Command Center at statement 100. After the user chooses the order (N), the coefficients are calculated and printed. The approximate standard deviation of the points (S) is also printed. Then the user is given a choice: $<A>$ do the calculation again with another order; $<R>$ (return) go to statement 100; $<S>$ calculate the exact standard deviation of the points (S, the first calculation was done in a way that could give spurious results, especially for very accurate data) and the standard deviations of the parameters. If the approximate S, the first one displayed, is followed by a "?," the approximate calculation failed and the exact calculation must be done. (However, the absence of the "?" does not necessarily mean the value is reliable. It would certainly be possible to do the correct sum of squares each time, but this is time-consuming, especially when you are playing around trying to find the best N to use for a given set of data. It will be faster to do the exact calculation after the optimum value of N is determined.)

SUBROUTINE PREG

4000 'POLYNOMIAL REGRESSION: M POINTS STORED IN DX(M),DY(M)

4010 'REQUIRES DIM STMT FOR DX(M),DY(M),BY#(2*N),SX#(2*N),
     and SY#(2*N) where M is the number of data points and N is the
     highest-order polynomial to be used. Data are in arrays DX and
     DY. Uses SLE subroutine 10000, coef. will be in BB(I).

4020 CLS' use DEFDBL Q for better accuracy. (Ref. 2, pp. 576-581)

```
4030 IF M<8
     THEN KK=M-2
     ELSE KK=6
4040 PRINT"......order of polynomial N<=";KK;
4050 INPUT K:IF K<=0
     THEN 100
     ELSE N=K
4060 DN=M-N-1 'DEGREES OF FREEDOM
4070 IF DN<=0
     THEN PRINT"? ? ?";:GOTO4040
4080 PRINT CHR$(27)"order N="N" points M="M" DF="DN" DET=";
4090 SY#=0: YY#=0
4100 FOR I=1 TO N
4110 SX#(I)=0 :SX#(N+I)=0 :SY#(I)=0 :NEXT I
4120 FOR I=1 TO M: X=DX(I): Y=DY(I)
4130 SY#=SY#+Y :YY#=YY#+Y*Y :DU#=1
4140 FOR J=1 TO N
4150 DU#=DU#*X :SX#(J)=SX#(J)+DU#
4160 SY#(J)=SY#(J)+Y*DU# :NEXT J
4170 FOR J=N+1 TO 2*N :DU#=DU#*X
4180 SX#(J)=SX#(J)+DU#
4190 NEXT J,I
4200 'COMPUTE COEFFICIENTS
4210 QM=1/CDBL(M) :BY#=YY#-SY#*SY#*QM
4220 FOR I=1 TO N :BY#(I)=SY#(I)-SY#*SX#(I)*QM
4230 QA(I,N+1)=BY#(I)
4240 FOR J=1 TO N
4250 QA(I,J)=SX#(I+J)-SX#(I)*SX#(J)*QM
4260 NEXT J,I
4270 FL%=1:GOSUB 10000 ' SLE QA(row,col),BB(I),N
4280 PRINT DT:IF DT=0
```

```
        THEN PRINT"DET=0":STOP:GOTO 100
4290 DU#=SY# :TE#=BY# :SA#=1
4300 FOR I=1 TO N: QX=SX#(I)*QM
4310 DU#=DU#-BB(I)*SX#(I)
4320 TE#=TE#-BY#(I)*CDBL(BB(I))
4330 FOR J= 1 TO N
4340 SA#=SA#+SX#(J)*QX*QA(I,J)
4350 NEXT J
4360 NEXT I
4370 AA=DU#*QM
4380 IF TE# >0
        THEN S=SQR(TE#/DN)
        ELSE S=-SQR(-TE#/DN)
4390 SA=S*SQR(QM*SA#)
4400 PRINT"A=";AA;"B(I)=";
4410 FOR I=1 TO N
4420 PRINT BB(I);
4430 NEXT: PRINT
4440 PRINT"S=";S;
4450 IF S<0
        THEN PRINT"?"
        ELSE PRINT"/"
4460 PRINT STRING$(18,45);"<Again,Return,Stat>";STRING$(18,45)
4470 B$=INKEY$:IF B$=""
        THEN 4470
4480 IF B$="S"
        THEN GOSUB 4500 :GOTO 4460
4490 IF B$="A"
        THEN PRINT CHR$(27);STRING$(56,95):GOTO 4040
        ELSE IF B$="R"
```

```
          THEN GOTO 100
          ELSE GOTO 4470
4500 S=0:PRINT TAB(15) CHR$(27);CHR$(27);"actual S=";
4510 FOR J=1 TO M:X=DX(J)
4520 GOSUB 9400 :Y=Y−DY(J)
4530 S=S+Y*Y : NEXT
4540 S=SQR(S/DN):PRINT S;
4550 IF N<>0
          THEN GOTO 4590
4560 SY=SQR(CSNG(YY#−QM*SY#*SY#)/(M−1))
4570 SX=SQR(CSNG(SX#(2)−QM*SX#(1)*SX#(1))/(M−1))
4580 R=SX*BB(1)/SY:PRINT" ","R=";R
4590 PRINT" Standard Deviations";:IF N<>1 THEN PRINT
4600 SA=S*SQR(QM*SA#) :PRINT"(A)";SA;"(B)";
4610 FOR I=1 TO N :PRINT S*SQR(QA(I,I)); :NEXT
4620 PRINT:RETURN
```

Note: The use of this program requires SLE (at 10000) and a subroutine at 9400 to evaluate the polynomial (see subroutine UPOLY, below). If your computer does not support the STRING$ function, delete them all. For an IBM PC, change all CHR$(27) to CHR$(30).

Once you have done the regression analysis, it is likely that you will want to do something with the results. Subroutine UPOLY, below, provides routines for interpolation, differentiation, and integration using the polynomial calculated by PREG.

SUBROUTINE UPOLY

```
9000 CLS' POLYNOMIAL EVAL, DIFFERENTIATION, INTEGRATION
9010 PRINT:PRINT"COMMANDS:Return,Function,Derivative,Integral";
9020 PRINT TAB(45);:INPUT A$: K=INSTR("FDIR",A$)
```

```
9030 ON K GOTO 9050, 9090, 9150, 100
9040 GOTO 9010
9050 INPUT"AT X=";X:PRINT TAB(20)CHR$(27);
9060 GOSUB 9400
9070 PRINT"F(";X;")=";Y;
9080 GOTO 9020
9090 INPUT"AT X=";Z:PRINT TAB(20)CHR$(27);: F=0
9100 FOR I=1 TO N
9110 F=F+I*BB(I)*Z^(I-1)
9120 NEXT
9130 PRINT"DF(";Z;")=";F;
9140 GOTO 9020
9150 REM
9160 PRINT"INT FROM";:INPUT Z1:PRINT TAB(20)CHR$(27);"TO";
9170 INPUT Z2: PRINT TAB(34)CHR$(27);"INT=";
9180 F=AA*(Z2-Z1)
9190 FOR I=1 TO N
9200 F=F+(BB(I)/(I+1))*(Z2^(I+1) -Z1^(I+1))
9210 NEXT
9220 PRINT F;
9230 GOTO 9020
9400 Y=0:' SUBROUTINE TO EVALUATE POLYNOMIAL-
9410 FOR K= N TO 1 STEP -1
9420 Y=Y*X+BB(K)
9430 NEXT
9440 Y=Y*X+AA
9450 RETURN
```

Assignment 4.5: Write a program (POLYREG) that incorporates SLE (which you should have already), PREG and UPOLY. You will need to supply a command center and code for data input: number of points = M, data arrays, DX(I) and DY(I). The following code must precede the program:

```
1 '                    PROGRAM POLYREG
4 CLEAR 1000 'NEEDED FOR TRS80/III;
       CHECK YOUR MANUAL
10 DEFDBL Q 'OPTIONAL
20 DEFINT I-N
30 DIM DX(50),DY(50),BY#(12),SX#(12),SY#(12)
40 DIM QA(6,7),BB(6),JC(6),IR(6),JO(6),VY(6) 'FOR SLE
90 ON ERROR GOTO 990
```

Error-handling statements must be placed at 990. The dimension statements above assume no more than 50 data points and a maximum order of 6 (7 = order + 1, and 12 = 2 times order). The test data used earlier for MULTIREG can be used to test your program. You should get exactly the same results.

Assignment 4.6: One of the major uses for polynomial regression is for extrapolation. For example, the extrapolation of equivalent conductances (Λ) to infinite dilution (Λ°). The data below are for the equivalent conductance of KCl; use them to determine the equivalent conductance at infinite dilution for this salt.

C (concentration)	Λ(Eq. Cond.)
0.0005	147.81
0.001	146.95
0.005	143.55
0.01	141.27
0.02	138.34
0.05	133.37

If you fit these data to a power series in concentration (C), the best fit will be (standard deviation in parentheses.): N = 3, Λ° = 148.065 (0.281), S = 0.338. (Your program may fail for N = 4; try it.) A better procedure is to regress *vs.* the square root of concentration, SQR(C); modify your program to do this (change the input statements, not the DATA statement). The best result for this method is: N = 3, Λ° = 150.01 (0.012), S = 5.74×10^{-3}. There are sound theoretical reasons for using the square root, and clearly this works best from the numerical point of view. The moral is that a computer is not a substitute for thinking. (These data are from S. Maron and J. Lando, *Fundamentals of Physical Chemistry*, 1974: New York, Macmillan Publishing Co., Inc., page 507, who give Λ° = 149.86 from the same data.)

Assignment 4.7: The following apparent equilibrium constants (K") for the dissociation of acetic acid were measured using conductance (Reference 1, Table 8.9).

$C \times 10^5$	$K'' \times 10^5$
11.135	1.7689
21.844	1.7694
136.340	1.7856
344.065	1.7922
599.153	1.7982
984.21	1.8036

C is the concentration of the acetic acid. Extrapolate these results *vs.* SQR(C) to C = 0 to determine the thermodynamic equilibrium constant (K, the intercept). Answer: 1.758×10^{-5} with third-order regression in SQR(C).

Assignment 4.8: Another common application of polynomial regression is for interpolation and integration of data tables. (These topics are discussed further in Chapters 5 and 6 of this book.) The data below are for the constant-volume molar heat capacity (C_{vm}) of carbon dioxide. Use these data to interpolate the value of C_{vm} at 500 K (Answer: 36.195 J/K with N = 3) and to calculate the change in the internal energy (ΔU) when this gas is heated from 500 to 1500 K (answer: 44833 J/mol with N = 3).

$$\Delta U = \int_{500}^{1000} C_{vm}\,dT \qquad (4.16)$$

T(K)	C_{vm} (J/K)
298.15	28.81
400	33.00
600	39.00
800	43.11
1000	45.98
1500	49.05
2000	52.02

(These data are from W. J. Moore, *Physical Chemistry*, 1972: Englewood Cliffs, N.J., Prentice-Hall, Inc., page 148. The datum at 1500 has been corrected for an apparent misprint.) You may find it necessary to use X = $T/100$ as your variable, in which case, you'll have to think carefully how to enter data and interpret results for the interpolation and integration.

Assignment 4.9: Use MULTIREG to fit the data above to an equation of the form of Eq. 4.1. The results should be: $A = 38.70$ (1.71), $B = 7.106E-3$ (1.2E-3), $C = 1.139E6$ (0.183E6) and $S = 1.425$. Interpolated heat capacity at 500 K, 37.70.

Assignment 4.10: Add code to POLYREG and MULTIREG for plotting the data points (arrays DX and DY) and the fitted curve. The following code will calculate a set of points in arrays AX and AY for plotting purposes:

```
5000 INPUT"X1,X2, and step size";X1,X2,XS: I=0
```

```
5010 FOR X=X1 TO X2+XS/2 STEP XS
5020 GOSUB 9400
5030 AX(I)=X: AY(I)=Y: I=I+1
5040 NEXT X
5050 MX=I−1 'Maximum points in calc. array
5060 GOTO 100
```

In statement 5010, the upper limit is set at X2+XS/2 to ensure that the last point is calculated. BASIC permits the use of noninteger variables in FOR . . . NEXT loops, but this feature must be used with caution because round-off error can cause problems.

Cautions about POLYREG

Polynomial regression is not a cure-all, and if done blindly (without plotting and inspecting the results), it can be highly deceptive. For that reason the reader is strongly encouraged to provide some sort of plot program for POLYREG. The point will be illustrated with data for the compressibility, $z = PV_m/RT$, for methane at 204 K (the data are from Reference 2, page 133, and are given in Chapter 5 of this book).

Figure 4.2 shows a graph of z vs. P for methane at 203 K. Compressibilities are often represented as power series vs. P or $1/V$. This is called the *virial series* (Reference 1, Chapter 1). An attempt to fit these data using POLYREG gave the following standard deviations of points (S) (X = P/1000 was used to keep the determinant from overflowing): N = 3, S = 0.15757; N = 4, S = 0.104052; N = 5, S = 0.0640624 with intercept A = 1.03404. Note that since all gases become ideal ($z = 1$) as $P \to 0$, the intercept should be equal to 1. This seems to be progressing satisfactorily, so trying N = 6 seems worthwhile: N = 6, S = 0.053508, A = 1.08531. It would appear reasonable to conclude that a 6th-order polynomial is satisfactory for representing these data − until you do the plot (solid line, Figure 4.2).

Perhaps the data of Figure 4.2 could be fit by a higher-order polynomial. The restriction to polynomials of order 6 in POLYREG is rather artificial; it could be increased by changing the DIM statements, and a few

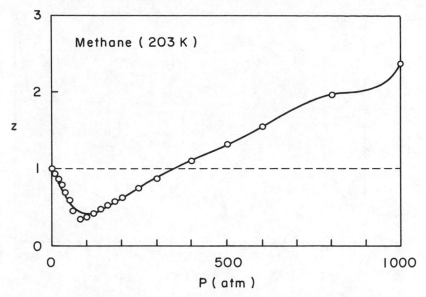

Figure 4.2: Compressibility of methane vs. P at 203 K.

others; however, this will exacerbate the inherent problems with precision and magnitude of numbers. Polynomials are inherently limited (and program execution times become very long), so the point of diminishing returns is soon reached.

Figure 4.3 shows a more pathological case. Here, a graph of $1000(z - 1)/P$ is shown *vs.* P (P/1000 was used for regression). (The purpose of this function is discussed in Chapter 5 of this book and in Reference 1, Chapter 6.) The 6th-order polynomial "fit" (S = 0.714) is clearly unreasonable. The moral is: *polynomial functions can give good sums of squares, and pass through or near all points, without necessarily giving a realistic or correct function.* (Even worse cases can be found than those shown; be especially suspicious if you get an excellent value for S only with one degree of freedom, DF = 1.)

Any reasonable person can see where the curves of Figures 4.2 and 4.3 should lie, but POLYREG cannot figure it out; it is clear that we have some information that we are not sharing with the computer. This information involves the smoothness of the function, and this involves the likely values for its derivatives. There are better ways; for example, *spline*

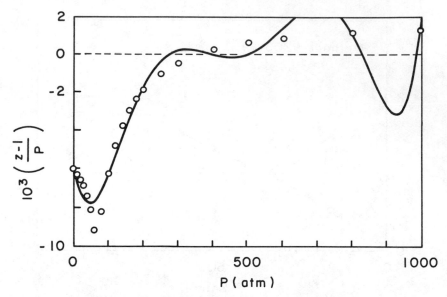

Figure 4.3: The failure of a polynomial fit.

functions will fit a set of points with a curve that has the least mean-squared curvature. This is a piece-wise method — that is, only the nearest points are used to interpolate the fitting function. Cubic splines will give a fitted curve that is continuous with a continuous first derivative. Other methods will be discussed in Chapter 6.

CHAPTER 5: NUMERICAL INTEGRATION

There are two types of problems for which numerical integration is useful. Sometimes the function to be integrated is represented by a data table (as opposed to an equation), and it is necessary to calculate the integral of this function. In this case, curve fitting, as described in Chapter 4, can be used to obtain a formula for integration, but it is also possible to integrate the table directly. In other applications, the function may be represented by a formula that cannot be integrated analytically using the methods of calculus. The simplest example of such a case is:

$$F(x) = e^{-x^2} \tag{5.1}$$

whose integral between finite limits must be calculated numerically. This chapter will discuss a number of numerical methods for calculating integrals, beginning with the simplest.

The Trapezoidal Rule

The geometrical meaning of an integral is that it is the area under the function. Suppose you know two points of some function, $y_0 = f(x_0)$ and $y_1 = f(x_1)$. The area under the function could be approximated as the area under the trapezoid defined by these points, which, in turn, is the area of a square whose height is the average of y_0 and y_1 (see Figure 5.1):

$$Area \approx \frac{1}{2}(y_1 + y_0)(x_1 - x_0) \tag{5.2}$$

If the function is defined by $N + 1$ points (numbered $I = 0$ to N), the area can be approximated by repeated application of Eq. 5.2 for each pair of points, and summing the areas of the N intervals (see Figure 5.2):

$$Area = \frac{1}{2} \sum_{i=1}^{N} (y_i + y_{i-1})(x_i - x_{i-1}) \tag{5.3}$$

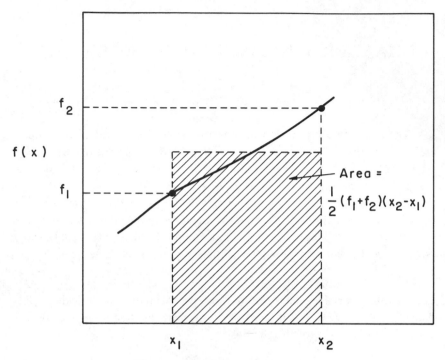

Figure 5.1: The trapezoidal rule.

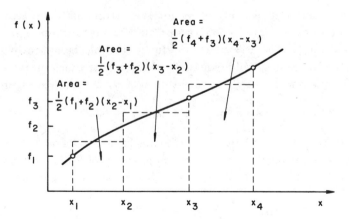

Figure 5.2: Integration over multiple intervals.

Equation 5.3 is the trapezoidal rule. This is more often given in books for the special case of equally spaced base points; if each successive pair of points is separated by an interval $h = \Delta x$, then Eq. 5.3 is easily shown to become:

$$Area = \frac{h}{2} \left[y_0 + 2y_1 + 2y_2 + \ldots + 2y_{n-1} + y_n \right] \qquad (5.4)$$

The last form is, no doubt, the one you would use for formula integration — that is, in the case that you have a formula for calculating the base points. However, in such a case, there are better methods, which will be described later in this chapter. The principal utility of the trapezoidal rule is for the integration of data tables, where an equation is not available, and, as such, Eq. 5.3 is the most generally useful.

The following program will READ sets of points, calculate the cumulative integral using Eq. 5.3, and print the results. (An INPUT statement could be used as well, but for the assignments to follow you will probably find the READ . . . DATA method of input to be the easiest.)

PROGRAM TRAP

```
400 A = 0 'AREA
410 READ X,Y
420 X1=X: Y1=Y 'FIRST POINT, SAVED
430 READ X,Y
440 A = A + 0.5*(Y+Y1)*(X−X1)
450 PRINT X,Y,"AREA=";A
460 GOTO 420
490 DATA ...
```

This program is as simple as it can be. Of course, it will end inelegantly with an "OUT OF DATA" error message. Note that the points must be in order with respect to the independent variable X. The trapezoidal rule is exact for linear functions, so TRAP can be tested using data from an equation such as $y = 4 + 2x$; for which the area from $x = a$ to b is:

$$Area = 4 \, (b - a) + (b^2 - a^2)$$

Using:

490 DATA 0,4, 1,6, 2,8, 5,14

the calculated area should be 45.

Applications: Data Table Integration

One application of data table integration is using measured heat capacities to calculate thermodynamic functions. For example, the enthalpy change (ΔH) on heating a material between T_1 and T_2 is:

$$\Delta H = n \int_{T_1}^{T_2} C_{pm}\, dT \tag{5.5}$$

where C_{pm} is the molar heat capacity. Similarly, the entropy change (ΔS) for the same process is:

$$\Delta S = n \int_{T_1}^{T_2} \frac{C_{pm}}{T}\, dT \tag{5.6a}$$

Using the relationship for the derivative of a logarithm, $d(\ln x) = dx/x$, this equation can be rewritten as:

$$\Delta S = n \int_{\ln T_1}^{\ln T_2} C_{pm}\, d(\ln T) \tag{5.6b}$$

It appears that the second form of Eq. 5.6 is generally more suitable for numerical analysis because C_{pm} vs. $\ln T$ is usually a smoother function than C_{pm}/T vs. T. This is something we shall test in the assignments below.

Assignment 5.1: The data below are for the heat capacity of solid benzene.

$T(K)$	C_{pm} (cal/K)	$T(K)$	C_{pm} (cal/K)	$T(K)$	C_{pm} (cal/K)
13	0.685	14	0.830	15	0.995
20	2.000	25	3.145	30	4.300
35	5.385	40	6.340	50	7.885
60	9.065	70	9.975	80	10.750
90	11.430	100	12.050	120	13.310
140	14.700	160	16.230	180	18.020
200	20.010	220	22.320	240	24.880
260	27.760	278.69(mp)	30.760		

Modify TRAP so the heat capacity is automatically converted to joules; this can be done by adding to statements 410 and 430, the statement $Y = 4.184 * Y$ (this must be separated from the current part of these statements by a colon).

(a) Use TRAP to calculate the enthalpy change for heating benzene from 13 K to its melting point (278.69 K). Answer: $\Delta H = 17659$ J/mol.

(b) Use TRAP to calculate the entropy change for heating benzene from 13 K to its melting point. Use both Eqs. 5.6a and 5.6b. (Modify only the input statements, *not* the DATA statements.) Answer: $\Delta S = 128.55$ J/K and 128.77 J/K respectively.

(c) If you have a PLOT program, make the graphs C_{pm}/T vs. T, and C_{pm} vs. $\ln(T)$. These are given by Reference 1, Figure 3.8. This will demonstrate that C_{pm} vs. $\ln(T)$ is the smoother function and, for this case at least, will be better for use with the trapezoidal rule.

Another application of numerical integration is calculating the fugacity coefficients (γ, Reference 1, Chapter 6) from measured compressibility factors, $z = PV_m/RT$. The ratio of the fugacity coefficients, γ_1 at P_1 and γ_2 at P_2 is given by:

$$\ln\left(\frac{\gamma_2}{\gamma_1}\right) = \int_{P_1}^{P_2}\left(\frac{z-1}{P}\right) dP \tag{5.7}$$

This, of course, gives only a ratio, so another method must be used to obtain the value of γ at one pressure. If the lower pressure is small (for example, 1 atm), the fugacity coefficient can be calculated using:

$$(low\ P) \qquad \gamma = e^{BP/RT} \tag{5.8}$$

where B is the second virial coefficient (which can be calculated as described in Chapter 2). Another method for doing this is described in Reference 1, section 6.6.

Assignment 5.2: Use the data below for the compressibility factor of methane at $70\,^\circ$C, and program TRAP, to calculate the fugacity coefficients of methane at $P = 10$ atm, 100 atm, 500 atm, and 1000 atm relative to its fugacity coefficient at 1 atm. Answers: 0.946, 0.477, 0.309, and 0.534. (These data are shown on Figures 4.2 and 4.3.)

P(atm)	z	P(atm)	z	P(atm)	z
1	0.9940	10	0.9370	20	0.8683
30	0.7928	40	0.7034	50	0.5936
60	0.4515	80	0.3429	100	0.3767
120	0.4259	140	0.4753	160	0.5252
180	0.5752	200	0.6246	250	0.7468
300	0.8663	400	1.0980	500	1.3236
600	1.5409	800	1.9626	1000	2.3684

Beyond the Trapezoidal Rule

For the integration of functions defined by formulas, there are a number of methods to obtain better accuracy over the trapezoidal rule; several of these will be discussed later in this chapter. However, for data table integration, the options are somewhat limited. The improved methods, such as Simpson's rule, place requirements on the number and location of the base points: for example, that there must be an odd number of equally spaced base points, which will not ordinarily be met by data tables.

One option, already discussed in Chapter 4, is to fit the data points to a polynomial. However, this method works well only for smoothly varying functions − precisely the case where the trapezoidal rule works well. The assignment above, the fugacity calculation for methane, is a good example of a case for which polynomial regression will not work.

Also, the calculation of the entropy of benzene using Eq. 5.6a also cannot be done using POLYREG. (The other two calculations, the enthalpy and the entropy using Eq. 5.6b, will work; but the results are not necessarily more accurate than those achieved with the trapezoidal rule.)

Assignment 5.3: Make a graph of $(z-1)/P$ *vs.* P for the methane data above. If your POLYREG program has a graphics routine, try to use it with these data and plot the resulting polynomial. The results for N = 6 are bizarre (*cf.* Fig. 4.3). Even if you do not have a way to plot functions on your computer, it would be worthwhile to print the calculated function and graph it by hand. You could do the same using Eqs. 5.6a and 5.6b with the benzene data above (see Reference 1, Figure 3.8).

There are formulas for calculating integrals with unequally spaced base points that have an accuracy comparable to Simpson's rule; however, the formulas are rather complicated (see Reference 1, Appendix I). A more attractive method, which will work if the data are reasonably precise and reasonably spaced over the integration interval, is to use interpolation to convert the unequally spaced base points into equally spaced base points required for Simpson's or Romberg's methods (below); this will be discussed in Chapter 6.

Simpson's Rule

If the base points of the function to be integrated are evenly spaced, and there are an odd number of these points (an even number of intervals in the calculation; see Figure 5.3), Simpson's rule offers an attractive improvement over the trapezoidal rule for the same amount of calculation. In fact, for function integration, when there is no restriction of the location of the base points (since they are calculated as you please), there is no reason to use a method less accurate than Simpson's rule. The formula for $n + 1$ points numbered $I = 0$ to n (n intervals, where n is an *even* number) is:

$$Area = \frac{h}{3}[y_0 + 4y_1 + 2y_2 + 4y_3 + \cdots + 4y_{n-1} + y_n] \quad (5.9)$$

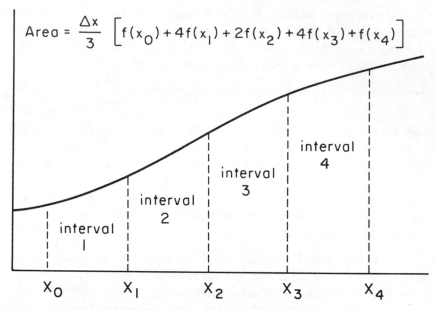

$$\text{Area} = \frac{\Delta x}{3}\left[f(x_0) + 4f(x_1) + 2f(x_2) + 4f(x_3) + f(x_4)\right]$$

interval 4

interval 3

interval 2

interval 1

x_0 x_1 x_2 x_3 x_4

Figure 5.3: Simpson's rule for 4 intervals (5 base points).

where $h = \Delta x$ is the spacing of the independent variable, x (see Figure 5.3). For programming Eq. 5.9, we note that the first and last points are multiplied by 1, while the points in between are multiplied by 4 if the index (I) is an odd number, and multiplied by 2 if I is even. Therefore, the first thing we must do is to train the computer to recognize the difference between odd and even numbers; this can be done using the INT function. The function INT(X) returns the integer part of the argument — that is, the argument is truncated to an integer. The following miniprogram will illustrate this:

Miniprogram 5.1

```
10 INPUT"ANY NUMBER"; K : PRINT INT(K)
20 PRINT "YOUR NUMBER IS ";
30 IF K<>INT(K) PRINT"NOT AN INTEGER": GOTO 10
40 IF K/2=INT(K/2)
```

> THEN PRINT"AN EVEN INTEGER"
> ELSE PRINT"AN ODD INTEGER"

50 GOTO 10

Try various inputs — positive, negative, integer or not — with this program and observe and explain the results. What is the effect of INT on negative numbers? For example, is −3.3 truncated to −3 or −4? Will the odd/even choice (above) work for negative integers?

Assignment 5.4: Write a program (named SIMPSON) to evaluate an integral using Simpson's rule. The function should be defined by:

30 DEF FNY(X) = · · · (insert code for appropriate function)

The limits for the integral (X1 and X2) should be checked to be certain that X2 > X1, and the number of intervals (N) should be checked to be certain that N is an even number (if not, print an appropriate admonition and go back to the INPUT statement). The summation variable (A) can be initialized with the first and last points: A = FNY(X1) + FNY(X2). Then, the summation of the other terms from I = 1 to N − 1 can be made. The following code demonstrates one way to do the alternating sum of Eq. 5.9.

740 FOR I=1 TO N−1: X=X1 + H∗I
750 IF I/2=INT(I/2)
> THEN A=A+2∗FNY(X)
> ELSE A=A+4∗FNY(X)

Can you think of a way of writing 750 without the IF . . . THEN . . . ELSE? (Hint: remember the trick used in MULTIREG.) Remember to multiply the result by (H/3), but do this after the summation to save time.

The function:

F(X) = X∗EXP(−X∗X)

provides a convenient test, since the integral can be done exactly. (Do it!) The following results can be used to test your program (all for X1 = 0):

Upper Limit	Integral
1	0.316060279
2	0.490842180
5	0.500000000

Note that the last case, X2 = 5, is the same as the integral to infinity — that is, the integral above X = 5 is effectively zero. Try various values for the number of intervals to get a feeling for the accuracy of this program. Your program should, at the end, provide the following options: <H> change intervals, <L> change limits, <R> return to 100.

Assignment 5.5: The function $F(X) = EXP(-X*X)$ cannot, as stated earlier, be done between finite limits. The integral from zero to infinity, however, can be calculated as $\sqrt{\pi}/2$. Use program SIMPSON to confirm this result. What is "infinity" for this function?

Assignment 5.6: The Maxwell-Boltzmann distribution function (Reference 1, Chapter 1) for the speeds (v) of molecules in a gas as a function of molecular weight (M) and temperature (T) is:

$$f(v)\, dv = \frac{4}{\sqrt{\pi}} e^{-w^2} w^2 dw \qquad (5.10)$$

with

$$w = v/\sqrt{2RT/M}$$

R is the gas constant (in erg/K or J/K, depending on the unit system you are using). Modify program SIMPSON to calculate the fraction of chlorine molecules ($M = 70.906$ g/mol) with speeds between 0 and 200 m/s, 200 and 400 m/s, and so forth, for T = 300 K and 1000 K. Some results are given below for testing your program:

speed (m/s)	at 300 K	at 1000 K
0 - 200	0.231871	—
200 - 400	—	—
400 - 600	0.191337	—
600 - 800	—	0.239766
800 - 1000	—	—
1000 - 1200	—	—
1200 - 1400	—	5.67×10^{-3}

[All calculated with N = 20 intervals.]

Assignment 5.7: Calculate the fraction of molecules in a gas that have kinetic energies greater than kT, if the gas is hydrogen or oxygen at $T = 300$ K or $T = 1000$ K.

Assignment 5.8: The diffusion equation:

$$\frac{\partial C}{\partial t} = D \frac{\partial^2 C}{\partial x^2} \tag{5.11}$$

relates the rate of change of concentration (C) with time (t) and distance (x) to the diffusion constant D. Typically, for a small molecule in a non-viscous solvent, $D \approx 1 \times 10^{-5}$ cm^2/sec. The solution to this equation for "step-function" initial $(t = 0)$ boundary conditions is:

(at $t = 0$, $C = C_0$ for $x < 0$ and $C = 0$ for $x > 0$)

$$C(x,t) = C_0 \left[\frac{1}{2} - \frac{1}{\sqrt{\pi}} \int_0^\xi e^{-\xi^2} d\xi \right] \tag{5.12}$$

where $\xi = x/\sqrt{4Dt}$ (see Reference 1, Figure 9.7).

For $C_0 = 1$ mol/liter, calculate the concentration at $t = 600$ sec and $x = 0.01$, 0.1, 0.2, and 0.5 cm. Answers: 0.463632, 0.180655, 0.0339447,

2.71×10^{-6}. What do you get for negative values of x? What is the concentration at $x = 1$ cm and -1 cm after one day?

Integration Errors: Richardson Extrapolation

Both the trapezoidal rule and Simpson's rule involve approximations and errors that disappear only as the interval h approaches zero. You have probably discovered by now that checking the accuracy of your results by using successively smaller values of h is rather tedious, to say the least. The error (E) for using the trapezoidal rule, Eq. 5.4, can be shown to be (Reference 2, Chapter 2):

$$E = (h^3/12)f''(\xi)$$

For Simpson's rule, the error is:

$$E = (h^5/90)f^{iv}(\xi)$$

where ξ is some value of x in the intergration interval, f'' is the second derivative of the function, and f^{iv} is the fourth derivative. Thus, the trapezoidal rule is exact for linear functions (for which $f'' = 0$), and Simpson's rule is exact for cubic polynomials.

Assignment 5.9: Use program SIMPSON with a cubic polynomial function to show that Simpson's rule is exact for such functions, regardless of the number of intervals used (N = 2 is, of course, the minimum).

The formulas above are of little practical use because the information required to calculate the errors is generally missing. However, they do suggest a way to improve accuracy. Consider the use of the trapezoidal rule for an interval H; the leading error term will be KH^3 where K is an unknown constant. If the interval is now halved to $h = H/2$, the error will be $2Kh^3$ (times two because there are two steps in the calculation). The areas and leading error terms are now:

> interval: $H = 2 \times h$ Area: A_0 Error: $8Kh^3$
> interval: h Area: A_1 Error: $2Kh^3$

If one now calculates:

$$A_2 = (4A_1 - A_0)/3 \qquad (5.13)$$

this estimate of the integral will be more accurate than the preceding ones because the leading error term has been canceled. This is called the Richardson extrapolation. In fact, the error is now on the order of that for Simpson's rule.

Assignment 5.10: Write a program (RICH) to use the trapezoidal rule and the Richardson extrapolation to integrate the function used earlier— X*EXP(−X*X). The evaluation of the integral by Eq. 5.4 should be a subroutine, because it has to be used twice for different values of H. Compare its speed and accuracy to SIMPSON. Sample data: For X1 = 0, X2 = 1, and number of steps = 20 (40 the second time through), the estimated areas are: A0 = 0.315775, A1 = 0.315989, A2 = 0.316060. What is the correct answer?

Romberg Integration

The Richardson extrapolation is still small comfort — it is as accurate as Simpson but not particularly faster. Also, we still do not know what the error is. Consider the following: The trapezoidal rule is used to calculate an area A_0 with an interval H ; then the interval is halved and another area (A_1) is calculated. These are used to calculate an extrapolated area (B_1) with Eq. 5.13. Then the interval is halved again and an area (A_2) is calculated; A_1 and A_2 are used to calculate an extrapolation B_2. The extrapolations B_1 and B_2 are then used to calculate another extrapolation (C_2). This procedure is continued until two successive estimates of the area are the same within some predetermined tolerance. This process can be diagrammed as follows:

Interval H: area A_0
Interval $H/2$: area A_1 extrap. B_1
Interval $H/4$: area A_2 extrap. B_2 extrap. C_2 (from B_1 and B_2)
etc.

This method is called Romberg integration. The program that follows implements this method (for details, see Reference 2, pages 90-93; also Reference 3).

PROGRAM ROMBERG

```
1 CLS'              PROGRAM ROMBERG
10 DEFINT I-N
20 DIM A(20,20)
30 DEF FNF(X)=X*EXP(-X*X)
80 T=1E-6 'TOLERANCE FOR ACCURACY OF INTEGRAL
1000 REM  Program ROMBERG  for integration of functions
1010 NC=6:N1=4' NC IS # CYCLES; N1 SETS INITIAL INTERVAL
1020 INPUT"X1,X2 ";X1,X2
1030 H=(X2-X1)/N1
1040  GOSUB 1190:A(0,0)=A:PRINT A
1050 FOR K=1 TO NC
1060 N1=N1*2: H=H/2
1070 GOSUB 1190:A(0,K)=A:PRINT A,
1080 FOR L=1 TO K
1090 A(L,K)=(4^L*A(L-1,K)--A(L-1,K-1))/(4^L-1)
1100 PRINT A(L,K),
1110 IF ABS((A(L,K)-A(L-1,K))/A)<T
        THEN 1160
1120 NEXT L
1130 PRINT
1140 NEXT K
1150 K=K-1:L=L-1
1160 PRINT
1165 PRINT"...FINI...AFTER ";N1;"INTERVALS:AREA=";A(L,K)
1170 END
```

1190 SU=(FNF(X2)+FNF(X1))/2

1200 FOR I=1 TO N1−1

1210 X=X2−I*H

1220 SU=SU+FNF(X)

1230 NEXT

1240 A=SU*H:RETURN

Comments on ROMBERG

The criterion for convergence (T) is set in statement 80. In statement 1010, the initial interval is set (N1) to 1/4 of the total interval; this is fairly arbitrary and you may want to experiment to find the most efficient method. The maximum number of cycles, NC, is arbitrarily set to 6, although the matrix (A) is dimensioned by statement 20 to hold up to 20 iterations; you may wish to change this as well. What is the purpose of the subroutine at 1190?

Assignment 5.11: Use program ROMBERG with the function X*EXP(−X*X), whose integral was given earlier. Compare its accuracy and speed with SIMPSON. Then modify ROMBERG, using statements 1000 onward as a subroutine, to do the diffusion calculation of Eq. 5.12. The test data given earlier can be used.

Assignment 5.12: The work of a reversible expansion ($-w$ with the convention used in Reference 1) of a gas is given by:

$$-w = \int_{V_1}^{V_2} P dV \qquad (5.14)$$

Use ROMBERG to calculate the work for a gas obeying the Beattie-Bridgeman equation of state:

$$P = \frac{nRT}{V} + C_1\left(\frac{n}{V}\right)^2 + C_2\left(\frac{n}{V}\right)^3 + C_3\left(\frac{n}{V}\right)^4 \qquad (5.15)$$

where

$$C_1 = -A_0 + B_0 R T - cR/T^3$$
$$C_2 = aA_0 - bB_0 R T - cB_0 R/T^2$$
$$C_3 = bcB_0 R/T^2$$

For carbon dioxide, the Beattie-Bridgeman constants are: $A_0 = 5.0065$, $a = 0.07132$, $B_0 = 0.10476$, $b = 0.07235$, $c = 66.0 \times 10^4$. (More values can be found in Reference 1, Table 1.2). You must use V in liters and P in atmospheres, with $R = 0.082057$ liter-atm/K. For testing the program, the ideal gas calculation can be done by using:

30 DEF FNF(V) = R*TE/V 'TE IS THE TEMPERATURE

and compared to the theoretical result:

$$-w = RT \ln \left(\frac{V_2}{V_1} \right) \tag{5.16}$$

The following results (for carbon dioxide) can be used for testing your program.

For volume change from 1 to 50 liters, work in liter-atm:

T	C_1	C_2	C_3	$-w$(ideal)	$-w$(BB)
400	-1.56883	0.0728272	0.0244894	128.404	126.915
650	0.580893	$-.060627$	0.00927409	208.656	209.206

For $T = 800$ K:

	V_1	V_2	$-w$(ideal)	$-w$(BB)
	1	100	302.309	304.099
	0.5	50	302.309	305.742

Note that the ideal and BB results are closest at 650 K, which is the Boyle temperature of carbon dioxide. (Since your program calculated the pressures, you may as well incorporate a statement to print the pressures at the upper and lower limits.)

Assignment 5.13: Debye's theory for the heat capacity of atomic solids gives the following formula:

$$C_{vm} = 9R \left(\frac{T}{\theta} \right)^3 \int_0^{\theta/T} \frac{u^4 e^u}{(e^u - 1)^2} \, du \qquad (5.17\text{a})$$

where T is the temperature in kelvins, and θ is the Debye characteristic temperature, which is determined empirically for each substance. For silver, $\theta = 229$ K. Modify ROMBERG to do this calculation. Several problems may arise. The first may occur when e^u is evaluated for low temperatures (when the upper limit of the integral is very large); if θ/T exceeds 87.5, overflow may result. The equation is better for numerical computation in the mathematically equivalent form:

$$C_{vm} = 9R \left(\frac{T}{\theta} \right)^3 \int_0^{\theta/T} \frac{u^4 e^{-u}}{(1 - e^{-u})^2} \, du \qquad (5.17\text{b})$$

Even so, a problem will occur when the lower limit of the integral is requested by ROMBERG; when $u = 0$, the integrand is indeterminate (0/0). The limit is easily shown to be zero, but the computer doesn't know that. One way around this problem is to make the lower limit small but nonzero; X1 = 1E−5 seems to work. A better solution is to modify the subroutine that calculates the integral so that FNF(X1) is automatically presumed to be zero. SIMPSON could also be used for this calculation, but because the limits of the integral and the number of steps required varies so much with temperature, ROMBERG will be the most convenient method. (Which calculation is the more difficult, high T or low T? Why?) Do the calculation for $T = 1$ to 1000 and graph the results (a log scale for T will be more revealing). Some results for testing are (for Ag):

T(K)	C_{vm} (J/K)	T(K)	C_{vm} (J/K)
1	1.619×10^{-4}	10	1.619×10^{-1}
20	1.2816	50	10.51
100	19.46	300	24.23
1000	24.89		

Rationalize your results with the law of Dulong and Petit and the Debye T-cubed law. Could this theory give reasonable results for Ag at 2000 K? Note that the calculations at 1 K and 10 K (above) have the same significant figures. Is this a coincidence? Try it for Al ($\theta = 375$ K) and Na ($\theta = 160$ K). Another interesting material you may wish to try is diamond, $\theta = 1860$ K. How do the heat capacities of Ag, Al, Na, and diamond compare at room temperature?

CHAPTER 6: INTERPOLATION

Suppose you have a set of experimental data — a set of measurements of some quantity (y) as a function of an independent variable (x): $y = f(x)$. This chapter will discuss the manipulation of these data for the following purposes: (1) Interpolation; this may be required because you need to know the value of y for some x for which it has not been measured. Also, you may need an evenly spaced set of (x,y) data for purposes of plotting a smooth curve through the data. (2) You may need to calculate the integral of the data. As we saw in the previous chapter, the best methods of integration require knowing the value of the function at arbitrary values of the independent variable — not necessarily the ones available. (3) You may need to calculate some quantity related to the differential of the data. (4) Interpolation would permit data table functions to be used in root problems such as those described in Chapter 3.

Interpolation *vs*. Curve Fitting

In this chapter you will learn how to solve by interpolation such problems as those stated above. Emphasis is placed on methods that do not require evenly spaced points; this is the only case worth doing, for it is not generally practical to obtain evenly spaced data. (Suppose you are measuring heat capacities. It would not be unreasonable to measure them at constant T intervals, but if you wanted to calculate entropies, you would need them in evenly spaced intervals of $\ln(T)$. Similarly, you would need to measure vapor pressures in evenly spaced intervals of $1/T$ in order to use the Clausius-Clapeyron equation. Anything is possible, of course, but sticking to methods that do not make such requirements seems like the best idea.) The interpolation methods covered in this chapter use a polynomial of degree N between $N + 1$ points.

Such problems can, as discussed in Chapter 4, also be solved by curve fitting. However, interpolation is generally a simpler and faster procedure and will be better in many cases. One of the disadvantages of interpolation is that it provides no smoothing — that is, noise (random fluctuations caused by experimental errors) is not removed as it would be in a least-squares fit. For that reason, interpolation is best suited for fairly precise data. On the other hand, polynomial curve fitting is, as we have seen, no panacea. If the data set is very large and changes sharply over the interval, polynomial regression is apt to fail. Of course, interpolation uses polynomials and could fail as well under the same circumstances; however, it is better suited for use in piece-wise fits where only the data nearest the interpolant are used. For example, if you needed to interpolate for a value of x in a data set of 20 points, the nearest 4 points could be used with a cubic interpolation; then only the smoothness of the data set over those 4 points will affect the calculation. (POLYREG could be used in such a piece-wise fashion, but this would be rather complicated and slow.)

Lagrangian Interpolation

The linear interpolant of $y = f(x)$ from two base points is given by:

$$y = y_1 + \left[\frac{y_2 - y_1}{x_2 - x_1}\right](x - x_1) \tag{6.1}$$

This is simply the point-slope formula for a straight line with $(y_2 - y_1)/(x_2 - x_1)$ as the slope. This can be rearranged as:

$$y = \frac{(x - x_2)\,y_1}{(x_1 - x_2)} + \frac{(x - x_1)\,y_2}{(x_2 - x_1)} \tag{6.2}$$

Equation 6.2 is the Lagrange formula for the two-point case. For three points, the formula is:

$$y = \frac{(x - x_2)(x - x_3)\,y_1}{(x_1 - x_2)(x_1 - x_3)} + \frac{(x - x_1)(x - x_3)\,y_2}{(x_2 - x_1)(x_2 - x_3)}$$
$$+ \frac{(x - x_1)(x - x_2)\,y_3}{(x_3 - x_1)(x_3 - x_2)} \tag{6.3}$$

(What is the value of the function when the interpolant x is one of the base points?) The general formula for Lagrange interpolation is:

$$y = \sum_{i=1}^{N} \frac{Q_i \, y_i}{P_i}$$

(6.4)

$$P_i = \prod_{i \neq j} (x_i - x_j) \qquad Q_i = \prod_{j \neq i} (x - x_j)$$

where the symbol $i \neq j$ means the product of factors for all values of j, excluding the case $i = j$. (Compare Eq. 6.4 to Eq. 6.3 to see what these symbols mean.) The following program implements this method:

PROGRAM LAGRANGE

```
10 DEFINT I-N
20 DIM DX(10), DY(10), P(10), Q(10)
200 READ L$,N 'LABEL AND NUMBER OF POINTS
210 FOR I=1 TO N
220 READ X,Y
230 DX(I)=X: DY(I)=Y: NEXT
300 'CALCULATE P FACTORS
310 FOR I=1 TO N
320 P(I)=1
330 FOR J=1 TO N
340 IF I=J
        THEN 360
350 P(I)=P(I)*(DX(I)-DX(J))
360 NEXT J
370 NEXT I
380 DATA HEAT CAPACITY OF BENZENE,4,200,83.7, 240,104.1
381 DATA 260,116.1, 278.69,128.7
400 PRINT"INTERPOLATION FOR ";L$
410 INPUT"VALUE OF X";X
420 FOR I=1 TO N: Q(I)=1
430 FOR J=1 TO N
```

```
440 IF I=J
      THEN 460
450 Q(I)=Q(I)*(X-DX(J))
460 NEXT J
470 NEXT I
480 Y=0 'SUMMATION TO GET Y
490 FOR I=1 TO N
500 Y=Y+DY(I)*Q(I)/P(I)
510 NEXT
520 PRINT"Y(";X;")=";Y
530 GOTO 410
```

Comments on LAGRANGE

The base points are stored in the arrays DX and DY. The "Q" factors must be calculated for each interpolant, but the "P" factors are calculated only once for the whole data set. This means that the program (as written) will be useful only for small data sets (6 or so). If LAGRANGE is used with, for example, 40 data pairs, you are in effect fitting them to a 40th-order polynomial. The problem with overflow or underflow discussed earlier (see POLYREG) will be encountered. One solution to this problem would be to modify LAGRANGE to use only the data points nearest the interpolant. This way is rather inefficient, since the "P" factors would need to be recalculated for each interpolant. A better way is to use the technique to be discussed in the next section: Newton's divided difference method.

Assignment 6.1: Use LAGRANGE as written (for the heat capacity of benzene, in J/K) to interpolate values at 220, 250 and 270 K. (Answers: 93.4, 109.7, 122.7) The experimental value at 20 K is 8.4 J/K; what does LAGRANGE say? Interpolation methods should not be used for extrapolation, calculating values outside the range of the base points, except for very small distances, and then only with caution and trepidation.

Assignment 6.2: Use the data below for the viscosity (η) of water as DATA for LAGRANGE:

$T(°C)$	$\eta(mp)$
0	17.921
10	13.077
20	10.05
30	8.007
40	6.560
50	5.494

The value interpolated at 25 °C should be 8.967 mp; the experimental value is 8.937 mp. Viscosities are known to be nearly linear on a $\ln(\eta)$ *vs.* $1/T$ plot; modify LAGRANGE to convert the input data to this scale, accept a temperature in degrees celsius, and print out the viscosity (not $\ln(\eta)$). Now recalculate the viscosity at 25 °C; now your answer should be much closer to the experimental value. Use the modified program to interpolate for the following temperatures (experimental viscosities in parenthesis): 5 (15.188), 45 (5.988), 55 (5.064), 100 (2.838). Note that the last two are extrapolations. Once again we encounter a situation in which an appropriate choice of variable can produce greatly superior results.

Newton's Divided Difference Method

Again, let's start with the linear case. Suppose you had a set of N data points; for each pair you calculated a slope (or divided difference):

$$D_i = \frac{y_{i+1} - y_i}{x_{i+1} - x_i} \tag{6.5}$$

Then, given a value for x, you would search through this table until you found two values that bracketed the interpolant, and the linear interpolation of Eq. 6.1 would be:

$$y = y_i + D_i(x - x_i) \tag{6.6}$$

The advantage of this method is that the difference table is calculated only once; however, it is exact only for linear function. This method could be made more accurate by calculating second divided differences from the table of D's:

$$S_i = \frac{D_{i+1} - D_i}{x_{i+1} - x_i} \quad \text{with} \quad D_{i+1} = \frac{y_{i+2} - y_{i+1}}{x_{i+2} - x_{i+1}} \tag{6.7}$$

Then, three points $(i, i+1$ and $i+2)$ can be used to interpolate for a value x in the range x_i to x_{i+2}:

$$y = y_i + D_i(x - x_i) + S_i(x - x_i)(x - x_{i+1}) \tag{6.8}$$

This interpolation will be exact for a quadratic polynomial. The procedure can be carried to higher differences, as far as the data permit. (For Nth-degree differences, a minimum of $N + 1$ points are required.)

The major advantage of the divided difference method, *vis-à-vis* the Lagrange method for example, is that the difference table is calculated only once. Then, for each interpolant, the program need only decide which entries on the table are closest and calculate the interpolated value.

The program below (DIVDIF) will do the divided difference interpolation described above and several other things as well; we shall discuss these extensions before describing the program. (A more detailed description of the method is provided by Reference 2, Chapter 1.)

Integration and Differentiation

Given a method that can, from an arbitrarily spaced data set, calculate values for any value of the independent variable, either Simpson's or Romberg's methods can be used for integration. In the program below, Simpson's method is used because the accuracy is limited, in any case, by the accuracy of the data and the interpolation. However, Romberg's method would work as well and perhaps better.

In Chapter 4, it was pointed out that the derivative in an interval $x - h$ to $x + h$ could be approximated by:

$$\frac{df}{dx} \approx \frac{f(x+h) - f(x-h)}{2h} \tag{6.9}$$

However, this method is somewhat limited because, if h is small enough for good accuracy, the subtraction in the numerator could lose precision.

Equation 6.9 is exact for quadratic functions. A somewhat better method, used in the program below, is to use four flanking points and calculate:

$$\frac{df}{dx} = \frac{f(x-2h) - 8f(x-h) + 8f(x+h) - f(x+2h)}{12h} \quad (6.10)$$

This formula is exact for polynomials up to 4th order. (*Cf.* Reference 1, Appendix I, and Reference 2, page 139; the latter also gives formulas for the second derivative.)

PROGRAM DIVDIF

```
1 '                   PROGRAM DIVDIF
2 'NEWTON DIVIDED DIFFERENCE INTERP W/ SIMP RULE
3 'INTEGRATION AND 4TH-ORDER DIFF
10 DEFINT I-N
20 DIM DX(50), DY(50), T(50,8)
99 GOTO 200
100 CLS: PRINT W$,"PTS="M,"DEGREE";ID;"/";ND
120 PRINT"<&> DATA INPUT <T> TABLE  <Q> QUIT"
122 PRINT"<F> FUNCTION  <D> DIFF  <I> INTEGRATE"
130 A$=INKEY$: IF A$=""
      THEN 130
      ELSE J=INSTR("&TQFDI",A$)
140 ON J GOTO 200,300,900,400,500,1000
199 GOTO 100
200 ND=0:' DATA INPUT
210 READ W$,M
220 FOR I=1 TO M
230 READ X: Y=COS(X)
240 DX(I)=X: DY(I)=Y: NEXT
260 GOTO 100
290 DATA COSINE TEST,15,-3.5,-3.0,-2.5,-2,-1.5,-1,
      -.5,0,.5,1,1.5,2,2.5,3,3.5
```

```
300 INPUT"DEGREE";ID: IF ID<=ND
      THEN 100
      ELSE GOSUB 9000
310 PRINT"DIFFERENCE TABLE"
320 FOR I=1 TO M-1
330 FOR J=1 TO I
340 IF J<=ND
      THEN PRINT T(I,J);
350 NEXT
360 PRINT
370 NEXT
380 GOTO 130
400 INPUT"VALUE OF X";X
410 GOSUB 9400
420 PRINT"EST Y=",Y,"EST ERROR",ABS(ER)
430 PRINT"ACTUAL ",COS(X),"ACT ERROR",ABS(Y-COS(X))
480 GOTO 130
500 INPUT"VALUE OF X";X1 'DIFFERENTIAL EVALUATION
510 S=0.01 ' INCREMENT FOR DERIVATIVE
520 IF ABS(X1)>S
      THEN H=X1*S
      ELSE H=S
530 X=X1-2*H: GOSUB 9400: DX=Y
540 X=X1-H  : GOSUB 9400: DX=DX-8*Y
550 X=X1+H  : GOSUB 9400: DX=DX+8*Y
560 X=X1+2*H: GOSUB 9400: DX=DX-Y
570 DX=DX/(12*H)
580 PRINT"DERIVATIVE",DX
590 PRINT"ACTUAL",-SIN(X1),"DIFF",ABS(DX+SIN(X1))
599 GOTO 130
```

```
900 END: GOTO 100
1000 INPUT"LOWER & UPPER LIMITS"; X1,X2
1005 IF X1>=X2
     THEN 1000
1010 INPUT"NUMBER OF INTERVALS";N
1020 IF N/2<>INT(N/2)
     THEN PRINT"EVEN NUMBER, STUPID":GOTO 1010
1030 H=(X2-X1)/N:X=X1:GOSUB 9400
1032 A=Y:X=X2:GOSUB 9400 : A=A+Y
1040 FOR K=1 TO N-1:   X=X1+K*H: GOSUB 9400
1050 A=A+2*Y*(1-(K/2<>INT(K/2)))
1060 NEXT
1070 A=A*H/3: PRINT
1080 PRINT"THE INTEGRAL IS";A;"(";N;" INTERVALS)"
1082 PRINT"ACTUAL INTEGRAL"; SIN(X2)-SIN(X1)
1090 PRINT"Type <H> to change interval,
     <L> to change limits,
     <R> to return"
1100 A$=INKEY$: IF A$=""
     THEN 1100
     ELSE K=INSTR("HLR",A$)
1110 ON K GOTO 1010 ,1000 , 100
1120 GOTO 1100
9000 'CALC OF TABLE FOR NEWTON DIVIDED DIFF
9010 IF ID>M OR ID>8
     THEN W$="DEGREE TOO BIG": GOTO 100
9020 ND=ID 'INTERPOLATION ORDER, ID, MAX ND
9030 IF ND<=1
     THEN PRINT "ND=";ND: STOP: GOTO 100
9040 FOR I=1 TO M-1
```

```
9050 T(I,1)= (DY(I+1)−DY(I))/(DX(I+1)−DX(I)):  NEXT
9060 FOR J=2 TO ND
9070 FOR I=J TO M−1
9080 T(I,J)=(T(I,J−1)−T(I−1,J−1))/(DX(I+1)−DX(I+1−J))
9090 NEXT I,J
9100 W$="TABLE READY": RETURN
9400 'INTERPOLATION BY NEWTONS DIVIDED DIFF
9410 IF W$<>"TABLE READY"
        THEN W$="TABLE NOT READY": GOTO 100
9420 IF ID>ND
        THEN PRINT"MAX DEGREE=";ND: GOTO 9410
9430 FOR I=1 TO M
9440 IF I=M OR X<=DX(I)
        THEN 9460
9450 NEXT
9460 MX=I+ID/2
9470 IF MX<=ID THEN MX=ID+1
9480 IF MX>=M
        THEN MX=M
9490 Y=T(MX−1,ID): ER=T(MX,ID)−T(MX−1,ID)
9500 IF ID<=1
        THEN 9540
9510 FOR I=1 TO ID−1: D=X−DX(MX−I)
9520 Y=Y*D+T(MX−I−1,ID−I): ER=ER*D
9530 NEXT
9540 Y=Y*(X−DX(MX−ID))+DY(MX−ID)
9550 ER=ER*(X−DX(MX−ID))
9550 PRINT"/";:RETURN
```

Comments on DIVDIF

The divided difference table is stored in the array T; it is dimensioned (statement 20) for up to 8th degree. For applications, an interpolation less than 8th degree will usually be appropriate. With limited precision numbers, the point of diminishing returns for increasing degree will soon be reached; after that, the successive subtractions become a random number generator, and no significant improvement will result.

The string W\$ is provided to display messages from the "program" along with the menu; initially this will show the label of the first data set. The menu has a command $<\&>$ for data input; this is in case you have included several sets. The data must be in order with respect to the independent variable (X), and points should not be too closely spaced or precision will be lost in the divisions. On the other hand, the data should include a number of points in any region where the function takes a sharp bend. The command $<T>$ calculates the table; this must be done before anything else. After the table is calculated, the degree (ID) can be changed using command $<T>$; if the new degree is less than the old one, the table is not recalculated. (ND in the program denotes the highest degree for which differences have been calculated. The table is printed when calculated.) Command $<F>$ calculates an interpolated value (Statements 400-480). Command $<D>$ calculates the derivative (statements 500-599). Command $<I>$ calculates the integral (statements 1000-1120). The subroutine for calculating $Y = f(X)$ is at 9400.

After each calculation, control is returned to statement 130 so the screen will not be erased; if you wish to restore the screen, hit the space-bar (or any key except those used for commands). You may wish to add routines for listing data (arrays DX and DY), plotting data, or plotting the interpolated function.

Test data: DIVDIF, as written, will interpolate the cosine function. Note that the data input is only for X; Y is calculated as COS(X). (This will need to be changed when you are ready to use DIVDIF for real problems.) The exact values for COS(X), and its differential and integral, are printed so you can judge the accuracy of the method for various values of X and various degrees of interpolation. (An approximate "error", ER, is calculated by the program. This is generally useful only as an order-of-magnitude guide; you can observe how well it works with the test program. Under no circumstances should it be used in the way one would use error estimates from least squares regressions — it is simply not that reliable.) The following is the difference table for X = −3.5, −3, −2.5, −2, −1.5, −1, −0.5, 0, 0.5, 1, 1.5, 2, 2.5, 3, 3.5, and degree 4:

−.107071			
.377698	.484769		
.769993	.392295	−.0616492	
.973768	.203775	−.12568	−.0320155
.939130	−.034638	−.158942	−.016631
.674560	−.26457	−.153288	2.82708×10^{-3}
.244835	−.429725	−.110104	.0215922
−.244835	−.489670	−.0399632	.0350701
−.674561	−.429726	.039963	.0399631
−.93913	−.26457	.110104	.0350705
−.973768	−.0346379	.153288	.0215919
−.769993	.203775	.158942	2.82705×10^{-3}
−.377698	.392295	.12568	−.0166309
.107073	.48477	.0616496	−.0320153

Test data: Interpolation for X = 2.25: Y = −0.628398, ER = 1.12554×10^{-4}. Actual values, Y = −0.628174, Error 2.24292×10^{-4} Differential for X = 2.5: −.597265 (actual −.598472). Integral from 0 to 2 (20 intervals): 0.908944 (actual 0.909298).

Try the program with various degrees and values of X, both within the range (−3.5 to 3.5) and outside. There is a general rule of thumb that, given an approximate function of a given accuracy, the derivative will be less accurate and the integral more accurate by an order of magnitude; check this. How many steps do you need for optimum utilization of Simpson's rule for various intervals and degrees of interpolation? (Roughly, the number of intervals should be about twice the number of data points in that range. More intervals may appear to give greater accuracy, but this is somewhat deceptive since, in a real-data situation (as opposed to this artificial test case) the error may come from the data, the interpolation, or the integration. It would be rare to have data accurate to the 7 significant figures that these test data have.

The original use of interpolation was for interpolating function tables (such as logarithms or cosines, as above); this may still have some application in cases where double-precision functions are needed, or if the function evaluation is very time-consuming. However, our principal interest in this method is for data tables for which the formula is unknown.

Applications

A material with surface area a, has an entropy and energy attributable to the surface:

$$S_s = \left(\frac{\partial S}{\partial a} \right)_{T,V} \qquad U_s = \left(\frac{\partial U}{\partial a} \right)_{T,V} \qquad (6.11)$$

Where U_s and S_s are the surface energy and entropy — that is, the energy and entropy per unit area due to the surface. These quantities can be calculated from surface tension (γ) *vs.* temperature data with the formulas (Reference 1, Chapter 4):

$$S_s = - \left(\frac{\partial \gamma}{\partial T} \right)_{V,a} \qquad (6.12a)$$

$$U_s = \gamma - T \left(\frac{\partial \gamma}{\partial T} \right)_{V,a} \qquad (6.12b)$$

Assignment 6.3: Use the data below for the surface tension of water to calculate the surface energy and entropy of water.

$t(^\circ C)$	γ(dynes/cm)
0	75.7
20	72.75
25	72.0
40	69.6
60	66.2
80	62.6
100	58.8

Sample results for degree = 4:

$t(^\circ C)$	γ(dynes/cm)	S (erg $K^{-1}cm^{-2}$)	U(erg/cm^2)
25	72.00	0.153	117.5
50	67.95	0.170	122.9
75	63.48	0.179	125.9

Assignment 6.4: The coefficient of thermal expansion (α) is defined as:

$$\alpha = \frac{1}{V}\left(\frac{\partial V}{\partial T}\right)_P \tag{6.13}$$

where V is the volume, T is the temperature and P is the pressure. Use the data below for the specific volume of water to interpolate the specific volume and calculate the coefficient of thermal expansion:

$t(^\circ C)$	$v(cm^3/g)$	$t(^\circ C)$	$v(cm^3/g)$
0	1.00160	2	1.00006
4	1.00003	6	1.00006
8	1.00015	10	1.00030
15	1.00090	20	1.00180
25	1.00297	30	1.00438
35	1.00601	40	1.00785
45	1.00988	50	1.01210

Sample results: at 25 $^\circ$C, $dv/dt = 2.586\times10^{-4}$, $\alpha = 2.58\times10^{-4}$. Interpolated volume at 37 $^\circ$C, 1.00672 cm^3/g, $\alpha = 3.62\times10^{-4}$.

Assignment 6.5: Use the heat capacity data for benzene given in Chapter 5, together with program DIVDIF, to calculate the enthalpy and entropy change for heating solid benzene from 13 K to its melting point (278.69 K). The best results achievable for these data are $\Delta H = 17611$ J, $\Delta S = 127.90$. How do the two methods for calculating ΔS compare when interpolation is used? What degree and integration interval give the best results in the least time?

The rate law for a chemical reaction is formulated in terms of the velocity of the reaction (v), which is related to the rate of change of the concentration, dC/dt. If C is the concentration of a reactant (whose stoichiometric coefficient is 1 — see Reference 1, Chapter 10 for the general case), the rate law is often of the form:

$$v = -\frac{dC}{dt} = kC^n \qquad (6.14)$$

where k is the rate constant and n is the order of the reaction. Usually it is the concentration that is measured as a function of time, so in order to determine the rate constant and reaction order, one must either differentiate the data or integrate the rate law; the relative merits of these approaches are discussed by Reference 1, Chapter 10. The problem with the differential method is, as mentioned earlier, that the effect of experimental error is exaggerated.

Given a set of velocities, calculated from $C(t)$ data, the order can be calculated by linear regression of:

$$\ln v = \ln k + n \ln C \qquad (6.15)$$

Further explanation of this method can be found in Reference 1, Chapter 10.

Assignment 6.6: Data for the decomposition of di-t-butyl peroxide (concentration relative to those at $t = 0$) are given below. Use DIVDIF to create a data set for $\ln v$ vs. $\ln C$; then use LINREG to analyze these data.

t(min)	C	t(min)	C	t(min)	C
0	1.0000	2	.9592	3	.9412
5	.9061	6	.8884	8	.8541
9	.8373	11	.8042	12	.7906
14	.7608	15	.7469	17	.7188
18	.7035	20	.6796	21	.6654

The results will depend on your choice of points. For 4th degree, and points at $t = $ 1, 2, 3, 5, 7, 9, 12, 15, and 18, $n = 1.12$ ($\sigma = 0.15$), $r = 0.940$. This is not a lot better than the results of Reference 1, where linear interpolation and two-point differentiation was used: $n = 1.04$($\sigma = 0.16$), $r = 0.8810$. This suggests that the problem is with the precision of the data rather than the interpolation method; in either case, a conclusion that the reaction is first-order is justified. The elegant way to do this problem would be to renumber LINREG and MERGE it onto DIVDIF; several variable names in LINREG may have to be changed, including the data arrays DX and DY.

Assignment 6.7: Use the compressibility data for methane given in Chapter 5 to create a divided difference table for interpolation of $(z - 1)/P$ *vs.* P. Make a graph of this function and compare it to the results of POLYREG in Figure 4.3.

Since the fugacity coefficient (γ) is equal to 1 at $P = 0$, its absolute value can be calculated using (compare Eq. 5.7):

$$\ln \gamma = \int\limits_{0}^{P} \left(\frac{z - 1}{P} \right) dP \tag{6.16}$$

Use DIVDIF to calculate the fugacity coefficient of methane. Sample results: 0.994 at 1 atm, 0.941 at 10 atm, 0.472 at 100 atm, 0.309 at 500 atm, and 0.539 at 1000 atm. (Because the earlier results were calculated relative to 1 atm, they can be compared to these results if they are multiplied by 0.994.)

Assignment 6.8: The free energy function (denoted here, as in Reference 1, Chapters 5 and 6, as $\phi\,^\circ$) is defined as:

$$\phi\,^\circ = -\frac{G^\theta - H_0}{T} \tag{6.17}$$

From this, the equilibrium constant for a reaction can be calculated using:

$$\ln K_a = \frac{\Delta\phi\,^\circ}{R} - \frac{\Delta H_0}{RT} \tag{6.18}$$

ΔH_0 is the enthalpy of reaction at $T = 0$ K. Use the data below for free energy functions involved in the dissociation of phosgene:

$$COCl_2 \leftrightarrows CO + Cl_2$$

to calculate the equilibrium constant at 100 degree intervals from 300 to 2000 K. For this reaction, $\Delta H_0 = 103.99$ kJ/K.

T	$\phi°(CO)$	$\phi°(Cl_2)$	$\phi°(COCl_2)$
298.15	168.4	192.2	240.6
500	183.5	208.6	266.2
1000	204.1	231.9	304.6
1500	216.6	246.2	331.1
2000	225.9	256.6	351.1

[Units: J/K]

Sample results: $K = 7.28 \times 10^{-8}$ at 400 K, 128.9 at 668 K, 350.6 at 1250 K.

Modify DIVDIF to find the value of T for which $K = 1$ (use Newton's method, Chapter 3). Answer: 797.777 with degree 3 (all figures are not significant). What is the answer for degree 4? Is it worthwhile doing 4th degree?

CHAPTER 7: DATA CONVOLUTIONS

Data Collection Using a Computer

In the previous chapters, we have frequently discussed manipulations of data tables — that is, the situation in which the functional dependence of some physical quantity on an independent variable was represented by a finite set of numbers. It was implicitly assumed that this data set was small and, in general, unevenly spaced in the independent variable. These data came, presumably, from some reference book or, perhaps, as the results of series of discrete measurements in the laboratory. In this chapter we shall discuss the manipulation of large data sets (thousands of points) that, presumably, are the result of an automated experiment.

The way many modern experiments are done, the data are in the form of a voltage that changes in time as the result of the systematic change of the independent variable. The prototype of such an experiment is a spectrometer in which the wavelength or frequency is varied systematically in time (preferably, linearly in time), and the light transmitted is changed to an electrical signal by some sort of transducer such as a phototube. Even the classic titration experiment can be done this way using an automatic titrator (making the volume of titrant a function of time) and the electrical output of a pH meter. Similarly, the spectrophotometric measurement of concentration during a kinetics experiment can be used for measuring rates of reactions. In such cases, the data are effectively a continuous function; the difficulty is that, if you need to manipulate these data with a computer, a computer can do only finite mathematics — that is, operations on a discrete set of points.

A continuously varying voltage is called an analog signal, as opposed to a digital representation of such a quantity by a computer. The device by which such a voltage is translated into a form that a computer can understand is called an analog-to-digital converter (ADC). The ADC, during a finite but short period of time called the sampling interval, measures the voltage and converts it into a binary number, proportional to the voltage, that can be stored in the computer's memory; successive measurements are stored in successive memory locations (an array), and these form the data table (or array). It is possible to sample at rates up to hundreds of thousands per second, and data tables of thousands of points are not at all unusual. Sampling times of microseconds are easily achieved, but with a microcomputer the time required for the computer to store the data will probably limit this time to 10 milliseconds or so.

With such large data tables, the methods discussed in earlier chapters are practically useless. The saving grace is that the points are usually evenly spaced (in time at least), so we are free to use techniques that require evenly spaced data. All the methods of this chapter make such a requirement.

What types of manipulations are likely to be desired? Such data will surely contain noise, random fluctuations because of the experimental apparatus and not related to the signal. The noise may, in some cases, totally obscure the signal. Therefore, data smoothing is likely to be useful. Also you may need to differentiate or integrate the data. Each of these will be discussed in turn. There are a number of other similar manipulations, for example, the Fourier transform operation used in modern nuclear magnetic resonance (NMR) and infrared (IR) spectroscopy, which will not be covered here.

In the ensuing discussions we shall assume that the independent variable is time. Often the interesting variable is secondarily related to time, for example, the wavelength of a swept spectrometer, but time is usually the fundamental variable. In any case, it will make the discussions simpler to assume that time is the variable.

Convolution Integrals and Sums

There are basically two types of convolutions: the unsymmetrical (backward or forward) convolutions and the symmetrical convolution. Given a function $F(t)$, the convoluted function, $G(t)$, is calculated as:

$$G(t) = \int_0^t C(t)F(t - t)d\tau \qquad (7.1)$$

where C is the convoluting function. The symmetrical form of Eq. 7.1 is:

$$G(t) = \int_{-t}^{t} C(\tau)F(t + \tau)d\tau \qquad (7.2)$$

If the functions are represented by a finite series of points, the integrals of Eqs. 7.1 and 7.2 are replaced by sums. The unsymmetrical convolution becomes:

$$G_i = \frac{1}{N} \sum_{j=1}^{m} C_j F_{i-j} \qquad (7.3)$$

where N is a scaling constant. This form of convolution can be used for integration or smoothing.

The symmetrical convolution is:

$$G_i = \frac{1}{N} \sum_{j=-m}^{m} C_j F_{i+j} \qquad (7.4)$$

This form of convolution is suitable for differentiation and is the preferred method for smoothing. For a five-point convoluting array, Eq. 7.4 is:

$$G_i = \frac{1}{N} \left[C_{-2} F_{i-2} + C_{-1} F_{i-1} + C_0 F_i + C_1 F_{i+1} + C_2 F_{i+2} \right] \qquad (7.5)$$

Of course, for Eq. 7.5 to represent a symmetrical convolution, the coefficients must be symmetrical or antisymmetrical; for example, C_i must be the same, or the negative, of its opposite number, C_{-i}. Also, when translating these equations into computer statements, it will be helpful to remember that BASIC (like most computer languages) will not tolerate negative indices in an array. Also, BASIC arrays may begin with an index of zero or one; either way is acceptable so long as you are reasonably consistent. (The writer recently was subjected to many hours of suffering as a result of being inconsistent in such a manner.)

Figure 7.1 shows, schematically, some convolution functions for various applications.

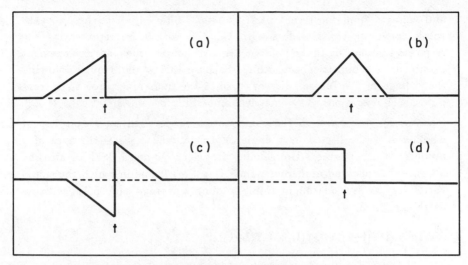

Figure 7.1: Convolution functions for (a) backwards smoothing, (b) symmetrical smoothing, (c) differentiation and (d) integration.

Data Smoothing

If you made a measurement that contained excessive random error (noise), you could improve the precision by repeating the measurement and averaging the results. This is a major application for computer data collection, which utilizes the computer's large memory capacity and long-term memory. An experiment is repeated numerous times and the results, provided to a computer via an ADC, are added together by the computer. Since the signal is, presumably, consistent in its changes, and the noise is randomly adding or subtracting from the signal, the signal will add while the noise will tend to cancel. The theory of random walks (Reference 1, Chapter 9) tells us that, after N measurements, the improvement in the rms signal-to-noise ratio will be proportional to $\sqrt{N}$.

Signal averaging can also be made a part of the experimental apparatus. Typically this involves the use of a resistance-capacitance (RC) circuit that stores the voltage for some time after it is applied. Thus, the voltage at any given time is an average of the present voltage.

and voltages from the recent past. The RC filter is, effectively, a backwards convolution of the data with Eq. 7.1, with $C(\tau)$ representing the response function of the RC filter. But, of course, such an arrangement cannot do a symmetrical smoothing because this would require knowing the voltage in the future. However, once the data are stored in a computer, such operations as symmetrical smoothing become practical.

Assume you have, in the computer, a single data set (regardless of whether it was collected in a single experimental run or is the sum of a number of such runs). How could its signal-to-noise (S/N) ratio be improved? If one had numerous points in a time frame in which the signal varies very slowly, one might think to simply average each point with its neighbors, giving:

$$AY(I) = (DY(I-1) + DY(I) + DY(I+1))/3$$

This is just a simple example of Eq. 7.5 with the three-point convolution array, $C = (1, 1, 1)$ and $N = 3$. However, some resolution will be lost by this procedure — that is, some information about the signal is lost because it is not really stationary. One might do better by predicting how the signal is likely to vary over some short time period. This was the idea of linear regression where it was assumed that the "signal," the experimental value as a function of the independent variable, was varying linearly. Polynomial regression was an extension of this concept to nonlinear functions.

Over a short enough interval, the change of any smoothly varying function can be represented by a low-degree polynomial, so one could "average" the data by a piece-wise polynomial regression. This approach would be very slow, and the preferred method is to represent this operation by a convolution function. This has been done by A. Savitzky and M. J. E. Golay, *Analytical Chemistry*, **36**, 1627 (1964). The convolution array they present are called Savitzky-Golay filters. A number of these are given in Table 7.1. (The original paper has some typographical errors.)

The Savitzky-Golay filters have recently been discussed by T. A. Nevius and H. L. Pardue [*Anal. Chem.*, **56**, 2249 (1984)] who point out some problems and suggest improvements.

Let us look at an example of how one could use these numbers to smooth data. We shall assume the the raw data are in arrays DY and DX,

Table 7.1 Savitzky-Golay Filters

N	m = −4	−3	−2	−1	0	+1	+2	+3	+4
Smoothing (quadratic/cubic)									
35			−3	12	17	12	−3		
21			−2	2	6	7	6	3	−2
231	−21	14	39	54	59	54	39	14	21
Smoothing (quartic/quintic)									
231		5	−30	75	131	75	−30	5	
429	15	−55	30	135	179	135	30	−55	15
First Derivative (cubic/quartic)									
12			1	−8	0	8	−1		
252		22	−67	−58	0	58	67	−22	
1188	86	−142	−193	−126	0	126	193	142	−86
Second Derivative (quartic/quintic)									
3			−3	48	−90	48	−3		
99		−117	603	−171	−630	−171	603	−117	

Source: A. Savitzky and M.J.E. Golay, *Analytical Chemistry*, **36**, 1627 (1964).

and that the convolute will go into the arrays AY and AX. (Because the independent variable is changing in a systematic and evenly spaced way, the DX and AX arrays are not strictly necessary; however, if you have set up your plotting routines to use two arrays, the most general method, it will be more convenient to keep them.) The first line of Table 7.1 gives the coefficients that would correspond to a regression fit of order 3 or 4. (The coefficients are the same for both.) The average, called a moving average, would be accomplished by the following BASIC statement:

$$AY(I) = (- 3*DY(I - 2) + 12*DY(I - 1) + 17*DY(I) \\ + 12*DY(I + 1) - 3*DY(I + 2))/35 \tag{7.6}$$

Such a moving average will still produce some distortion of the data, but these filters are designed to provide the maximum improvement in S/N with minimum distortion. A Savitzky-Golay filter of quartic accuracy would smooth a noisy, quartic polynomial function with no distortion of the underlying function. Any function that contained higher-order polynomial components would be distorted. Any smoothly varying function can be represented over a short interval by a low-order polynomial, and such cases will not be distorted excessively. However, sharply varying functions can, and will, be distorted.

Assuming that there are M points in the DY array, the statement above must be in a FOR . . . NEXT loop from I = 3 TO M − 2; otherwise and illegal array reference will result (that is, you will use array elements that do not exist, such as DY(−2), or array elements that do not contain data, such as DY(M + 2)). This means that the new array will be shorter by 4 points. There are several alternatives: (1) The first and last two elements could be simply replaced by the unaveraged values of DY. (2) A forward or reverse average could be used to calculate these elements. (3) The arrays AY and AX could be simply shortened to length M − 4; in this case, it may be better to shift the points down so they run from 1 to M − 4 rather than from 3 to M − 2. (It is assumed here that DX and DY were indexed from 1 to M.) The following code would accomplish this:

```
850 FOR I=3 TO M−2
860 AY(I−2)=(−3*DY(I−2)+12*DY(I−1)+17*DY(I)
      +12*DY(I+1)−3*DY(I+2))/3
870 AX(I−2)=DX(I)
880 NEXT
```

Assignment 7.1: Write BASIC code to do the 7 point quadratic/cubic average. Make it a complete program except for input and output.

Data Simulation: The RND Function

The procedure used in earlier chapters, in which you were given a set of data for analysis, is not too practical here — neither of us wants to type 200 pairs of points. It will be better to simulate a set of data. One way to do this is to use the Gaussian function, a reasonable representation of line shapes in many spectroscopic experiments:

$$y(x) = e^{-wx^2} + noise \qquad (7.7)$$

Use this to generate perhaps 200 points for $-1 < x < 1$, and $w = 25$. The width of the function will be $1/\sqrt{w}$. Figure 7.2 shows an example of this function. (You will get more out of this chapter if you have a routine for plotting, for the screen at least.)

The random "noise" can be generated using the BASIC RND(d) function. In this function, the argument (d, above) is often a dummy — that is, it doesn't matter what you put in the parentheses, but you must put something there. On a TRS80/III, the argument determines the range of the random numbers. In the discussion to follow, it will be assumed that RND(0) generates a random number between 0 and 1; check your manual to see how this is done on your computer. With this function, the "noise" in Eq. 7.7 could be given by:

$$\text{noise} = \text{F}*(\text{RND}(0)-0.5)$$

where F is a factor with values such as 0.01, 0.05, 0.10. (Why is it necessary to subtract one-half?) But this would produce noise with equal probability of all amplitudes between $+\text{F}/2$ and $-\text{F}/2$: this is not particularly realistic. A better method is to use:

$\text{G} = \text{RND}(0)-0.5$
$\text{noise} = \text{F}*\text{G}*\text{EXP}(-2*\text{G}*\text{G})$

which will give noise with, roughly, a Gaussian distribution of intensity.

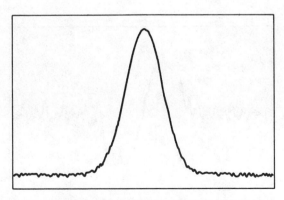

Figure 7.2: The Gaussian curve.

Assignment 7.2: Generate a set of Gaussian data as described above (see Figure 7.2) with a noise factor (F) of approximately 0.10. Try out the various smoothing functions of Table 7.1 and observe and compare their results. Use a large value of W to get a very sharp peak, and watch for distortion caused by the smoothing functions. Make this the basis for a program (SGFILTER), to which you will later add differentiation, integration, and other refinements.

Differentiation

Table 7.1 also provides convolution coefficients for the first and second derivative of a function. The first set of coefficients, which give:

$$d_i = \frac{(f_{i-2} - 8f_{i-1} + 0f_i + 8f_{i+1} - f_{i+2})}{12} \tag{7.8}$$

will be recognized as the form used in DIVDIF. Of course, for Eq. 7.8 to be exactly the derivative, it would need to be divided by the interval H (see Eq. 6.10); this is not always necessary — often a curve that is simply proportional to the derivative is sufficient. Figure 7.3 shows the numerical derivative of the curve of Figure 7.2, as calculated using the seven-point first-derivative convolution of Table 7.1. The increase in noise level is, as

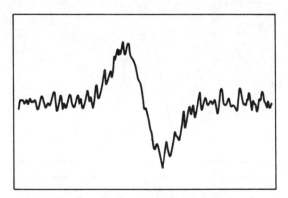

Figure 7.3: Derivative of the Gaussian curve of Figure 7.2.

stated before, to be expected in numerical differentiation. For that reason, the higher-order methods are strongly recommended.

Assignment 7.3: Modify SGFILTER to calculate the first derivative of the Gaussian data you generated earlier. Try the various methods given in Table 7.1. Try smoothing the data before and/or after differentiation. (For consistency's sake, it is suggested that for all examples you use the arrays DX and DY for the raw data, and the arrays AX and AY for the convoluted data, such as the derivative function of this example. This will be particularly convenient if you have a plotting routine, because it can be used with minimal changes for all examples.)

One application of numerical differentiation is the determination of end points in titrations. Figure 7.4 shows a typical result for the emf of a pH meter *vs.* volume of titrant. Students who have studied analytical

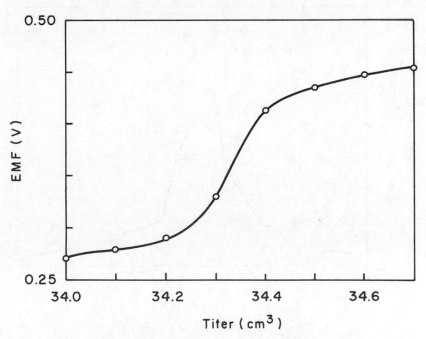

Figure 7.4: Emf *vs.* volume for a titration.

chemistry should have no difficulty in recogizing the end point for this titration. But what about your poor dumb computer? The end point will be at the point of maximum slope, so it would seem to be a good idea to differentiate the pH data. Figure 7.5 shows this result — the maximum in the derivative curve is the end point. Even so, it is somewhat easier for a computer to find roots (zero-crossings) than maxima, so the second derivative is recommended.

Assignment 7.4: Use the data below (from which Figures 7.4 and 7.5 were constructed) to calculate the second derivative function. Have the computer find the zero-crossing, and calculate the end-point volume by linear interpolation.

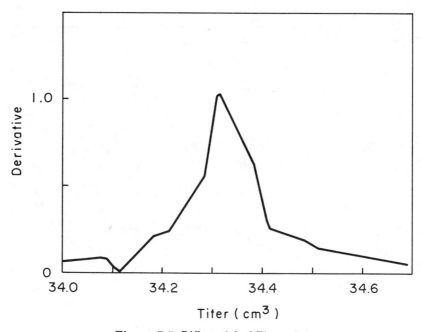

Figure 7.5: Differential of Figure 7.4.

Volume of titrant (cm^3)	Meter Reading (millivolts)
34.00	0.271
34.10	0.279
34.20	0.290
34.30	0.330
34.40	0.413
34.50	0.435
34.60	0.447
34.70	0.454

[Data from Reference 6, page 184.]

Integration

We define a function $g(x)$ as the integral of the function $f(x)$ by:

$$g(x) = \int_0^x f(x')dx' \qquad (7.9)$$

It is assumed here that the variable x begins at zero; if this is not convenient, simply replace, in Eq. 7.9, x by $x - a$, where a is the desired starting point. Comparing Eq. 7.9 to Eq. 7.1, we see that integration is simply a backward convolution with the convolution function equal to 1 (or some other constant as convenient; as for derivatives, it is often sufficient to get a curve that is only proportional to the integral).

For a finite data set, indexed from 1 to N, Eq. 7.9 becomes:

$$g_i = H \sum_{j=1}^{i} f_j \qquad (7.10)$$

with $H = \Delta x$ and $i = 1$ to N. This is, effectively, the trapezoidal-rule integration of the function $f(x)$.

Simpson's rule can also be used, but its use will result in an integrated array with half the points as the data array. The following code will do this:

```
1250 MX = 0 'INDEX FOR NEW ARRAYS, AX AND AY
1252 SU=0 'SUMMING VARIABLE
1254 AY(0)=0: AX(0)=DX(1) 'FIRST POINT IN NEW ARRAY
1260 FOR J=2 TO M-1 STEP 2 'M IS # DATA POINTS
1270 SU=(DY(J-1)+4*DY(J)+DY(J+1))*H/3 'H IS DELTA X
1280 AX(J/2)=DX(J): AY(J/2)=SU
1290 NEXT
1300 MX=J/2-1 'NUMBER OF POINTS IN ARRAYS AX,AY
1310 · · ·
```

Figure 7.6 shows the integral of the Gaussian curve of Figure 7.2. Note the decrease in noise level. It is generally unnecessary, indeed undesirable, to smooth data before integration; integration itself is a smoothing convolution.

Assignment 7.5: Modify SGFILTER to include code to integrate the Gaussian curve. Use a lot of noise and observe the effect. Vary the width parameter (W) to see its effect on the Gaussian curve and its integral.

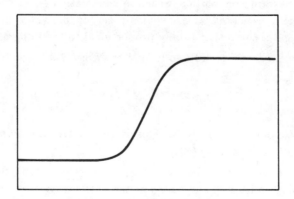

Figure 7.6: Integral of the Gaussian curve of Figure 7.2.

Assignment 7.6: A more realistic simulation of spectroscopic data can be obtained by using several Gaussian curves with (possibly) different widths and centers. The following formula shows how to do this for two curves.

$$y(x) = A_1 e^{-w_1(x - c_1)^2} + A_2 e^{-w_2(x - c_2)^2} + noise \qquad (7.11)$$

In Eq 7.11, the coefficients c_1 and c_2 determine the centers of the peaks, w_1 and w_2 determine the widths, and A_1 and A_2 determine the maximum amplitudes. Use this with your differentiation and integration programs and observe the effect of various separations and widths. Does differentiation/integration change the resolution? If one had two peaks of greatly differing widths that were heavily overlapped, which form of presentation (function, differential, or integral) is more suitable for discovering that fact?

Assignment 7.7: Try several of the assignments above with the Lorenzian curve:

$$y(x) = \frac{A^2}{A^2 + (x - c)^2} \qquad (7.12)$$

What is the meaning of the constant c? How is the constant A related to the width? How does the Lorenzian curve compare to the Gaussian curve in shape, resolution, and so on? This assignment can be done with relatively minor modifications to SGFILTER.

Random Number Generators

Although it is only tangentially relevant to this chapter, this seems as good a place as any to discuss how computers generate random numbers. As mentioned earlier, most microcomputers have the RND function or some equivalent; but there are times when it may be better for you to write your own random number generator and, in any case, you should probably know something about how the computer is doing it.

The first thing you must understand is that there is nothing random about a computer. The numbers produced are properly called "pseudorandom" numbers. They are perfectly predictable, given the algorithm that produces them, and they will repeat the same sequence periodically. To get a set of numbers that are reasonably random, it is important that the repetition period be large compared to the number of such random numbers to be generated.

A typical random number algorithm is:

$$x = (ax + b) \pmod{m} \tag{7.13}$$

Here, a number x (called the seed) produces a new number x, which will be the seed for generating the next number. (The built-in random number generators of microcomputers seem to hide the seed effectively from the user — or, at least, from those users not initiated into the mysteries of PEEK and POKE). The constants a and b are moderately small numbers (4 to 6 significant figures) and, preferably, primes. (A number of reference books give lists of prime numbers.) According to Reference 2 (page 545), the constant a should differ from the nearest multiple of 200 by one of these numbers: 3, 11, 13, 19, 21, 27, 29, 37, 53, 59, 61, 67, 69, 77, 83, or 91.

In Eq. 7.13, "mod m" means modulus m — the remainder upon division by m. The following miniprogram will illustrate this technique:

Miniprogram 7.1: Modulus/Remainder

```
10 INPUT"NUMBER";N: N=INT(N)
20 INPUT"MODULUS";M: M=INT(M)
30 R = INT(N−M*INT(N/M))
40 PRINT"THE REMAINDER IS ";R
50 GOTO 10
```

For example, 103 (mod 3) = 1. Check this, and other examples, by hand and with the miniprogram above.

The random numbers will repeat in a period $m/20$ or less; optimal results will be achieved with prime seed numbers, but the repetition will always occur after $m/20$ numbers. However, there is a limit on the upper size of the modulus that is imposed by the finite word size of the computer. If two 6 digit numbers are multiplied together, a 12 digit number results. The purpose of the modulus operation is to take the least significant digits of this multiplication as the next pseudorandom number. If the modulus is 1×10^6, the last 6 figures of the 12-digit product will be used. However, this presumes that your computer has 12 digit accuracy. If you have a computer with only 7 digits of accuracy, the modulus should probably be no larger than 1000; therefore, the sequence will repeat after 50 numbers. In such cases, double precision is required — with 15 significant figures, a modulus of 1×10^7 (for double precision, enter it as 1D7) can be used, and the repetition period will be 500,000 — good enough for most purposes.

The following subroutine will produce pseudorandom numbers between 0 and 1 with a uniform distribution. The calling program must define the modulus (M# if your computer has double precision) and the first value for X# (the seed); the random number (single precision) is returned as A, with $0 < A < 1$:

SUBROUTINE RANDOM

```
1000 X#=X#*7259+317
1010 X#=ABS(INT(X#−M#*INT(X#/M#)))
1020 A=X#/M#
1030 RETURN
```

This routine has been found to work well with M#=1D6 and up to several thousand cycles.

Assignment 7.8: Write a program (RANDOM) to generate random numbers, permitting the user to input both the seed and the modulus. Observe the results when the modulus is 100. For larger moduli, you may prefer to make a bar chart on your screen. The code below will, if suitably adapted for your specific computer, accomplish this:

10 DIM Y(100)

150 A=INT(A∗100)

      'CREATES TWO-DIGIT RANDOM NUMBERS

160 Y(A)=Y(A)+1

      'COUNTING HOW OFTEN THIS ONE HAS HAPPENED

170 SET(A+1,LY−Y(A))

      'COMMAND MAY BE PSET, HPLOT, etc.; SEE YOUR MANUAL

171 ' LY ABOVE IS THE MAXIMUM PIXEL NUMBER IN Y DIRECTION

− SEE CHAPTER 2 AND/OR YOUR MANUAL

FOR DETAILS ON SCREEN PLOTTING

180 NEXT'END OF FOR ... NEXT LOOP

      FOR 100 TO 1000 RANDOM NUMBERS.

This will give you a pictoral view of the randomness of the numbers generated with various seeds and moduli. Try other coefficients in the subroutine. What happens if you use $X\# = X\#∗100 + 20$? Try to find some really poor combination of modulus, seed, and generating constants. (Reference 2 has some suggestions on what to avoid in order to get a good generator.)

CHAPTER 8: NONLINEAR LEAST SQUARES

Curve Fitting, Revisited

Given a set of experimental points, x_i, y_i, the problem is to fit these data to an equation that relates y functionally to x:

$$y = f(x,a,b,c, \cdots) \tag{8.1}$$

where a, b, c, . . . are constants that are chosen for best fit. This is done by treating the "constants" as "variables" in order to find the minimum in the sum of squares of the deviations of the observed points from the calculated points:

$$SS = \sum_{i=1}^{M} w_i[y_i - f(x_i, a, b, c, \cdots)]^2 \tag{8.2}$$

where M is the number of points. The factors w_i are the weighting factors that can be used to take into account error distributions that are nonuniform; in this chapter we shall always use an unweighted sum of squares; that is, all weighting factors will be equal to one. The procedure is to vary the constants until the sum of squares is a minimum.

These types of problems can be divided into two classes. If the function is linear in the coefficients, then the methods outlined in Chapter 4 will work (program MULTIREG). If the function is a polynomial, POLYREG demonstrates the technique to be used. If the equation is nonlinear in the coefficients, a different approach is needed. A common example of a simple, but nonlinear, formula is:

$$y = \frac{ax}{b + x} \tag{8.3}$$

This equation arises in enzyme kinetics (the Michaelis-Menten mechanism; x is the substrate concentration and y is the reaction velocity) and in Langmuir's theory of surface adsorption (x is the pressure of the gas, y is proportional to the amount of gas adsorbed). It is well known that Eq. 8.3 can be linearized by changing the variables to $1/y$ and $1/x$; in biochemistry this is called the Lineweaver-Burk plot. Other linearization techniques have been used for both gas adsorption and enzyme kinetics. However, it is generally a bad practice to use such variable transformations, because this alters the error distributions and weighting of the experimental points. We shall discuss other examples of this type later in this chapter.

The Response Surface

The problem is more general than curve fitting. Suppose you had a piece of experimental apparatus with a set of knobs labeled $a, b, c, \ldots$ You wish to adjust these knobs to obtain a optimum response. An example of this type occurs in nuclear magnetic resonance (NMR). For NMR, the magnetic field must be as homogeneous as possible. The homogeneity can be adjusted by use of a set of electrical shims. The response is the intensity of a reference resonance, and it must be maximized by adjusting the knobs. Typically, there may be a dozen or so knobs.

In curve fitting, you must adjust a set of parameters, "knobs" in a sense, to minimize the "response" that could be, for example, the sum of squares of Eq. 8.2. We shall prefer to deal with the standard deviation of the points rather than the sum of squares, and define the response (R) as:

$$R = \left[\frac{SS}{M - 1} \right]^{1/2} \tag{8.4}$$

The reason for doing this is that you are more likely to have an intuitive feeling for what constitutes a "good" response when it is defined this way. For example, if the variable y has an accuracy of 0.01, then any response that is better than 0.01 is good. R is, in effect, the standard error for using the fitted equation for calculating the dependent variable (y).

Whether you are doing experimental adjustments, or fitting data to a function, the response as a function of the adjustable parameters, $R(a, b, c, \ldots)$ can be thought of as a surface. This is most easily visualized when there are two parameters $(a$ and $b)$ for then $R(a, b)$ can be graphed *vs.* a and b; see Figure 8.1. The problem can then be stated as finding the minimum (or, perhaps, the maximum) of this surface.

To find the minimum in the surface, you go downhill. The direction that goes down could be discovered by calculating the derivatives of the functions $R(a, b)$; this is equivalent to the root-finding methods discussed

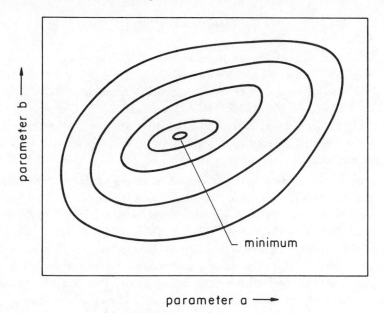

Figure 8.1: The response surface.

in Chapter 3, and the same sort of techniques can be used. The problem is that the surface may have local minima that could mislead you (root-finding had the same problem). Furthermore, because you are dealing with experimental data, the surface is rough; it will have bumps and pits caused by random noise. Thus it is possible to get isolated in one of these pits and to be unable to find the global minimum that will tell you the best values for the parameters.

Newton's iteration has been generalized for functions of several variables and can be used for such cases (with numerical differentiation if the derivatives are difficult to calculate otherwise). Newton's method is very fast but rather unstable. D. W. Marquardt ("An Algorithm for Least-Squares Estimation of Nonlinear Parameters," *Journal of the Society of Industrial and Applied Mathematics*, 11, 431 (1963)) has developed a general technique that combines Newton's method with the method of steepest descent. This algorithm is implemented on most mainframe computers and has been widely used. However, the computer code required is rather complex for use on a microcomputer.

The Simplex Method

The simplex algorithm was proposed by J. A. Nedler and R. Mead in 1965. References discussing this method, including improvements on the original method, include: C. L. Shavers, M. L. Parsons and S. N. Deming, *J. Chem. Educ.*, 56, 307 (1979), M. S. Caceci and W. P. Cacheris, *BYTE*, May 1984, and J. Cooper, Reference 7, Chapter 18. The method used here is that of Caceci and Cacheris. Cooper gives a well-documented PASCAL program for simplex.

A simplex is a figure that has one more vertex than the dimension of the space in which it exists. For two dimensions, the space for two parameters (a, b), the simplex is a triangle. If there are NP parameters, the number of vertices of the simplex (NV) is NV = NP + 1. The initial locations of the vertices are determined somewhat arbitrarily. It is helpful to have some idea of the value of the parameters before starting; this will also help to avoid false minima. Such estimates can sometimes be obtained by some other method; for example, for Eq. 8.3 the double reciprocal plot could be used for this purpose. Often a thoughtful inspection of the data will produce reasonable estimates. Then, for each vertex, the response is calculated and the best response (BR) and worst response (WR) are identified.

This is most easily pictured with two parameters; see Figure 8.2. For two parameters, there are 3 vertices that can be ranked as to response as best (B), second best (S), and worst (W). The centroid (C) of all points but the worst is calculated as the sum of coordinates $(a$ or $b)$ of the points:

$$C_a = \frac{1}{(NV-1)} \sum_{i \neq w} a_i \; ; \qquad C_b = \frac{1}{(NV-1)} \sum_{i \neq w} b_i \qquad etc. \quad (8.5a)$$

The worst point is then reflected through the centroid to produce the reflected point (1); for each coordinate, we calculate the reflected value:

$$\text{reflected coordinate} = C + F(C - W) \qquad (8.5b)$$

$(F = 1$ in Eq. 8.5b, at this stage). The response is then calculated at the reflected point. Calling this response R1, the procedure below is followed:

If the reflected point is better than the best (R1 < BR), then the simplex is expanded using Eq. 8.5b with F = 2 (point 2 on Figure 8.2). The

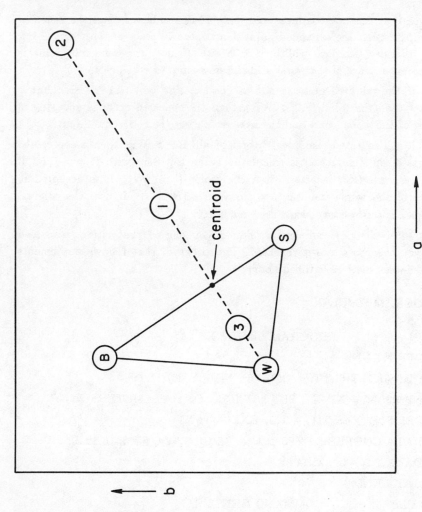

Figure 8.2: The Simplex.

response at this point is measured (R2). If this is better than the reflected point, R2<R1, the expanded point is accepted in place of the worst point, and the new simplex will be (*B, S*, 2). If not, the reflected point is accepted in place of the worst and the new simplex is (*B, S*, 1).

If the reflected point is not as good as the best (R1 > BR), but is better than the worst (R1 < WR), then the reflected point is accepted in place of the worst point and the new simplex is (B, S, 1).

If the reflected response is worst of all, R1 > WR, then a contracted point (3, on Figure 8.2) is calculated using Eq. 8.5b with F = −0.5. If this response (R3) is better than the worst (R3<WR), it is accepted in place of the worst and the new simplex is (*B, S*, 3). If not, the original simplex is contracted toward the best point.

After the new simplex is defined (by one of the criteria discussed above), the procedure is repeated. The program that follows implements the simplex method outlined above:

PROGRAM SIMPLEX

```
1 '              PROGRAM SIMPLEX
10 DEFINT I-N
20 DIM S(6,7),T(6),TT(6),R(7),C(6), X(30),Y(30)
30 NP=3: NV=NP+1 ' SET NUMBER OF PARAMETERS = NP
40 DEF FNY(X)= T(1) + T(2)*EXP(T(3)*X)
50 DATA COOPER,8,1,2.80, 2,3.74, 3,5.01, 4,6.74, 5,9.06, 6,12.2
51 DATA 7,16.43, 8,22.14
59 DATA END,0
100 CLS'          COMMAND CENTER
110 PRINT"ITER=";KI;"/";KX,"R=";BR;"/";EP,"PTS";M,TI$
120 PRINT"PARAMETERS:";:FOR I=1 TO NP: PRINT S(I,JB),:NEXT
130 PRINT"
        <I> DATA INPUT
        <G> INPUT GUESSES
        <P> PRINT RESULTS
```

```
          <C> CALCULATE
          <F> FUNCTION CALC
          <Q> QUIT"
140 PRINT"?";:GOSUB 190: J=INSTR("IGPCQF",A$)
150 ON J GOTO 200,300,400,1000,900,800
160 GOTO 100
190 A$=INKEY$: IF A$=""
          THEN GOTO 190
          ELSE PRINTA$;":";: RETURN
200 READ TI$,M: IF TI$="END"
          THEN GOTO 100
210 FOR I=1 TO M: READ X,Y
220 X(I)=X: Y(I)=Y
230 NEXT
240 GOTO 100
300 FOR I=1 TO NP:PRINT I;":";: INPUT"VALUE, INC";Z,D
310     FOR J=1 TO NV
320     S(I,J)= Z − D*(I>=J)−D/2
330     NEXT
340 NEXT
344 GOSUB 350: GOTO 400
350 FOR I3=1 TO NV
360     FOR J3=1 TO NP: T(J3)=S(J3,I3): NEXT
370 GOSUB 500: R(I3)=R
380 NEXT: RETURN
400 PRINT"RESPONSE/PARAMETERS"
405 FOR I=1 TO NV:PRINT R(I);"/",
410     FOR J=1 TO NP
420     PRINT S(J,I);",";: NEXT
430 PRINT: NEXT
```

```
480 PRINT"?":GOSUB 190
490 GOTO 100
500 R=0 'CALCULATE RESPONSE"
510 FOR I5=1 TO M
520 R=R+(Y(I5)-FNY(X(I5)))^2
530 NEXT
540 R=SQR(R/(M-1)): RETURN
600 '        FIND NEW VERTEX (T)
610 FOR J6=1 TO NP: SU=0
615 IF F<>1
        THEN GOTO 660
620 FOR K6=1 TO NV 'CALC CENTROID
630 IF K6<>JW
        THEN SU=SU+S(J6,K6)
633 NEXT
640 C(J6)=SU/NP
660 T(J6)= C(J6)*(1+F)-F*S(J6,JW)
670 NEXT
680 GOSUB 500: PRINT"/ F=";F;"R=";R;
690 RETURN
700 ' EXCHANGE T FOR WORST
710 FOR I7=1 TO NP
720 S(I7,JW)=T(I7)
730 NEXT
740 R(JW)=R
750 GOTO 1050
800 INPUT "X=";X
810 PRINT FNY(X)
820 GOTO 140
900 END: GOTO 100
```

```
1000 KI=0'         ITERATION
1010 IF M=0 OR R(1)=0
         THEN GOTO 100
1020 INPUT"MAX # ITER";KX
1030 EP=1E-6
1040 IF BR<>0 AND BR<EP
         THEN EP=EP/10: GOTO 1040
1050 WR=R(1):BR=WR: JW=1: JB=1
1060 FOR I=2 TO NV
1070 IF R(I)>=WR
         THEN WR=R(I): JW=I
1080 IF R(I)<BR
         THEN BR=R(I): JB=I
1090 NEXT
1150 IF KI>=KX OR BR<EP
         THEN PRINT"END":GOSUB 190: GOTO 100
1160 IF (WR-BR)/BR < EP
         THEN PRINT: GOTO 400
1170 IF INKEY$="Q"
         THEN GOTO 100
1200 PRINT: KI=KI+1: PRINT"#";KI;
1210 IF BR<>PR
         THEN PR=BR:PRINT"!!!NEW BEST";BR;"WORST";WR
1220 F=1: GOSUB 600     'NEW VERTEX
1230 IF R<=BR
         THEN GOTO 1400 'EXPAND VERTEX
1240 IF R<=WR
         THEN GOTO 700: 'EXCH FOR WORST
1250 F=-0.5: GOSUB 600     'CONTRACT
1260 IF R<=WR
```

```
     THEN GOTO 700 'EXCHANGE FOR WORST
1270 PRINT"CONTRACT";' CONTRACT ALL VERTICES
1280 FOR I=1 TO NP
1290 FOR J=1 TO NV
1300 IF J< >JB
     THEN S(I,J)=(S(I,JB)+S(I,J))/2
1310 NEXT J,I
1380 GOTO 1050
1400 RT=R:FOR I=1 TO NP: TT(I)=T(I): NEXT 'SAVE VERTEX
1410 F=2: GOSUB 600 ' EXPANDED VERTEX
1420 IF R<=RT
     THEN GOTO 700 'ACCEPT EXPANDED VERTEX
1430 R=RT:FOR I=1 TO NP: T(I)=TT(I): NEXT 'RESTORE
1440 GOTO 700   'EXCHANGE W/ WORST
```

Discussion of SIMPLEX

The coordinates of the vertices are stored in the array S. The first column of S contains the coordinates $(a, b, c, \ldots)$ of the first vertex, the second column for the second vertex, and so forth. The array T contains the coordinates of the point whose response (R) is being calculated; thus the function statement (40) must use $T(1)$, $T(2)$, $T(3)$, and so forth, as the parameters.

Data input is via READ . . . DATA statements. A title (TI$) is read first, then the number of data pairs (M), then the x, y pairs.

After the data are read, the initial guesses must be entered. For each parameter (in turn), you must enter an initial guess and an increment (separated by a comma). Increments should not be too small or you may get caught in a local minimum or pit on the response surface; increments of about an order of magnitude less than the parameter seem to work. If you wish to "freeze" a parameter — that is, keep it fixed while the others are optimized — simply enter an increment of zero for that parameter. The way the initial vertices are generated is crucial. The obvious method of adding the increments successively to the starting values will produce a set of points that lie on a straight line. This may be evident on inspection of Figure 8.2. Instead (see statements 300-340), the increments are added to the points in the upper half of the array S and subtracted from the lower half. This is accomplished with a direct logical statement (320), (I >= J), whose numerical value, you may recall, will be zero if false, and −1 if true. The initial vertices and their responses can be displayed from the main menu using the command <P>.

With the data entered and the initial vertices in place, you are ready to start the calculation using command <C>. There are four ways the iteration may end: (1) At the start, you provide a maximum number of iterations to be performed; it will stop after this number. You can always resume the iteration if this is insufficient. (2) If the response R<EP, the iteration will stop. In statement 1030, EP is set to 1E−6; with such a small value for EP, the iteration is unlikely to end by this route; but, generally, it seems better to keep EP small and to end the iteration by one of the other routes. (3) If the best and worst response (BR, WR) are closer than EP (statement 1160), the iteration will end. This indicates that the iteration has converged to some point that, one hopes, is the correct answer. (4) Push the PANIC button; that is, hit the <Q> key. This will cause a return to 100 at the end of the current calculation. The responses are displayed throughout the calculation; watch them and push <Q> if you don't seem to be making any progress. (Don't get too impatient, SIMPLEX sometimes dawdles.)

The data in the program are from Reference 7, for the equation:

$$y = a + b \, e^{cz} \tag{8.6}$$

With initial guesses and increments of 1 and 0.1, respectively, for all parameters, the program should converge to parameters = 0.092734, 2.00283, 0.299835 with R = 3.3E−3 in 150 to 200 iterations. This will take about 5 minutes, so pull up a comfortable chair. (These answers are not quite the same as given by Cooper; this may simply be a matter of which "pit" on the surface you land in − different ways of generating the initial points, and different initial guesses, give slightly different answers.)

The virtues of the simplex method are its stability (it will not diverge) and the simplicity of its code. It is not necessary to know anything about the derivatives of the response function, nor do they need to

be calculated numerically. It is extremely flexible; any function that can
be coded can be used. It has even been used in NMR for adjusting magnet
homogeneity (as suggested above); in an hour, or so, it can achieve results
comparable to those obtainable by a trained technician in 5 minutes.

Against these virtues, the principal complaint is its slowness. Clearly
this is one place where a compiler would be welcomed. Bad initial guesses
and/or increments can produce fruitless and possibly endless iterations; if
this happens, hit $<Q>$ and start over. In order to avoid false minima,
you must have a reasonable initial estimate of the values of the parameters. However, this is a common feature of all nonlinear least-squares
methods. The program as written provides no error estimates for the
parameters, and no convergence criterion based on the parameters. From
the main menu, the command $<P>$ will list the current vertices and their
responses; this will give you some idea of how well they have converged.

Command $<F>$ will calculate the function for a given X; this can be
used to check the results after the iteration is complete.

Applications

As mentioned earlier, Eq. 8.3 can be applied to enzyme kinetics and
Langmuir adsorption (Reference 1, Sections 10.10 and 10.9 respectively).

Nonlinear regression can also be used to determine intermolecular
potential constants from experimental second virial coefficients (Reference
1, Section 1.7). For example, the square-well potential, $U(r)$, is defined
as:

$$
\begin{aligned}
U(r) &= \infty & &\text{for } 0 < r < \sigma \\
U(r) &= -\epsilon & &\text{for } \sigma < r < R\sigma \\
U(r) &= 0 & &\text{for } R\sigma < r < \infty
\end{aligned}
\tag{8.7}
$$

where R is a unitless constant that measures the width of the well in mul-
tiples of the molecular diameter parameter, σ. The second virial coefficient
for the square-well potential can be shown to be:

$$
B(T) = b_0 \left[1 - (R^3 - 1)(e^{\epsilon/kT} - 1) \right]
\tag{8.8}
$$

with

$$
b_0 = 2\pi L \sigma^3 / 3
$$

(k is Boltzmann's constant, and L is Avogadro's number.) The three parameters, b_o, ϵ/k, and R, can be determined from experimental second virial coefficients by nonlinear least squares. For most gases, the best value of R is about 1.8, and this value is often presumed if the data are insufficient for determining 3 parameters. The value of b_0 will be about the same as the van der Waals b. The well depth, ϵ/k in units of kelvins, can be estimated as 0.56 times the Lennard-Jones well depth, provided this quantity is known.

The viscosity of gases as a function of temperature is given by the Sutherland equation:

$$\eta = \frac{k_s\, T^{3/2}}{T + S} \tag{8.9}$$

The first constant, k_s, can be calculated from kinetic theory (Reference 1, Chapter 9). The second constant, S, is called the Sutherland constant and can be related to the intermolecular potential. Determining these constants from experimental viscosity values can be done by linearizing Eq. 8.9, but nonlinear least squares is probably preferable.

The concentration of a reactant as a function of time, $C(t)$, for a first-order reaction is given by:

$$C(t) = C(0)e^{-kt} \tag{8.10}$$

where $C(0)$ is the initial concentration and k is the rate constant. Frequently, one measures some quantity that is proportional to C, not C itself. For example, one may measure absorbance, conductivity, pressure or the volume (*via* a dilatometer). Let us call this property λ with the value at $t = 0$, λ_0, and at infinite time, λ_∞. Then:

$$C = p(\lambda - \lambda_\infty)$$
$$C(0) = p(\lambda_0 - \lambda_\infty) \tag{8.11}$$

where p is a proportionality factor. With this, Eq. 8.10 becomes:

$$\lambda = \lambda_\infty + (\lambda_0 - \lambda_\infty)e^{-kt} \tag{8.12}$$

Of course, Eq. 8.12 can be linearized as a plot of $\ln(\lambda - \lambda_\infty)$ *vs.* t, provided, of course, that the infinity value is known. Therein lies the rub. Since the infinity value is approached asymptotically, one must wait many half-lives before making that measurement — and that without knowing the value of the rate constant. This is slow and uncertain. Even if the infinity value is known, the subtraction $\lambda - \lambda_\infty$ will exaggerate the errors of the later points, and the use of the logarithmic scale will give these points (whose relative error is greater than that of the earlier points) an excessive weight; the comments made earlier regarding the undesirability of linearizing data apply here with a vengeance. With a nonlinear least squares fit to Eq. 8.12, the infinity value need not be known in advance, and the need to change variables from λ to $\ln(\lambda - \lambda_\infty)$ is avoided. It is generally best to leave the initial value to be determined as well, making this a three parameter model. The reason for doing this is that, otherwise, the initial value (λ_0), which is measured no more accurately than the others, is given excessive weight in determining the parameters. (Similar equations can be derived for other orders of reaction.)

Equation 8.12 arises also in the measurement of spin-lattice relaxation times in NMR. Then the measurable quantity (λ) is the peak intensity, which is proportional to the magnetization at time t. The same problems occur: One must wait a very long time to determine the infinity value, and the initial value is uncertain. For that reason, nonlinear least squares is greatly preferred over the traditional semilogarithmic plots.

Assignment 8.1: Fit the data below to (see Eq. 8.12):

Y = A + B*EXP(−C*X)

X	Y	X	Y
1	8.17	2	7.12
3	6.48	4	6.10
5	5.86	6	5.72
7	5.63	8	5.58
9	5.55	10	5.53

From inspection of the data, we see that, at large X, Y is approaching a value of about 5; therefore, a good guess for A is 5 (increment 0.5). At X = 0, Y = A + B, and this value is greater than 8; therefore, a guess of 5 for B is also reasonable (increment 0.5). With an initial guess for C of 1 (increment 0.1), the calculation should converge in 50 to 70 iterations (about 5 minutes) to:

A = 5.49969, B = 4.40149, C = 0.499768, R = 1.996E−3

Assignment 8.2: Fit the following data to Eq. 8.3:

X	Y	X	Y
1	2.06	2	3.14
3	3.81	4	4.26
5	4.58	6	4.83
7	5.02	8	5.18
9	5.30		

Starting with guesses (increments) of 6(1) and 2(0.5), the calculation should converge in about 50 iterations (about 2 minutes) to A = 6.60102, B = 2.20193, R = 2.73E−3.

Assignment 8.3: Use the data below ("obs.") for the second virial coefficient of carbon tetrafluoride to determine the parameters of the square-well potential, Eq. 8.8.

$T(K)$	$B(\text{obs.,cm}^3)$	$B(\text{calc.,2})$	$B(\text{calc.,3})$
273	−111	−109	−111
373	−44	−47	−43
473	−10	−14	−12
673	17	21	18

Rather than using R as a parameter, use $(R^3 - 1)$. Because there are only four experimental points, start out assuming $R = 1.8$ ($R^3 - 1 = 4.8$) and fix this parameter by setting the increment to zero. After determining reasonable values for the other two parameters, turn the third parameter loose and determine the optimum value for R. (Best response: 1.16)

Command <F> in SIMPLEX permits you to calculate $y = f(x)$, the theoretical value of the dependent variable, for any value of x input. This will also serve for interpolation/extrapolation, and could be used to obtain points for plotting the fitted function. The table above gives calculated values of B for a two-parameter fit ("calc.,2") and a three-parameter fit ("calc.,3") to the data given.

One could argue that fitting 4 points to a 3 parameter model is unsound, and there is some truth to that. On the other hand, there is one degree of freedom and a good fit is not guaranteed (three points do not necessarily fit a straight line) unless the model has some degree of validity. However, to get really trustworthy results, one should have at least twice as many points as parameters to be fit. In this case, the value obtained for R in the three-parameter fit (1.33) is a good bit smaller that that found for other molecules.

Assignment 8.4: Fit the data below, for the viscosity of sulfur dioxide, to the Sutherland equation (Eq. 8.9). The values in parentheses were calculated with the best-fit parameters.

T(K)	η(micropoise)	(calculated)
273	117	(117.134)
293	126	(126.506)
323	140	(140.389)
373	163	(163.019)
423	186	(184.981)
473	207	(206.272)
523	227	(226.904)
573	246	(246.903)

The same source that gave these data, claimed that the Sutherland constant was $S = 306$ K. Do you agree?

Assignment 8.5: The kinetics of hydration of isobutene in perchloric acid was determined by measuring the solution volume with a dilatometer.

This reaction was used as an example by A. A. Frost and R. G. Pearson (*Kinetics and Mechanism*, 1953: New York, John Wiley and Sons, pages 38-49); consult this reference for further details. Selected data are given below:

Time (minutes)	Dilatometer Reading
0	18.84
5	18.34
10	17.91
15	17.53
20	17.19
25	16.86
30	16.56
35	16.27
40	16.00
120 (after lunch)	13.50
130	13.19
140	13.35

Fit these data to Eq. 8.12 and compare your results to those given by Frost and Pearson (infinity reading $= 12.16$, rate constant $k = 1.322 \times 10^{-2}$). It is worth reading this reference to see the involved method required to obtain infinity readings without computers (Guggenheim's method, page 48); your results will be significantly different.

Next, eliminate the first $(t = 0)$ point and run SIMPLEX again; you will find that the response decreases drastically (to about 8×10^{-3}). If a reaction has a multistep mechanism, there is often an initial transient or induction period, and the first point will not fit the same curve as the later points. See Reference 1, Chapter 10, for details. For that reason, it is often a good idea not to use the initial point in kinetic curve fitting, even if it is known.

Assignment 8.6: When computer data collection (*cf.* Chapter 7) is used, in NMR for example, a problem that frequently occurs is that the peak (or resonance) is often defined by only a few points. This makes difficult the determination of important parameters such as the peak height, width, area, and the actual position of the peak maximum. If the theoretical line shape function is known, these can be determined accurately by curve fitting. In NMR, the theoretical line shape (which is not always observed in practice) is the Lorenzian function:

$$y = \frac{AB^2}{B^2 + (x - C)^2} \tag{8.13}$$

In Eq. 8.13, y is amplitude of the peak, and x is the frequency offset. The parameters to be determined are the maximum amplitude of the peak (A), the width parameter (B, the full width at half maximum intensity is $2B$), and the value of x at the maximum (C). Use the data below to determine these parameters:

X	Y	X	Y
16	2.55	21	32.53
17	2.94	22	9.40
18	6.00	23	4.17
19	17.77	24	2.41
20	88.65		

A thoughtful inspection of these data will tell you reasonable guesses for the values of the parameters A, B, and C. You should converge to a response of about 0.4 in 60 to 70 iterations.

Assignment 8.7: Use the PV data below (for $T = 203$ K) to estimate the van der Waals constants for the gas.

P(atm)	V(liters)	P(atm)	V(liters)
1	16.56	10	1.561
20	0.7232	30	0.4402
40	0.2929	50	0.1978

Because of the nature of the van der Waals equation, it will be necessary to use P as the dependent variable (Y) and V as the independent variable (X). Use the constants so derived to estimate the critical temperature of this gas. Answers: $a = 2.46$, $b = 0.0502$, R = 0.0285 in about 40 iterations. Critical temperature is 177 K. (These data are for methane; you will find these numbers are quite different from the literature values.)

Multivariate Regression

To this point we have considered only the case of regression of a dependent variable *vs.* a single independent variable. The last example, fitting the Van der Waals equation, is an example of a case for which multivariate regression is needed. That is, one wishes to find a set of parameters (a and b) to fit $P(V,T)$. Program SIMPLEX is easily adapted to such uses. The following changes are necessary:

Statement 20 (DIM) — add Z(30)

Statement 30 NP = 2: . . .

Statement 40 DEF FNP(T,V)=0.08206*T/(V−T(2)) − T(1)/(V*V)

    (T(1) is the van der Waals *a*, T(2) is *b*.)

Statement 50 etc: change data statements, of course.

Statement 210 FOR I = 1 TO M: READ P,V,T

Statement 220 Z(I)=P: X(I)=T: Y(I)=V

Statement 520 R=R+(Z(I5)−FNP(X(I5),Y(I5))

Assignment 8.8: Fit the data below (for nitrogen) to van der Waals equation.

P(atm)	T(K)	V(liters)	P(calculated)
1	223.15	18.28340	1.00007
5	223.15	3.63436	5.00256
10	223.15	1.80389	10.0098
20	223.15	0.889748	20.0355
1	273.15	22.4046	0.99903
10	273.15	2.23174	9.99186
20	273.15	1.11189	19.9730
50	273.15	0.44191	50.0017
5	373.15	6.13064	4.99820
20	373.15	1.53844	19.9777
50	373.15	0.621118	49.9670
5	473.15	7.77970	4.99961
10	473.15	3.89744	9.998
20	473.15	1.95651	19.9966
50	473.15	0.792572	50.04

You should converge to a response of about 0.02 with answers near to, but not exactly equal to, the "accepted values": $a = 1.39$, $b = 0.039$. Some difference is to be expected, since the values given in reference books are usually calculated from the critical constants and, thus, are effectively "fit" to PVT data near the critical point. The parameters you get are the best ones for representing PVT data in the temperature range used, *i.e.* 223 to 473 K.

Assignment 8.9: Use the data from the previous assignment to determine the parameters of the Berthelot equation:

$$P = \frac{RT}{(V - b)} - \frac{a}{TV^2} \qquad (8.14)$$

Answers: $R = 0.0138$ (better than van der Waals!), $a = 213.1$, $b = 0.0267$.

Concluding Remarks

The most impressive feature of SIMPLEX is its flexibility. By changing only the function and DATA statements, a wide variety of problems can be solved. Indeed, there are a great number of problems that chemists still solve by linearization that would be better solved using nonlinear regression. No doubt, many people continued to use stone axes after the iron age began.

One of the applications of nonlinear regression mentioned was the analysis of enzyme-kinetic data (Eq. 8.3). Another notable feature of this equation is that the variable (Y) is actually a derivative — that is, Eq. 8.3 as applied to the Michaelis-Menten mechanism is really:

$$-\frac{dx}{dt} = \frac{ax}{b + x} \tag{8.15}$$

where x is the substrate concentration and t is time (see Eq. 4.3). This equation is readily integrated to give:

$$kt = b \ln (x_0 / x) + (x_0 - x) \tag{8.16}$$

where x_0 is the initial concentration of the substrate. Enzyme kinetics is one of the few areas in which the differential method for determining rate constants is used; most kineticists avoid this method because of the problems inherent in the differentiation of experimental data. Perhaps this is because the integrated equation (8.16) is difficult to handle by traditional methods. On the other hand, SIMPLEX can handle this problem with ease. Equation 8.16 is easily solved for t, which would have to be the "dependent" variable, and the parameters determined in the usual manner. (It is probably best to use a three-parameter fit with x_0, the initial concentration of the substrate, left to be determined, for reasons explained above.)

One of the major limitations of SIMPLEX is that it does not provide confidence limits for the parameters determined. Caceci and Cacheris (*op. cit.*) recommend a Monte Carlo sensitivity analysis. Another way to estimate the errors in the parameter could be to vary each parameter (one at a time, with the others fixed) until the response increases by some fraction. Since the response used in this version of SIMPLEX is actually the standard deviation of the points, the limits of the parameters that double the response should correspond to something like 90% confidence limits.

CHAPTER 9: DIFFERENTIAL EQUATIONS

The need for solving differential equations arises in many areas of physical chemistry; for example, quantum theory, the study of transport processes (diffusion, viscosity, and so on), and the study of molecular dynamics (scattering, for example). The only applications to be discussed in this chapter are those that arise in the study of the rates of chemical reactions — that is, chemical kinetics.

The solution of differential equations is a very broad subject, and, since only certain limited types of differential equations can be solved analytically, the numerical solution of differential equations is an equally wide area. In this chapter we shall discuss only one limited aspect of this topic, namely the solution of sets of coupled first-order differential equations of the type one encounters in chemical kinetics.

Problem Statement

A first-order differential equation has the general form:

$$\frac{dy}{dx} = f(x,y) \tag{9.1}$$

If the right-hand side is a function of x only, for example

$$\frac{dy}{dx} = ax^n \tag{9.2}$$

the equation can be solved by direct integration. If the right-hand side is a function of y only, for example

$$\frac{dy}{dx} = by^n \tag{9.3a}$$

the equation can be integrated, after a simple separation of variables, in the form:

$$\frac{dy}{y^n} = b \, dx \tag{9.3b}$$

This form of equation occurs frequently in chemical kinetics. In fact, the general case, Eq. 9.1, for which the right-hand side depends explicitly on the independent variable (x, in kinetics this is time, so we shall usually call the independent variable t) is not the usual case. However, such a case could arise in situations where one or more of a set of coupled equations can be solved analytically. In the discussion to follow, it will generally be assumed that the right-hand side depends only on y (that is, concentration) and not x (that is, time). Differential equations that must be solved numerically generally occur when the equations result from complex, multistep, reaction schemes, involving non-first-order reactions; in such cases, the variables usually cannot be separated either directly or through any simple transformation of variables.

Equations of Chemical Kinetics

An elementary reaction, a chemical reaction that occurs in a single step, will generally have a rate law of the form:

$$\frac{dC}{dt} = -kC^n \tag{9.4}$$

where C is the concentration of the reactant, and n is the order of the reaction. Most often such reactions are first order ($n = 1$) or second order ($n = 2$). Very few chemical reactions are of this type. More often the reaction will proceed via a variety of intermediates and steps. The set of reactions whose overall effect is to turn reactants into products, is called the *mechanism* of the reaction. (See Reference 1, Chapter 10 for further discussion of this point.)

The simplest scheme of this type is consecutive first-order reactions:

$$A \xrightarrow{1} B \xrightarrow{2} P \tag{9.5}$$

for which the differential equations governing the concentrations of the species A, B and C are:

$$\frac{d[A]}{dt} = -k_1[A]; \quad \frac{d[B]}{dt} = -k_1[A] - k_2[B]; \quad \frac{d[P]}{dt} = k_2[B] \tag{9.6}$$

This set of equations can be solved analytically and the solutions can be found in most physical chemistry texts. Since we shall need them later, they will be presented here:

$$[A] = A_0 e^{-k_1 t} \tag{9.7a}$$

$$[B] = \frac{k_1 A_0}{k_2 - k_1} \left[e^{-k_1 t} - e^{-k_2 t} \right] \quad (k_1 \neq k_2) \tag{9.7b}$$

$$[B] = k_1 A_0 t e^{-k_1 t} \quad (k_1 = k_2) \tag{9.7c}$$

where A_0 is the initial concentration of A and the initial concentrations of B and P were presumed to be zero. The concentration of the product (P) can be obtained by material balance:

$$[P] = A_0 - [B] - [A] \tag{9.7d}$$

The reason that the consecutive first-order scheme is discussed in so many texts is that it is mathematically simple. But it is not especially interesting from the chemical kinetics point of view since second-order elementary reactions are generally more common than first-order.

The simplest chemically interesting reaction scheme:

$$A + B \underset{2}{\overset{1}{\rightleftharpoons}} C \overset{3}{\rightarrow} P \tag{9.8}$$

is already a candidate for numerical methods. (To ward off nit pickers, let it be admitted that this scheme can be solved analytically. However, since even advanced texts do not generally give the solution, it must be presumed that it is complicated. An analytical solution is usually more valuable than a numerical solution, but the advantage diminishes as the analytical solution becomes more complicated. In any case, the numerical method is the only one that works in general, so the question as to whether any particular scheme can be solved analytically will, henceforth, be dismissed as irrelevant.)

Euler's Method

As an introduction, let us solve the simplest of the kinetic equations, the one-step first-order reaction, by the simplest method. Since the analytical solution is known, it will be possible to check the accuracy of the method.

$$\frac{dC}{dt} = -kC \quad \text{(solution)} \quad C = C_0 e^{-kt} \tag{9.9}$$

This is an example of a first-order initial-value problem — that is, the initial concentration and the initial rate (dC/dt) are known. Given the initial concentration $C(0)$, the simplest estimate of the concentration a short time $(t = h)$ later is a linear extrapolation using the slope at $t = 0$:

$$C(h) = C(0) + \left(\frac{dC}{dt} \right) = C(0) - hkC(0)$$

where dC/dt can be calculated using the rate law (in this case, Eq. 9.9). This process can be continued, with the general step being:

$$C(t + h) = C(t) + h\left(\frac{dC}{dt} \right) = C(t) - hkC(t) \tag{9.10}$$

with dC/dt being calculated from the rate law at time t (Eq. 9.9 in this case). The miniprogram below will solve Eq. 9.9 by this method and print both the exact and estimated answers.

Miniprogram 9.1

```
10 K=0.01
20 C=1
30 FOR T=1 TO 100 STEP 1
40 D=−K∗C
50 C=C+D
60 PRINT T,C,EXP(−K∗T)
70 NEXT
```

The last value, when K∗T=1, is of course, $1/e = 0.367879441$. Your answer will be in error by approximately 0.5%. Try this program using other step sizes and observe the effect on the accuracy. Note that in this and other such methods the accuracy will not improve limitlessly with decreasing step size. The reason is that your computer is doing finite mathematics — that is, the number of significant figures is limited — and the increase in the number of steps needed as the step size is decreased will result in increased problems with round-off errors. Clearly the more significant figures you have the better, but some limit will be reached eventually in any case.

Runge-Kutta Methods

The major fault of Euler's method is its use of the slope at the beginning of the interval for extrapolation. If $S = dC/dt$ were known at the end of the interval as well, it would clearly be better to use the average slope to make the extrapolation:

$$C(t + h) = C(t) + \left[S(t + h) + S(t) \right] \frac{h}{2} \qquad (9.11)$$

but, of course, we can't calculate *S(t+h)* without knowing *C(t+h)*. This dilemma can be resolved by using Eq. 9.10 to estimate *C(t+h)* which can then be used to calculate the slope needed in Eq. 9.11. This two-step method is one of the second-order Runge-Kutta methods. Of the various Runge-Kutta methods, the fourth-order method is preferred. Since this is the method we shall be using, we shall defer its discussion until later.

Other Methods

There are a number of criticisms that can be made of Runge-Kutta methods. First, there is no built-in accuracy test, and the choice of step size, a very critical point in the compromise between speed and accuracy, is left to the intuition of the user. Also it is, among the commonly used methods, the least efficient in terms of the computational time required to obtain a given accuracy.

Runge-Kutta uses only the current point to estimate the next point. Predictor-corrector methods use information that the Runge-Kutta method ignores, namely, the most recent points before the current one. For example, one could use the three most recent points (*i*, *i*−1, and *i*−2, where *i* is the index of the current point), fit them to a quadratic polynomial, and use this to predict the value of the next point (*i*+1). Of course, you must first get some points as starters, and this is usually done using the Runge-Kutta method. This predicted value is then used with the two most recent points (*i* and *i*−1) to calculate a corrected value for the new point. Acton (Reference 3) has a good, if somewhat opinionated, discussion of this, and other, methods. The major criticism of predictor-corrector methods is that they tend to be unstable — especially with equations of the type found in chemical kinetics.

The problem of optimizing speed *vs.* accuracy can be solved by using methods such as the Richardson extrapolation; which that was discussed in Chapter 5. As can be seen from that chapter (compare programs ROMBERG and SIMPSON), such methods require rather complicated code; however; the guaranteed accuracy provided is surely worth the effort. The fourth-order Runge-Kutta method used below is easy to implement and has been found to perform satisfactorily in all cases tested. Put another way, it's not glamorous, but it works (the VW "beetle" of numerical methods).

Systems of Kinetic Equations

A general system of kinetic equations for the concentration of N species, C_i, $i = 1$ to N, can be written as:

$$\frac{dC_i}{dt} = f_i(C_i \cdots C_N) \qquad (9.12)$$

There will be as many as N equations of this type, but because some concentrations can usually be obtained from material balance (for example, Eq. 9.7d), a smaller number may be adequate. (In the program below, it is assumed that $N-1$ equations will be needed.)

Given a set of concentrations C at time t, the calculation requires the following steps:

(1) Calculate from equations 9.12, the slopes

$$k_{1i} = f_i(C) \qquad (9.13a)$$

With these slopes, estimate the concentrations $(C_i^{(1)})$ at $t + h/2$ with:

$$C_{i_{(1)}} = C_i + \frac{1}{2}hk_{1i} \qquad (9.13b)$$

(These steps are done for all concentrations, C_i .)

(2) Calculate from equations 9.12 with the new concentrations, the slopes:

$$k_{2i} = f_i(C^{(1)}) \qquad (9.13c)$$

These slopes are used to get a new estimate of the concentrations at $t+h/2$:

$$C_i^{(2)} = C_i + \frac{1}{2}hk_{2i} \qquad (9.13d)$$

(3) Calculate the slopes with these new concentrations:

$$k_{3i} = f_i(C^{(2)}) \qquad (9.13e)$$

These slopes are used to estimate the concentrations at $t+h$:

$$C_i^{(3)} = C_i + hk_{3i} \qquad (9.13f)$$

(4) Calculate the slope at $t+h$ with these new concentrations:

$$k_{4i} = f_i(C^{(3)}) \qquad (9.13g)$$

Finally, the concentrations at t+h are calculated as:

$$C_i(t+h) = C_i(t) + \frac{h}{6}\left(k_{1i} + 2k_{2i} + 2k_{3i} + k_{4i}\right) \qquad (9.14)$$

This procedure is then repeated for the next interval.

The procedure explained above is implemented below in program RUNGE.

PROGRAM RUNGE

```
1 '                    PROGRAM RUNGE
2 ' TEST PROGRAM FOR CONSECUTIVE FIRST-ORDER REACTIONS
20 DEFINT I,J,L,M,N
30 REM DEFDBL H,C, D
40 FOR I=1 TO 6: W(I)=1: NEXT
100 CLS:'COMMAND CENTER
110 PRINT"T=";T,"H=";H:GOSUB 9400
120 C1=C0*EXP(-K1*T)
122 IF K1=K2 OR T=0 THEN C2=K1*C0*T*EXP(-K1*T)
        ELSE C2=K1*C0*(EXP(-K1*T)-EXP(-K2*T))/(K2-K1)
123 C3=C0-C1-C2
```

```
124 PRINT"THEORETICAL",C1,C2,C3
130 PRINT"<1> NEW CALCULATION"
140 PRINT"<2> CONTINUE CALCULATION"
150 PRINT"<3> QUIT"
154 PRINT"<4> SET WEIGHTS"
160 GOSUB 771: K=VAL(A$): IF K=0 THEN 160
170 ON K GOSUB 1000, 1100, 900, 200
180 GOTO 100
200 PRINT"INPUT WEIGHTS"
210 FOR I=1 TO 6
220 INPUT"W=";W(I)
230 NEXT
240 RETURN
600 IX=127*(T-T1)/(T2-T1) 'SCREEN PLOT FOR TRS80III
610 FOR I=1 TO NQ: Y=C(I)*W(I)
620 IY=47*Y*(Y>=0)*(Y<=1)
630 SET(IX,47-IY)
640 NEXT
650 RETURN
771 A$=INKEY$
775 IF A$="" THEN 771 ELSE RETURN
900 STOP: GOTO 100
1000 T=0: T1=0
1010 GOSUB 9000
1030 GOSUB 9500
1040 FOR I=1 TO NQ: CT(I)=C(I): NEXT
1100 INPUT"CALCULATE TO T=";T2
1110 INPUT"TIME INTERVAL";TS
1120 INPUT"NUMBER OF STEPS PER INTERVAL";NR
1130 NS=INT((T2-T1)/TS+0.499)
```

```
1134 CLS
1140 H=TS/NR: PRINT"H=";H
1200 FOR J=1 TO NS
1230 FOR L=1 TO NR
1240 A=0.5:B=1:GOSUB 9100
1250 B=2:     GOSUB 9100
1260 A=1:     GOSUB 9100
1270 A=0: B=1: GOSUB 9100
1280 FOR I=1 TO NQ-1
1290 C(I)=C(I)+H*DS(I)/6
1300 CT(I)=C(I): DS(I)=0
1310 NEXT I
1320 NEXT L
1330 T=T1+J*TS: C(NQ)=C0
1333 FOR I=1 TO NQ-1: C(NQ)=C(NQ)-C(I): NEXT
1340 GOSUB 600
1343 IF INKEY$="Q" THEN T1=1: RETURN
1350 NEXT J
1360 T1=T
1370 GOSUB 771: RETURN
8000 FOR IS=1 TO NQ-1
8010 CT(IS)=C(IS)+H*DK(IS)*A
8020 DS(IS)=DS(IS)+DK(IS)*B
8030 NEXT IS
8040 RETURN
9000 ' CHANGE THIS PART TO CHANGE THE PROBLEM BEING
     SOLVED
9010 NQ=3: C0=1: C(1)=C0
9020 FOR I=2 TO NQ: C(I)=0: NEXT
9090 RETURN
```

9100 DK(1)=−K1*CT(1)

9110 DK(2)=+K1*CT(1)−K2*CT(2)

9190 GOTO 8000

9400 PRINT"K1=";K1,"K2=";K2

9410 PRINT"CONCENTRATION",C(1),C(2),C(3)

9420 RETURN

9500 INPUT"K1=";K1

9510 INPUT"K2=";K2

9520 RETURN

Comments on RUNGE

The program as written solves the consecutive first-order system described earlier (Eqs. 9.6 and 9.7); the analytical solutions given by Eq. 9.7 are computed for purposes of comparison. Since the decay of species A is simple first-order (like Eq. 9.9), the accuracy in its calculation can be compared to the results you obtained earlier using Euler's method. The results given below were obtained using a 7 digit computer (single-precision); your results may differ slightly if you are using a different type of computer.

Test data for K1 = 0.01, K2 = 0.02					
Method	T	H	C(1)	C(2)	C(3)
Euler	100	1	0.366032	−	−
RUNGE	100	20	0.367879	0.232544	0.399576
RUNGE	100	10	0.367880	0.232540	0.399580
exact	100	−	0.367879	0.232544	0.399580
RUNGE	200	20	0.135346	0.116972	0.747682
RUNGE	200	10	0.135336	0.117019	0.747646
exact	200	−	0.135335	0.117020	0.747645

The fact that the accuracy at T=100 is better for the larger increment (H) suggests that the error is primarily round-off error; note that deleting "REM" from statement 30 will make the calculation double-precision.

Computers such as the Apple II, which has nine significant figures (but no double precision), should do better on this example.

Statements 600-650 are for plotting on a TRS80 model III; if you are using another type of computer you will surely need to change these. If your computer cannot do screen plotting (or you don't know how), you can always replace these statements with PRINTs; for example:

600 PRINT T,

610 FOR I=1 TO NQ

620 PRINT C(I),

630 NEXT

640 PRINT

650 RETURN

The main computation is done in statements 1200-1350. Note that there is a double loop in the event that you do not wish to print/plot the data at each point; you are asked for a "time interval" (TS), and a "number of steps" (NR); the increment is H = TS/NR.

To do another type of calculation, the changes needed are mostly in statements 9000- end. (A few things in the earlier parts of the program may need to be changed; for example, the material balance condition of statement 1330-1333.) Note that it is assumed (in statements 1333 and 8000) that there will be NQ-1 equations for NQ concentrations; there is no reason not to use all NQ equations for the rates of change of all concentrations, and sometimes this is necessary, but if a material balance condition is available, this way will probably be faster. The subroutine at 9000 sets up the initial conditions. The one at 9500 permits input of the rate constants. The one at 9400 prints the data. The main computation is done in the subroutine beginning at 9100; the factors k of Equations 9.13 are called DK(I); the array DS(I) is used to make the sums needed in Eq. 9.14. The array CT(I) is used to hold the intermediate concentration estimates of Eqs. 9.13. What is the purpose and meaning of the constants A and B in statements 1240-1270?

A caution about RUNGE: Usually, when an error is made in writing a program, this becomes evident when you get obviously bad answers. A feature of RUNGE, noted with sorrow by this author on several occasions, is that many errors may cause a subtle loss in performance rather than total failure. For example, the computational error for a given increment may be 0.01% rather than 0.00001%. Thus, while with a different computer you should not expect to get precisely the same answers as given here, treat any major loss in accuracy with suspicion, and check your program again, and again.

The weights (set by command <4>; initially they are all equal to one) are used in the event you wish to plot the various concentrations on different scales. This will be very useful if you modify the program to save the calculations in an array for plotting (or replotting) later.

Assignment 9.1: Modify RUNGE to do a series of consecutive first-order reactions such as:

$$A \xrightarrow{1} B \xrightarrow{2} C \xrightarrow{3} D \xrightarrow{4} E \qquad (9.15)$$

This system gives particularly interesting results if the rate constants become smaller from the first to the last steps; try, for example, values 4, 3, 2, and 1. You will need to modify the following code segments of Runge:

9100-9199, add code for the derivatives of two more species: C(3) and C(4).

9400-9499, add code to print added rate constants (K3, K4) and concentrations.

9500-9599, add code to input added rate constants: K3 and K4.

Be certain all concentrations are properly initialized in statements 9000-9099.

Change NQ to 5 in statement 9010.

Assignment 9.2: Modify RUNGE to solve the system of equations given by Eq. 9.8. The differential equations for equal initial concentrations of A and B, (C_1) are:

$$\frac{dC_1}{dt} = -k_1 C_1^2 + k_2 C_2 \tag{9.16a}$$

$$\frac{dC_2}{dt} = -k_1 C_1^2 + k_2 C_2 - k_3 C_3 \tag{9.16b}$$

$$\frac{dC_3}{dt} = k_3 C_3 \tag{9.16c}$$

(The third equation is not needed, since C_3 can be calculated by difference.) In the equations above, C_2 is the concentration of the intermediate C, and C_3 is the concentration of the product, D. Test data follows: $k_1 = 1$, $k_2 = 0.1$, $k_3 = 1$

T	H	C(1)	C(2)	C(3)
0.1	0.05	0.909516	0.0859638	0.004521
1.0	0.10	0.51380	0.272820	0.21338
5.0	0.20	0.186995	0.0496945	0.763311
10	0.20	0.102777	0.0118281	0.885395
20	0.20	0.0535181	2.86836E-3	0.943614

Assignment 9.3: Systems of equations such as 9.8 are frequently solved using the steady-state approximation — that is, by setting the time derivative of the concentration of the intermediate, Eq. 9.16b, equal to zero. It can be shown (Reference 1, Eq. 10.74) that, in the steady-state, the rate of reaction will be second-order:

$$-\frac{d[\text{A}]}{dt} = k_e [\text{A}][\text{B}] \quad \text{with} \quad k_e = \frac{k_1 k_2}{k_2 + k_3} \tag{9.17}$$

Use your modification of RUNGE to test the limits of the validity and accuracy of this approximation. Reference 1, Figure 10.15, shows several such calculations.

Assignment 9.4: Solve the following system of kinetic equations using both the steady-state approximation and RUNGE:

$$A + B \underset{2}{\overset{1}{\rightleftarrows}} C$$

$$A + C \overset{3}{\rightarrow} P$$

Since the overall stoichiometry is $2A + B = P$, it will be simplest if you choose initial concentrations $A:B = 2:1$. It can be shown that, in the steady state, this reaction may be either second-order or third-order, depending on the relative values of k_2 and k_3. Use your calculations to test this conclusion. Reference 1, Figure 10.16, shows some sample computations.

Step Size and Stiffness

As mentioned earlier, the choice of step size (h) is critical when using the Runge-Kutta method — too small and tedium and round-off error set in, too large and the errors can be so large that the calculation is meaningless. Fortunately, with kinetic equations, excessive errors usually show up as wildly unrealistic behavior. For example, the concentration of a reactant or intermediate, slowly approaching zero at long times as it properly should, will suddenly veer off toward infinity and your computer will rudely announce "OVERFLOW ERROR."

A reasonable criterion for the choice of step size can be obtained from the concept of the mean lifetime of a species. For a species that is decaying by a first-order reaction, the lifetime is simply the reciprocal of the rate constant, $1/k$. For a second-order reaction, the lifetime is $1/kC$, where C is the concentration. Since C is changing in an initially unpredictable manner, a conservative estimate is $1/kC_0$, where C_0 is the largest initial concentration (of any species, not necessarily the one in question). Thus for any step for which a rate constant is specified, a minimum lifetime can be calculated. The rule is that h must be smaller than the shortest lifetime in the reaction scheme. It should be shorter by at least a factor of 2; 5 or 10 is safer.

In a system of reactions that has rates that differ by an order of magnitude or more, one is faced with a dilemma in the choice of step size. The overall progress of the reaction will be governed by the slowest step, but the step size must be determined, as described above, to satisfy the fastest step. There is a strong temptation, as the calculation grinds slowly, ever so slowly, towards its conclusion, to increase the step size; if this is done disaster is likely; the program you wrote for Eqs. 9.16 can demonstrate this readily — make k_3 much smaller (slower) than the other two. But with calculations required to very large times, with very small step sizes, a large number of steps will be necessary and round-off error is likely to become a problem. Such systems of differential equations are referred to as stiff. In such a case, double precision is highly recommended. Edleson, *J. Chem. Ed.*, **52**, 643 (1975) has a discussion of this problem and gives references to good algorithms for stiff differential equations.

This is the important conclusion: in a set of chemical reactions, the step size for computation is determined by the lifetime of the fastest step, not by the overall rate of change of the reactants.

Numerical Methods in Chemical Kinetics

The major advantage of numerical solutions for kinetic equations is that relatively few approximations are necessary, and mechanisms of any complexity can, in principle, be handled. However, such a solution is inferior to analytical solutions, even if approximate, in one respect. You can, with a program such as RUNGE, calculate the concentrations of all reactants, products, and intermediates given the mechanism and values for the rate constants. But that is backwards — more often you know the concentrations and are trying to discover the mechanism and to calculate values for the rate constants. Thus you are reduced to trial and error. However, one could envision coupling a program such as RUNGE with a program such as SIMPLEX to determine the rate constants. Nevertheless, you still must make an educated guess about the mechanism. Since RUNGE and SIMPLEX are the slowest programs in this book, the program we imagine may be unimaginably slow.

Perhaps the best use of such programs is in conjunction with approximate methods, in order to test the validity of those approximations. It is such an application that is suggested by Assignments 9.3 and 9.4. The steady-state approximation is often the only alternative suggested by texts for solving complex systems of kinetic equations. Yet there are fairly rigorous limitations on its validity. The steady-state approximation consists of assuming that the rate of change of the concentration of some or all intermediates in a chemical reaction is small compared to the rates for disappearance of reactants or appearance of products. This generally is valid if the intermediates are reactive and short-lived, in which case there never is any significant concentration of intermediate. A little exploration with the program written for the reaction scheme 9.8 will find many situations for which the steady-state solutions are flat-out wrong.

There are at least two other situations for which the steady-state approximation is inappropriate. In chain reactions that have branching steps, the concentration of an intermediate may, in certain situations, far from reaching a steady-state, undergo uncontrolled growth. In such cases, and explosion will usually result. It should be quite practical to simulate such a case using RUNGE, and this illustrates another utility for numerical computation in chemical kinetics — it allows you to "play" chemistry and explore the effect of various conditions on a given reaction scheme, all from the safety of your computer console.

Grass, Deer, and Wolves

Another situation in which reactions fail to reach a steady state is the recently discovered case of oscillating chemical reactions. In these reactions, the concentrations, rather than decaying or increasing calmly, will oscillate in time. When this oscillation is accompanied by a color change, the result is a spectacular sight. Jordan (*Chemical Kinetics and Transport*, Plenum Press, N.Y., 1979) gives a more extensive discussion and further references on this subject. Here we shall only discuss a mathematically related problem in wildlife management.

Oscillations of animal populations are well known and can be explained by a relatively simple mathematical model. We have three parameters: grass (G) which is eaten by deer (D) which are eaten by wolves (W). It is assumed that the rate of increase of the animal populations is proportional to their food supply, which is, as a result, depleted by population growth. These ideas can be expressed mathematically by the following differential equations:

$$\frac{dG}{dt} = k_1 - k_2 D \tag{9.19}$$

$$\frac{dD}{dt} = k_3 GD - k_4 W - k_5 D \tag{9.20}$$

$$\frac{dW}{dt} = k_6 DW - k_7 W \tag{9.21}$$

The constants in these equations (recommended values in parentheses) follow. (Note that the units are arbitrary, so the numbers given have no physical significance. The unit of grass could be square miles, the unit of deer could be thousands, the unit of wolves could be hundreds, or they could be something else.)

K1:   The rate of growth of the grass. (1.0)

K2:   Rate at which grass is eaten by a unit of deer population. (0.5)

K3:   Rate of increase of deer population (birth rate). (0.002)

K4:   Rate that a unit population of wolves eats deer. (0.40)

K5:   Natural death rate of deer. (0.02)

K6:   Birth rate of wolves. (0.2)

K7:   Death rate of wolves. (0.4; wolves lead short but active lives.)

Assignment 9.5: Modify RUNGE (name the new program "DEER") to solve the equations above. Since there is no material balance condition, you will need to solve all three equations; this involves changing NQ-1 to NQ in statements 1280 and 8000. Also delete the "C(NQ)=C0" part of statement 1330 and delete statement 1333 entirely.

If you use the following initial populations together with the constants given above, the equations will be in a steady-state — that is, all derivatives will be equal to zero and the populations will not change: $G = 20$, $D = 2$, $W = 0.1$ (arbitrary units). However, it is an unstable steady-state, and any change of constants or initial conditions will start the oscillations. For example, try changing the initial W to 0.12 or the initial D to 1.8. You should find that the populations oscillate several times for $T < 200$, but the amplitude of the oscillations is increasing; at or about $T = 200$, the system goes out of control (wolves die?), and the curves take off to infinity or (worse) negative infinity.

Clearly, this is a more interesting program if you can present the results graphically; this is a case where you will appreciate (or wish you had) a color graphics monitor. With this, you are ready to play "wild life management."

The results indicate some sort of stability problem, since the populations not only oscillate but tend to oscillate out of control. There are several possible explanations. (1) There could be a numerical problem in solving the equations. This seems unlikely since varying the step size by a factor of 5 seemed to have no effect. (2) Wildlife populations are inherently unstable. This seems unlikely since some such populations have survived for a long time; on the other hand, some animals have become extinct. (3) The mathematical model is inadequate. Nothing could be more true! It is certainly oversimplified. Even uneaten grass will not grow indefinitely. Are birth rates directly proportional to food supply? Is this a good way to take the starvation factor into account? Since this book is not about wildlife management, all of these questions will be left unanswered. The lesson of this assignment is that some sets of equations, even those found in chemical kinetics, may oscillate or be unstable. This may be caused by a physically significant effect (chemical reactions and wild life populations can really oscillate — reactions can explode) or merely a mathematical artifact.

POSTSCRIPT

The Role of the Microcomputer in Chemistry

The rapid advance in technology that has changed computers from an esoteric and expensive tool into a consumer product is not yet complete, and speculations about its future are risky at best. The microcomputer has found a secure and well-defined niche in business; although one occasionally gets the impression that the world is being overrun by pie charts and bar graphs. Its role in scientific research and teaching is not as yet so clear.

Microcomputers are used, of course, for education, but at this time these uses appear to be primarily in teaching facts to students. This is surely a worthwhile objective, but one that has been accomplished with books for generations, and more cheaply at that. Computers can play a unique role in education if what they do is help the student to experiment, explore and create. The programs of this book, which in general have emphasized simplicity over accuracy and efficiency, can play such a role for students in science and engineering.

It will be admitted freely that all of the techniques discussed in this book are discussed more thoroughly in numberless texts on numerical analysis. Furthermore, all are available on mainframe computers with better, more accurate and more efficient algorithms. But this has been true for many years, yet the majority of chemists still do not use computers extensively and often are not aware of numerical methods that could help them in their research. Outdated methods of data analysis still survive. At the very least it can be hoped that the personal computer, personal, private and always available, will break down this barrier. If the end result of this book is that its readers abandon microcomputers for a mainframe, and simple techniques for better ones, it will not have been a failure.

In the proximate issue to which this book is primarily addressed, the teaching of physical chemistry, there are many unresolved problems. How should such material be included in the curriculum and what types of problems and assignments are most appropriate? While some suggestions have been made in this book, there is much to be done, and only time and only experience will tell us the best course.

REFERENCES

1. J. Noggle, *Physical Chemistry*, 1985: Boston, Little, Brown and Company.

2. B. Carnahan, H. A. Luther and J. O. Wilkes, *Applied Numerical Methods*, 1969: New York, John Wiley and Sons, Inc.

3. F. S. Acton, *Numerical Methods That Work*, 1970: New York, Harper and Row, Publishers.

4. I. Guttman and S. S. Wilkes, *Introductory Engineering Statistics*, 1965: New York, John Wiley and Sons.

5. N. Draper and H. Smith, *Applied Regression Analysis* (2nd Ed.), 1981: New York, John Wiley and Sons.

6. T. R. Dickson, *The Computer and Chemistry*, 1968: San Francisco, W. H. Freeman and Company.

7. J. W. Cooper, *Introduction to PASCAL for Scientists*, 1981: New York, John Wiley and Sons.

APPENDIX I: APPLE II PROGRAMS

```
1   REM   MINIPROGRAM 2.5
2   REM   APPLESOFT VERSION
4   REM   TRANSLATED BY DJC
5   REM
100   PRINT "THIS IS THE COMMAND CENTER:ENTER COMMAND"
120   PRINT "<I> INPUT DATA"
122   PRINT "<C> CALCULATE"
124   PRINT "<P> PLOT"
126   PRINT "<Q> QUIT
130   GET A$: IF A$ = "" THEN   GOTO 130
140 J% = 0: FOR I = 1 TO 4:
      IF A$ =   MID$ ("ICPQ",I,1) THEN J% = I
145   NEXT : IF J% = 0 THEN   GOTO 130
150   ON J% GOTO 200,300,400,900
199   GOTO 100
200   PRINT "STATEMENT 200": GOTO 100
300   PRINT "STATEMENT 300": GOTO 100
400   PRINT "STATEMENT 400": GOTO 100
900   PRINT "STATEMENT 900": GOTO 100
```

```
1   REM   SUBROUTINE FOR SCREEN PLOTTING X,Y
2   REM   APPLESOFT VERSION
4   REM   TRANSLATED BY DJC
5   REM
50 LX% = 279:LY% = 159
60   HGR : HOME
140   HGR
200 X1 = 0:X2 = 1:Y1 = 0:Y2 = .30
210   FOR X = X1 TO X2 STEP 0.01
220 Y = X * (1 - X)
230   GOSUB 600
240   NEXT
250   VTAB 23: PRINT "HIT ANY KEY": GET A$
260   TEXT : END
600   REM   SUBROUTINE FOR SCREEN PLOTTING X,Y
610 IX% = LX% * (X - X1) / (X2 - X1)
```

```
620 IY% = LY% * (Y - Y1) / (Y2 - Y1)
630  IF IX% < 0 OR IX% > LX% THEN  RETURN
640  IF IY% < 0 OR IY% > LY% THEN  RETURN
650  HPLOT IX%,LY% - IY%
660  RETURN
```

```
1   REM   PROGRAM FAC
2   REM   APPLESOFT VERSION
4   REM   TRANSLATED BY DJC
5   REM
10 PI = 3.1415926
200  INPUT P,Q
210 N% = P + Q:WL =  - N% *  LOG (2)
220 M% = N%: GOSUB 1000:WL = WL + FL
240 M% = Q: GOSUB 1000:WL = WL - FL
250 M% = P: GOSUB 1000:WL = WL - FL
260 W =  EXP (WL): PRINT "PROBABILITY=";W
270  END
1000   REM   SUBROUTINE TO CALCULATE LOG FACTORIAL (FL)
1005  IF M% < 0 THEN  PRINT "ILLEGAL INPUT": GOTO 200
1010  IF M% = 0 THEN FL = 0: RETURN : REM  ZERO FACT
1020   IF M% < NX% THEN 1100
1030 FL = 0.5 *  LOG (2 * PI) + (M% + 0.5) *  LOG (M%) -
     M% + 1 / (12 * M%)
1040   RETURN
1100 PR = 1
1110   FOR I% = 1 TO M%:PR = PR * I%: NEXT
1120 FL =  LOG (PR): RETURN
```

```
1   REM   PROGRAM VDW, VANDERWAALS GAS LAW CALCULATIONS
2   REM   APPLESOFT VERSION
4   REM   TRANSLATED BY DJC
5   REM
20 R = 0.082057:G$ = "NITROGEN":F$ = "NO"
30 A = 1.39:B = 0.0391
100   HOME
110   PRINT "G=";G$,"A=";A,"B=";B,F$
120   IF T <  > 0 THEN Z = P * V / (R * T):
     REM  COMPRESSIBILITY FACTOR
130   PRINT "P=";P,"T=";T
135   PRINT "V=";V,"Z=";Z
```

```
140    PRINT "TYPE VARIABLE NAME TO CHANGE-
                 ENTER O TO CALCULATE"
145    PRINT "(TYPE <C> FOR CELSIUS,<Q> TO QUIT)"
150    GET A$: IF A$ = "" THEN  GOTO 150
160    J% = O: FOR I = 1 TO 8:
       IF A$ =  MID$ ("GABPVTCQ",I,1) THEN J% = I
162    NEXT I: IF J% = O THEN  GOTO 150
170    ON J% GOTO 200,300,400,500,600,700,750,900
199    GOTO 100
200    INPUT "NAME OF GAS,A,B:";G$,A,B: GOTO 100
300    INPUT "A=";A: GOTO 100
400    INPUT "B=";B: GOTO 100
500    INPUT "P=";P: IF P <  > O THEN F$ = "NO": GOTO 100
510 P = R * T / (V - B) - A / (V * V)
520 F$ = "OK": GOTO 100
600    INPUT "V=";V: IF V <  > O THEN F$ = "NO": GOTO 100
610 V1 = R * T / P:K = O
620 V = R * T / (P + A / (V1 * V1)) + B
630    IF  ABS (V - V1) < 1E - 6 THEN F$ = "OK": GOTO 100
640 K% = K% + 1:V1 = V: IF K% < 100 THEN  GOTO 620
650 F$ = "NOT CONV": GOTO 100
700    INPUT "T=";T: IF T <  > O THEN F$ = "NO": GOTO 100
710 T = ((P + A / (V * V)) * (V - B)) / R
720 F$ = "OK": GOTO 100
750    INPUT "DEGREES CELSIUS=";C
760 T = C + 273.15:F$ = "NO"
770    GOTO 100
900    END




1    REM   PROGRAM NEWTON
2    REM   APPLESOFT VERSION
3    REM   TRANSLATED BY DJC
4    REM
20   DEF  FN Y(X) = A + X * (B + X * (C + D * X))
30   DEF  FN D(X) = B + X * (2 * C + 3 * D * X)
40 T = 1E - 6: REM  CONVERGENCE CRITERION
100    INPUT "CONSTANTS,A,B,C,D:";A,B,C,D
110    INPUT "INITIAL X:";X
200    REM  NEWTON ITERATION
210 K% = O
220 X1 = X
230 X = X1 -  FN Y(X1) /  FN D(X1)
240 K% = K% + 1
250    IF  ABS ((X - X1) / (X + X1)) < T THEN  GOTO 300
260    IF K% < 100 THEN 220
```

```
270   PRINT "TRIED 100 ITERATIONS W/O FINISHING"
280   PRINT "LAST TWO VALUES ";X;",";X1
290   PRINT "PERHAPS..."
300   PRINT "THE ROOT IS ";X
310   END




1     REM   PROGRAM ROOTS
2     REM   APPLESOFT VERSION
4     REM   TRANSLATED BY DJC
5     REM
6     HOME
10    T = 1E - 6
12    PRINT "ROOTS BY REGULA FALSI- TOL=";T
15    PRINT "FUNCTION DEFINED AT STATEMENT 20"
20    DEF   FN Y(X) = X ^ 3 + 913 * X ^ 2 - 1023
22    PRINT "TYPE <M> FOR MANUAL SEARCH, <A> FOR AUTO"
23    GET A$
24    IF A$ = "M" THEN  GOTO 600
25    IF A$ <  > "A" THEN   GOTO 23
30    PRINT "LOWER LIMIT FOR SEARCH";
32    INPUT X1:Y1 =  FN Y(X1):X = X1
40    PRINT   TAB( 30): VTAB  PEEK (37):
      PRINT "UPPER";: INPUT XB
50    INPUT "STEP?";XS
70    X = X + XS: IF X > XB + XS / 2 THEN
      PRINT "NO ROOT IN THIS RANGE": GOTO 30
80    Y =  FN Y(X): IF  SGN (Y) =  SGN (Y1) THEN
      X1 = X:Y1 = Y: GOTO 70
90    X2 = X:Y2 = Y
100    PRINT X1;"<ROOT<";X2;: GOSUB 500: REM  CALC NEW X,Y
110    IF Y = 0 THEN  PRINT "ROOT=";Y: STOP : GOTO 10
120    IF  SGN (Y) =  SGN (Y2) THEN X2 = X:Y2 = Y: GOTO 130
125   X1 = X2:Y1 = Y2:X2 = X:Y2 = Y
130   IT = 0
140    GOSUB 500: IF  ABS (X1 - X) < T THEN 200
150   X1 = X:Y1 = Y:IT = IT + 1: IF IT < 10 THEN 140
160    PRINT : PRINT "CHOOSE:SWITCH PIVOT,RESTART,CONTINUE"
170    GET A$
180    IF A$ = "C" THEN   GOTO 130
182    IF A$ = "R" THEN   GOTO 30
185    IF A$ <  > "S" THEN   GOTO 170
190   X = X2:Y = Y2:X2 = X1:Y2 = Y1:X1 = X:Y1 = Y: GOTO 130
200    PRINT : PRINT "THE ROOT IS "X"(TOL="T")": END
500   X = (X1 * Y2 - X2 * Y1) / (Y2 - Y1):Y =  FN Y(X):
      PRINT
```

```
510    PRINT "Y("X")="Y;: RETURN
600    INPUT "VALUE OF X=";X
602    VTAB  PEEK (37): PRINT "Y("X")=" FN Y(X);"
610    PRINT "MORE?(Y/N)": GET A$: IF A$ = "Y" THEN
       GOTO 600
620    GOTO 30




1   REM   PROGRAM SYNDIV
2   REM   APPLESOFT VERSION
4   REM   TRANSLATED BY DJC
5   REM
6   REM   REAL ROOTS OF A POLYNOMIAL BY SYNTHETIC DIVISION
7   REM
8 T = 1E - 6: REM  TOLERANCE, TEST FOR CONVERGENCE
9   HOME
10    INPUT "ORDER OF POLYNOMIAL=";N
20    PRINT "ENTER COEFFICIENTS A(I)"
30    FOR I = O TO N
40    PRINT "A("I")=";
42    INPUT A(I)
44    NEXT
50    B(N) = A(N):C(N) = B(N)
55 K = O: INPUT "INITIAL GUESS FOR R";R
60    FOR I = N - 1 TO O STEP  - 1
70 B(I) = B(I + 1) * R + A(I)
80 C(I) = C(I + 1) * R + B(I)
90    NEXT
95    IF C(1) = O THEN DR = 1: GOTO 110
100 DR =  - B(O) / C(1)
105   IF  ABS (DR) < T THEN  GOTO 200
110 R = R + DR:K = K + 1
114   IF K > 100 THEN  PRINT "ITER=";K: GOTO 250
120   PRINT R,: GOTO 60
200   PRINT : PRINT "THE ROOT IS ";R
210   FOR I = 1 TO N:A(I - 1) = B(I): NEXT
220 N = N - 1
230   PRINT "COEFFICIENTS OF REDUCED POLYNOMIAL"
240   FOR I = O TO N
242   PRINT "A(";I;")=";A(I)
244   NEXT
250   PRINT : PRINT "TYPE <C> TO CONTINUE": GET A$
260   IF A$ = "C" THEN  GOTO 50
270   END
```

```
1    REM    PROGRAM LINBAR
2    REM    APPLESOFT VERSION
4    REM    TRANSLATED BY DJC
5    REM
6    REM    ROOTS OF POLYNOMIAL BY LIN-BAIRSTOW METHOD
7    REM
30   T = 1E - 8: REM TOLERANCE,CRITERION FOR CONVERGENCE
70    FOR I = O TO N
100   INPUT "N=";N%
110   PRINT "ENTER COEFFIECIENTS,A(O)...A("N%")"
120   FOR I = O TO N%: INPUT A(I): NEXT
122   IF A(N%) = O THEN N% = N% - 1: PRINT "ZERO ROOT":
      GOTO 122
124   IF N% < 3 THEN  GOTO 280
130   B(N%) = A(N%):C(N%) = A(N%):K% = O
140   K% = K% + 1: IF K% > 20 THEN
      K% = O:T = T * 10: PRINT "CONV???";T" ";EP
150   B(N% - 1) = A(N% - 1) + U * B(N%)
152   C(N% - 1) = B(N% - 1) + U * C(N%)
154   IF N% = 2 THEN  GOTO 210
160   FOR I = N% - 2 TO O STEP  - 1
170   B(I) = A(I) + U * B(I + 1) + V * B(I + 2)
200   C(I) = B(I) + U * C(I + 1) + V * C(I + 2): NEXT
210  F = C(2) * C(2) - C(1) * C(3)
212   IF F = O THEN
      PRINT "#";:DU = DU + 1:DV = DV + 1: GOTO 235
220  DU = (B(O) * C(3) - B(1) * C(2)) / F
230  DV = (C(1) * B(1) - C(2) * B(O)) / F
235  U = U + DU:V = V + DV
240  EP =  SQR (DU * DU + DV * DV)
245   IF EP > T THEN  GOTO 140
250  D = U * U + 4 * V: IF D < O THEN  GOTO 300
255   GOTO 400
260  N% = N% - 2
270   FOR I = O TO N%
272  A(I) = B(I + 2)
274   NEXT
276  A(O) = A(O) + B(O)
278  A(1) = A(1) + B(1)
280   IF N% > 2 THEN  GOTO 130
282   IF N% < 2 THEN  GOTO 500
285  U =  - A(1) / A(2):V =  - A(O) / A(2): GOTO 250
300   REM   COMPLEX ROOTS
310  RE = U / 2:W =  SQR ( - D) / 2
320   PRINT "ROOTS: REAL,";RE;"  IMAG,";W
330   GOTO 260
400   REM   REAL ROOTS
410  R1 = U / 2 +  SQR (D) / 2:R2 = U / 2 -  SQR (D) / 2
420   PRINT "REAL ROOTS:";R1","R2
```

```
430   GOTO 260
500   IF N% = 1 THEN  PRINT "LAST ROOT "; - A(O) / A(1)
510   PRINT "TOL=";T,"END OF ROOTS"
520   END




1   REM   PROGRAM LINREG: LINEAR REGRESSION
2   REM   APPLESOFT VERSION
4   REM   TRANSLATED BY DJC
5   REM
40   DIM DX(20),DY(20)
50   READ M%
60   FOR I = 1 TO M%: READ X,Y
70  DX(I) = X:DY(I) = Y
80  SX = SX + X:SY = SY + Y
82  PX = PX + X * X:PY = PY + Y * Y
84  PC = PC + X * Y
90   NEXT
100  D = M% * PX - SX * SX
110  A = (SY * PX - PC * SX) / D
120  B = (M% * PC - SX * SY) / D
130  VX = (PX - SX * SX / M%) / (M% - 1)
140  VY = (PY - SY * SY / M%) / (M% - 1)
150  RR = B * B * VX / VY
152  R =   SQR (RR)
154  E =   SQR ((1 - RR) / (M% - 2)) / R
160  RE = (M% - 1) * VY * (1 - RR): REM   APPROX RESIDUAL
170  GB =   ABS (E * B): REM   STANDARD DEVIATAION OF SLOPE
180  GA = GB *   SQR (PX / M%): REM   STANDARD DEVIATION
                                      INTERCEPT
190  GP =   SQR (RE / (M% - 1)): REM   STD DEV OF POINTS
195   HOME : PRINT   TAB( 10);"ANALYSIS"
200   PRINT "INTCPT=";A
205   PRINT "  (STD DEV=";GA;")"
210   PRINT "SLOPE=";B
215   PRINT "  (STD DEV=";GB;")"
220   PRINT "R=";R,"E=";E
222   PRINT "STD DEV PTS=";GP
230   PRINT "SUM OF SQUARES=";RE
240   PRINT "THE INDIVIDUAL RESIDUALS ARE:"
242  RA = O
250   FOR I = 1 TO M%
252  D = DY(I) - A - B * DX(I)
254  RA = RA + D * D: PRINT D,
256   NEXT
```

```
260   PRINT "SUM OF SQUARES";RA
270   DATA  8,1,1.01,2,2.02,3,3.0,4,4.01,5,5.0,6,6.02,7,
      7.01,8,8.01




1     REM   PROGRAM SIMLINEQ
2     REM   APPLESOFT VERSION
4     REM   TRANSLATED BY DJC
5     REM
6     REM   DRIVER PROGRAM FOR SLE
7     REM
50    DIM QA(9,10),BB(9),JC%(9),IR%(9),JO%(9),VY(9)
200   READ N%: REM  NUMBER OF EQUATIONS
210   FOR I = 1 TO N%
220   FOR J = 1 TO N% + 1
230   READ QA(I,J)
240 A(I,J) = QA(I,J)
250   NEXT
260   NEXT
280 FL% = O: GOSUB 10000
290   PRINT "SOLUTIONS:";
300   FOR I = 1 TO N%: PRINT BB(I);" ";: NEXT
310   PRINT
320   PRINT "INVERTED MATRIX"
330   FOR I = 1 TO N%
340   FOR J = 1 TO N%: PRINT QA(I,J),: NEXT
350   PRINT : NEXT
360   PRINT "DETERMINANT=";DT
400   PRINT "UNIT MATRIX CHECK"
410   FOR I = 1 TO N%
420   FOR J = 1 TO N%
430 U = O
440   FOR K = 1 TO N%
450 U = U + A(I,K) * QA(K,J)
460   NEXT K
470   PRINT U;"/";
480   NEXT J
490   PRINT
500   NEXT I
700   DATA  3,   0,-7,4,1,   1,9,-6,1,   -3,8,5,6
800   DATA  3,   2,-7,4,9,   1,9,-6,1,  -3,8,5,6
900   DATA  3,   -3,8,5,6,   2,-7,4,9,   1,9,-6,1
990   GET A$: GOTO 200
```

```
10000   REM   SUBROUTINE SLE
10001   REM   APPLESOFT VERSION
10003   REM   TRANSLATED BY DJC
10004   REM
10010   REM    N% IS THE NUMBER OF EQUATIONS,QA(N%,N%+10)
        IS THE MATRIX OF COEF.,RHS IN LAST COLUMN.
10020   REM SET FLAG FL%:-1 MATRIX INV ONLY,+1 SLE ONLY,
        FL%=0 FOR SLE WITH INVERSE IN PLACE.
10050   REM   SOLUTIONS RETURNED AS BB(N),DETERMINANT AS DT
10055   REM    DIMENSION STMT REQUIRED FOR QA(N%,N%+1),
        BB(N%),JC%(N%),IR%,(N%),JO%(N%),VY(N$).
10060 DT = 1:MZ% = N%: IF FL% > = 0 THEN MZ% = N% + 1
10070 EP = 1E - 12: REM   SMALLEST PERMITTED VALUE OF DET
10080   FOR K = 1 TO N%
10090 PV = 0
10100   FOR I = 1 TO N%
10110   FOR J = 1 TO N%
10120   IF K = 1 THEN 10180
10130   FOR IS = 1 TO K - 1
10140   FOR JS = 1 TO K - 1
10150   IF I = IR%(IS) THEN 10200
10160   IF J = JC%(JS) THEN 10200
10170   NEXT JS,IS
10180   IF  ABS (QA(I,J)) < = ABS (PV) THEN 10200
10190 PV = QA(I,J):IR%(K) = I:JC%(K) = J
10200   NEXT J,I
10210   IF  ABS (PV) < EP THEN DT = 0:
        PRINT "DETERMINANT ZERO": RETURN
10220 DT = DT * PV
10230   FOR J = 1 TO MZ%:
        QA(IR%(K),J) = QA(IR%(K),J) / PV: NEXT J
10240 QA(IR%(K),JC%(K)) = 1 / PV
10250   FOR I = 1 TO N%
10260 QA = QA(I,JC%(K))
10270   IF I = IR%(K) THEN 10320
10280 QA(I,JC%(K)) =  - QA / PV
10290   FOR J = 1 TO MZ%
10300   IF J < > JC%(K) THEN
        QA(I,J) = QA(I,J) - QA * QA(IR%(K),J)
10310   NEXT J
10320   NEXT I,K
10330   FOR I = 1 TO N%:JO%(IR%(I)) = JC%(I)
10340   IF FL% = > 0 THEN BB(JC%(I)) = QA(IR%(I),MZ%)
10350   NEXT I
10360 IN% = 0
10370   FOR I = 1 TO N% - 1
10380   FOR J = I + 1 TO N%
10390   IF JO%(J) > = JO%(I) THEN 10410
```

```
10400 JT% = JO%(J):JO%(J) = JO%(I):JO%(I) = JT%:
      IN% = IN% + 1
10410  NEXT J,I
10420  IF 2 *  INT (IN% / 2) <  > IN% THEN DT =  - DT
10430  IF FL% > O THEN  RETURN
10440  FOR J = 1 TO N%
10450  FOR I = 1 TO N%
10460 VY(JC%(I)) = QA(IR%(I),J)
10470  NEXT I
10480  FOR I = 1 TO N%
10490 QA(I,J) = VY(I): NEXT I
10500  NEXT J
10510  FOR I = 1 TO N%
10520  FOR J = 1 TO N%
10530 VY(IR%(J)) = QA(I,JC%(J)): NEXT J
10540  FOR J = 1 TO N%
10550 QA(I,J) = VY(J): NEXT J
10560  NEXT I
10570  RETURN




1   REM   PROGRAM MULTIREG
2   REM   APPLESOFT VERSION
4   REM   TRANSLATED BY DJC
5   REM
6   HOME
20   DIM QA(4,5),BB(4),JC%(4),IR%(4),JO%(4),VY(4)
30   DIM SX(4),SY(4),VA(4),DX(30),DY(30)
40   DEF  FN F(K) =  + (K = 1) * X + (K = 2) * X ^ 2 +
     (K = 3) * X ^ 3
50 N% = 2: REM   NUMBER OF TERMS TO USE IN FNF(STMT 40)
100   HOME : REM   COMMAND CENTER
105   IF M% > O THEN  GOSUB 2900: PRINT
110   PRINT  TAB( 5);" COMMANDS:"
115   PRINT  TAB( 5)"<R> FOR DATA INPUT AND REGRESSION"
120   PRINT  TAB( 5)"<I> TO INTERPOLATE"
130   PRINT  TAB( 5)"<Q> TO QUIT"
150   GET A$
160   IF A$ = "R" THEN  GOTO 2000
170   IF A$ = "I" THEN  GOTO 3000
180   IF A$ = "Q" THEN  GOTO 900
190   GOTO 150
900   END : GOTO 100
2000   HOME : READ M%: PRINT " X"," Y",M%;"POINTS"
2010   FOR I = 1 TO M%: READ X,Y
2012 DX(I) = X:DY(I) = Y
```

```
2014   PRINT X,Y
2020 SY = SY + Y:SX = SX + X:YY = YY + Y * Y
2030   FOR K = 1 TO N%
2040 SX(K) = SX(K) +  FN F(K)
2050 SY(K) = SY(K) + Y *  FN F(K)
2060   FOR L = K TO N%
2070 QA(K,L) = QA(K,L) +  FN F(K) *  FN F(L)
2080   NEXT L,K,I
2100   FOR K = 1 TO N%
2105   FOR L = K TO N%
2110 QA(K,L) = QA(K,L) - SX(K) * SX(L) / M%
2120 QA(L,K) = QA(K,L)
2130   NEXT L
2140 QA(K,N% + 1) = SY(K) - SY * SX(K) / M%
2150   NEXT K
2160 FL% = 0: GOSUB 10000:A = SY / M%
2170   FOR I = 1 TO N%:A = A - BB(I) * SX(I) / M%: NEXT
2172 SS = 0: PRINT "DEV OF PTS"
2174   FOR I = 1 TO M%:X = DX(I):
       GOSUB 9500:D = DY(I) - Y
2176   PRINT D,:SS = SS + D * D: NEXT
2178 SS = SS / (M% - N% - 1): PRINT
2180   FOR I = 1 TO N%:VA(I) = QA(I,I) * SS
2200   FOR J = 1 TO N%:
       SA = SA + SX(I) * SX(J) * QA(I,J) / M%
2210   NEXT J,I
2218 SA = SA * SS / M%
2230   GOSUB 2900
2300   PRINT "HIT ANY KEY TO RETURN"
2310   GET A$: GOTO 100
2500   DATA  6,1,6,2,11.01,3,17.99,4,27.01,5,37.99,6,51.01
2900   PRINT "INTERCEPT ";A;" (STD DEV "; SQR (SA);")"
2910   FOR I = 1 TO N%:
       PRINT "B(";I;")=";BB(I);" ("; SQR (VA(I));")"
2920   NEXT : PRINT "STD DEV OF PTS "; SQR (SS): RETURN
3000   REM   INTERPOLTATION
3010   INPUT "VALUE OF X";X: GOSUB 9500
3020   PRINT "Y(";X;")=";Y
3030   PRINT "<R> TO RETURN, ELSE TO CONTINUE"
3040   GET A$
3050   IF A$ = "R" THEN  GOTO 100
3060   GOTO 3010
9500 Y = A: REM  SUBROUTINE FOR CALCULATING Y=F(X)
9519   FOR K = 1 TO N%:Y = Y +  FN F(K) * BB(K): NEXT
9520   RETURN
```

```
1    REM    PROGRAM POLYREG
2    REM    APPLESOFT VERSION
4    REM    TRANSLATED BY DJC
5    REM
30   DIM DX(50),DY(50),BY(12),SX(12),SY$(12)
40   DIM QA(6,7),BB(6),JC%(6),IR%(6),JO%(6),VY(6)
100   HOME : REM   COMMAND CENTER
102   PRINT "NUMBER OF DATA POINTS=";M%;" ,ORDER=";N%:
      IF N% = O THEN 110
104   PRINT "INTERCEPT ";AA;"(";SA;")"
106   FOR J = 1 TO N%:
      PRINT "B(";J;")=";BB(J);"(";S * SQR (QA(J,J));")": NEXT
110   PRINT "COMMANDS:"
111   PRINT  TAB( 5);"<D>   DATA INPUT"
112   PRINT  TAB( 5);"<R>   REGRESSION"
113   PRINT  TAB( 5);"<E>   EVALUATE POLYNOMIAL, INTEGRAL,"
114   PRINT  TAB( 5);"      DERIVATIVE"
115   PRINT  TAB( 5);"<Q>   QUIT"
116   PRINT "?";
120 J% = O: GET A$: FOR K = 1 TO 4:
    IF A$ =  MID$ ("DREQ",K,1) THEN J% = K
125   NEXT : IF J% = O THEN 116
130   PRINT A$;: ON J% GOTO 2000,4000,9000,900
199   GOTO 120
900   END
2000  REM   DATA INPUT
2010  READ M%
2020  FOR I = 1 TO M%
2030  READ X,Y:X = X / 100
2040 DX(I) = X:DY(I) = Y: NEXT
2050  GOTO 100
2505  DATA   7,1,1,2,4,3,9,4,16,5,25,6,36,7,49
2510  DATA   7, 298.15,28.81, 400,33.00, 600,39.00, 800,
      43.11,1000,45.98,1500,49.05,  2000,52.02




4000  REM
4001  REM   SUBROUTINE PREG
4002  REM   APPLESOFT VERSION
4004  REM   TRANSLATED BY DJC
4005  REM
4010  REM REQUIRES DIM STMT FOR DX(M%),DY(M%),BY(2*N%),
      SX(2*N%), AND SY(2*N) WHERE M IS THE NUMBER OF DAT
      POINTS AND N IS THE HIGHEST-ORDER POLYNOMIAL TO BE
      USED. DATA ARE IN ARRARY DX AND DY. USES SLE
      SUBROUTINE 10000,COEF. WILL BE IN BB(I).
```

```
4020   HOME
4030   KK% = 6: IF M% < 8 THEN KK% = M% - 2
4040   PRINT "...ORDER OF POLYNOMIAL N<=";KK%;
4050   INPUT K%: IF K% <  = O THEN 100
4055   N% = K%
4060   DN = M% - N% - 1: REM   DEGREES OF FREEDOM
4070   IF DN <  = O THEN   PRINT "???";: GOTO 4040
4080   VTAB   PEEK (37):
       PRINT "ORDER N="N%" POINTS M="M%" DF="DN" DET=";
4090   SY = O:YY = O
4100   FOR I = 1 TO N%
4110   SX(I) = O:SX(N% + I) = O:SY(I) = O: NEXT I
4120   FOR I = 1 TO M%:X = DX(I):Y = DY(I)
4130   SY = SY + Y:YY = YY + Y * Y:DU = 1
4140   FOR J = 1 TO N%
4150   DU = DU * X:SX(J) = SX(J) + DU
4160   SY(J) = SY(J) + Y * DU: NEXT J
4170   FOR J = N% + 1 TO 2 * N%:DU = DU * X
4180   SX(J) = SX(J) + DU
4190   NEXT J,I
4200   REM   COMPUTE COEFFICIENTS
4210   QM = 1 / M%:BY = YY - SY * SY * QM
4220   FOR I = 1 TO N%:BY(I) = SY(I) - SY * SX(I) * QM
4230   QA(I,N% + 1) = BY(I)
4240   FOR J = 1 TO N%
4250   QA(I,J) = SX(I + J) - SX(I) * SX(J) * QM
4260   NEXT J,I
4270   FL% = 1: GOSUB 10000: REM   SLE QA(ROW,COL),BB(I),N%
4280   PRINT DT: IF DT = O THEN
       PRINT "DET=O": STOP : GOTO 100
4290   DU = SY:TE = BY:SA = 1
4300   FOR I = 1 TO N%:QX = SX(I) * QM
4310   DU = DU - BB(I) * SX(I)
4320   TE = TE - BY(I) * BB(I)
4330   FOR J = 1 TO N%
4340   SA = SA + SX(J) * QX * QA(I,J)
4350   NEXT J
4360   NEXT I
4370   AA = DU * QM
4380   IF TE > O THEN S =   SQR (TE / DN): GOTO 4390
4385   S =   -   SQR ( - TE / DN)
4390   SA = S *   SQR (QM * SA)
4400   PRINT "A=";AA: PRINT "B(I)=";
4410   FOR I = 1 TO N%
4420   PRINT BB(I);" ";
4430   NEXT : PRINT
4440   PRINT "S=";S;
4450   IF S < O THEN   PRINT "?": GOTO 4460
4455   PRINT "/"
```

```
4460    PRINT "<AGAIN,RETURN,STAT>"
4470    GET B$
4480    IF B$ = "S" THEN   GOSUB 4500: GOTO 4460
4490    IF B$ = "A" THEN   GOTO 4040
4495    IF B$ = "R" THEN   GOTO 100
4497    GOTO 4470
4500 S = 0: PRINT  TAB( 15): VTAB  PEEK (37) - 1:
        PRINT "ACTUAL S=";
4510    FOR J = 1 TO M%:X = DX(J)
4520    GOSUB 9400:Y = Y - DY(J)
4530 S = S + Y * Y: NEXT
4540 S =  SQR (S / DN): PRINT S
4550    IF N% <  > 1 THEN  GOTO 4590
4560 SY =  SQR ((YY - QM * SY * SY) / (M% - 1))
4570 SX =  SQR ((SX(2) - QM * SX(1) * SX(1)) / (M% - 1))
4580 R = SX * BB(1) / SY: PRINT " ","R=";R
4590    PRINT " STANDARD DEVIATIONS";: IF N <  > 1 THEN
        PRINT
4600 SA = S *  SQR (QM * SA): PRINT "(A)";SA;"(B)";
4610    FOR I = 1 TO N: PRINT S *  SQR (QA(I,I));: NEXT
4620    PRINT : RETURN




9000    REM   PROGRAM SUBROUTINE UPOLY
9001    REM   APPLESOFT VERSION
9003    REM   TRANSLATED BY DJC
9004    REM
9006    HOME
9010    PRINT :
        PRINT "COMMANDS:RETURN,FUNCTION,DERIV.,INTEGRAL"
9020    GET A$:K% = 0: FOR I = 1 TO 4:
        IF A$ =  MID$ ("FDIR",I,1) THEN K% = I
9025    NEXT I
9030    ON K% GOTO 9050,9090,9150,100
9040    GOTO 9010
9050    INPUT "AT X=";X: PRINT  TAB( 20): VTAB  PEEK (37)
9060    GOSUB 9400
9070    PRINT "F(";X;")=";Y
9080    GOTO 9020
9090    INPUT "AT X=";Z: PRINT  TAB( 20):
        VTAB  PEEK (37):F = 0
9100    FOR I = 1 TO N%
9110 F = F + I * BB(I) * Z ^ (I - 1)
9120    NEXT
9130    PRINT "DF(";Z;")=";F
9140    GOTO 9020
```

```
9150   REM
9160   PRINT "INT FROM";: INPUT Z1: PRINT   TAB( 20);:
       VTAB   PEEK (37): PRINT "TO";
9170   INPUT Z2: PRINT "INT=";
9180 F = AA * (Z2 - Z1)
9190   FOR I = 1 TO N%
9200 F = F + (BB(I) / (I + 1)) * (Z2 ^ (I + 1) -
       Z1 ^ (I + 1))
9210   NEXT
9220   PRINT F
9230   GOTO 9020
9400 Y = O: REM   SUBROUTINE TO EVALUATE POLYNOMIAL-
9410   FOR K = N% TO 1 STEP   - 1
9420 Y = Y * X + BB(K)
9430   NEXT
9440 Y = Y * X + AA
9450   RETURN




1   REM   PROGRAM TRAP
2   REM   APPLESOFT VERSION
4   REM   TRANSLATED BY DJC
5   REM
400 A = O: REM   AREA
410   READ X,Y
420 X1 = X:Y1 = Y: REM   FIRST POINT, SAVED
430   READ X,Y
440 A = A + .5 * (Y + Y1) * (X - X1)
450   PRINT X,Y,"AREA=";A
460   GOTO 420
490   DATA  ...




1   REM   PROGRAM ROMBERG
2   REM   APPLESOFT VERSION
4   REM   TRANSLATED BY DJC
5   REM
20   DIM A(20,20)
30   DEF  FN F(X) = X *  EXP ( - X * X)
80 T = 1E - 6
1000   REM   PROGRAM ROMBERG FOR INTEGRATION OF FUNCTIONS
1010 NC% = 6:N1% = 4:
       REM   NC% IS # CYCLES, N1% SET INITIAL INTERVAL
```

```
1020    INPUT "X1,X2:";X1,X2
1030 H = (X2 - X1) / N1%
1040    GOSUB 1190:A(0,0) = A: PRINT A
1050    FOR K = 1 TO NC%
1060 N1% = N1% * 2:H = H / 2
1070    GOSUB 1190:A(O,K) = A: PRINT A,
1080    FOR L = 1 TO K
1090 A(L,K) = (4 ^ L * A(L - 1,K) -
     A(L - 1,K - 1)) / (4 ^ L - 1)
1100    PRINT A(L,K),
1110    IF   ABS ((A(L,K) - A(L - 1,K)) / A) < T THEN 1160
1120    NEXT L
1130    PRINT
1140    NEXT K
1150 K = K - 1:L = L - 1
1160    PRINT
1165    PRINT "...FINI...AFTER "N1%" INTERVALS"
1167    PRINT "AREA=";A(L,K)
1170    END
1190 SU = ( FN F(X2) +  FN F(X1)) / 2
1200    FOR I = 1 TO N1% - 1
1210 X = X2 - I * H
1220 SU = SU +  FN F(X)
1230    NEXT
1240 A = SU * H: RETURN




1    REM    PROGRAM LAGRANGE
2    REM    APPLESOFT VERSION
4    REM    TRANSLATED BY DJC
5    REM
20   DIM DX(10),DY(10),P(10),Q(10)
200    READ L$,N%: REM   LABEL AND NUMBER OF POINTS
210    FOR I = 1 TO N%
220    READ X,Y
230 DX(I) = X:DY(I) = Y: NEXT
300    REM   CALCULATE P FACTORS
310    FOR I = 1 TO N%
320 P(I) = 1
330    FOR J = 1 TO N%
340    IF I = J THEN 360
350 P(I) = P(I) * (DX(I) - DX(J))
360    NEXT J
370    NEXT I
380    DATA   HEAT CAPACITY OF BENZENE,4,200,83.7,240,104.1
381    DATA   260,116.1,278.69,128.7
```

```
400    PRINT "INTERPOLATION FOR ";L$
410    INPUT "VALUE OF X ";X
420    FOR I = 1 TO N%:Q(I) = 1
430    FOR J = 1 TO N%
440    IF I = J THEN 460
450 Q(I) = Q(I) * (X - DX(J))
460    NEXT J
470    NEXT I
480 Y = O: REM  SUMMATION TO GET Y
490    FOR I = 1 TO N%
500 Y = Y + DY(I) * Q(I) / P(I)
510    NEXT
520    PRINT "Y(";X;")=";Y
530    GOTO 410




1   REM   PROGRAM DIVDIF
2   REM   APPLESOFT VERSION
4   REM   TRANSLATED BY DJC
5   REM
6   REM   NEWTON DIVIDED DIFFERENCE INTERP W/ SIMP RULE
7   REM   INTEGRATION AND 4TH-ORDER DIFF
8   REM
20   DIM DX(50),DY(50),T(50,8)
99   GOTO 200
100    HOME : PRINT W$,"PTS=";M%;"    DEGREE";ID%;"/";ND%
120    PRINT "<&> DATA INPUT <T> TABLE <Q> QUIT"
122    PRINT "<F> FUNCTION, <D> DIFF, <I> INTEGRATE"
130    GET A$:J = O: FOR I = 1 TO 6:
       IF A$ =  MID$ ("&TQFDI",I,1) THEN J = I
135    NEXT
140    ON J GOTO 200,300,900,400,500,1000
199    GOTO 100
200 ND% = O: REM    DATA INPUT
210    READ W$,M%
220    FOR I = 1 TO M%
230    READ X:Y =  COS (X)
240    DX(I) = X:DY(I) = Y: NEXT
260    GOTO 100
290    DATA  COSINE TEST,15,-3.5,-3.0,-2.5,-2,-1.5,-1,-.5,
       0,.5,1,1.5,2,2.5,3,3.5
300    INPUT "DEGREE ";ID%: IF ID% < = ND% THEN 100
305    GOSUB 9000
310    PRINT "`DIFFERENCE TABLE"
320    FOR I = 1 TO M% - 1
330    FOR J = 1 TO I
```

```
340   IF J < = ND% THEN   PRINT T(I,J);" ";
350   NEXT
360   PRINT
370   NEXT
380   GOTO 130
400   INPUT "VALUE OF X ";X
410   GOSUB 9400
420   PRINT "EST Y=",Y," EST ERROR ", ABS (ER)
430   PRINT "ACTUAL ", COS (X),"ACT ERR", ABS (Y - COS (X))
480   GOTO 130
500   INPUT "VALUE OF X ";X1: REM   DIFFERENTIAL EVALUATION
510 S = .01: REM   INCREMENT FOR DERIVATIVE
520 H = S: IF  ABS (X1) > S THEN H = X1 * S
530 X = X1 - 2 * H: GOSUB 9400:DX = Y
540 X = X1 - H: GOSUB 9400:DX = DX - 8 * Y
550 X = X1 + H: GOSUB 9400:DX = DX + 8 * Y
560 X = X1 + 2 * H: GOSUB 9400:DX = DX - Y
570 DX = DX / (12 * H)
580   PRINT "DERIVATIVE",DX
590   PRINT "ACTUAL", - SIN (X1),"DIFF", ABS (DX + SIN (X1))
599   GOTO 130
900   END : GOTO 100
1000   INPUT "LOWER&UPPER LIMITS ";X1,X2
1005   IF X1 > = X2 THEN 1000
1010   INPUT "NUMBER OF INTERVALS ";N%
1020   IF N% / 2 < > INT (N% / 2) THEN
       PRINT "EVEN NUMBER, STUPID": GOTO 1010
1030 H = (X2 - X1) / N%:X = X1: GOSUB 9400
1032 A = Y:X = X2: GOSUB 9400:A = A + Y
1040   FOR K = 1 TO N% - 1:X = X1 + K * H: GOSUB 9400
1050 A = A + 2 * Y * (1 + (K / 2 < > INT (K / 2)))
1060   NEXT
1070 A = A * H / 3
1080   PRINT "THE INTEGRAL IS ";A;"(";N%;" INTERVALS)"
1082   PRINT "ACTUAL INTEGRAL IS "; SIN (X2) - SIN (X1)
1090   PRINT "TYPE <H> TO CHANGE INTERVAL,
1091   PRINT "     <L> TO CHANGE LIMITS,"
1092   PRINT "     <R> TO RETURN"
1100   GET A$
1102   IF A$ = "H" THEN   GOTO 1010
1104   IF A$ = "L" THEN   GOTO 1000
1106   IF A$ = "R" THEN   GOTO 100
1120   GOTO 1100
9000   REM   CALC OF TABLE FOR NEWTON DIVIDED DIFF
9010   IF ID% > M% OR ID% > 8 THEN
       W$ = "DEGREE TO BIG": GOTO 100
9020 ND% = ID%: REM   INTERPOLATION ORDER, ID%, MAX ND%
9030   IF ND% < = 1 THEN
       PRINT "ND=";ND%: STOP : GOTO 100
```

```
9040  FOR I = 1 TO M% - 1
9050  T(I,1) = (DY(I + 1) - DY(I)) / (DX(I + 1) - DX(I)):
      NEXT
9060  FOR J = 2 TO ND%
9070  FOR I = J TO M% - 1
9080  T(I,J) = (T(I,J - 1) - T(I - 1,J - 1)) /
      (DX(I + 1) - DX(I + 1 - J))
9090  NEXT I,J
9100  W$ = "TABLE READY": RETURN
9400  REM   INTERPOLATION BY NEWTONS DIVIDED DIFF
9410  IF W$ < > "TABLE READY" THEN
      W$ = "TABLE NOT READY": GOTO 100
9420  IF ID% > ND% THEN
      PRINT "MAX DEGREE=";ND%: GOTO 9410
9430  FOR I = 1 TO M%
9440  IF I = M% OR X < = DX(I) THEN 9460
9450  NEXT
9460  MX% = I + ID% / 2
9470  IF MX% < = ID% THEN MX% = ID% + 1
9480  IF MX% > = M% THEN MX% = M%
9490  Y = T(MX% - 1,ID%):ER = T(MX%,ID%) - T(MX% - 1,ID%)
9500  IF ID% < = 1 THEN 9540
9510  FOR I = 1 TO ID% - 1:D = X - DX(MX% - I)
9520  Y = Y * D + T(MX% - I - 1,ID% - I):ER = ER * D
9530  NEXT
9540  Y = Y * (X - DX(MX% - ID%)) + DY(MX% - ID%)
9550  ER = ER * (X - DX(MX% - ID%))
9560  PRINT "/";: RETURN




1   REM   PROGRAM SIMPLEX
2   REM   APPLESOFT VERSION
4   REM   TRANSLATED BY DJC
5   REM
20  DIM S(6,7),T(6),TT(6),C(6),X(30),Y(30)
30  NP% = 3:NV% = NP% + 1: REM NUMBER OF PARAMETERS =NP%
40  DEF  FN Y(X) = T(1) + T(2) *  EXP (T(3) * X)
50  DATA   COOPER,8,1,2.80,2,3.74,3,5.01,4,6.74,5,9.06,
      6,12.2
51  DATA   7,16.43,8,22.14
59  DATA   END,0
100 HOME : REM   COMMAND CENTER
110 PRINT "ITER=";KI%;"/";KX%,"R=";BR;"/";EP,"PTS";
      M%,TI$
120 PRINT "PARAMETERS:";: FOR I = 1 TO NP%:
      PRINT S(I,JB%): NEXT
```

```
130    PRINT "<I> DATA INPUT"
132    PRINT "<G> INPUT GUESSES"
134    PRINT "<P> PRINT RESULTS"
136    PRINT "<C> CALCULATE"
138    PRINT "<Q QUIT"
140    PRINT "?";: GET A$:J% = 0: FOR I = 1 TO 5:
       IF A$ =  MID$ ("IGPCQ",I,1) THEN J% = I
145    NEXT : IF J% = 0 GOTO 140
147    PRINT A$
150    ON J% GOTO 200,300,400,1000,900
160    GOTO 100
200    READ TI$,M%: IF TI$ = "END" THEN  GOTO 100
210    FOR I = 1 TO M%: READ X,Y
220 X(I) = X:Y(I) = Y
230    NEXT
240    GOTO 100
300    FOR I = 1 TO NP%: PRINT I;":";:
       INPUT "VALUE,INC ";Z,D
310    FOR J = 1 TO NV%
320 S(I,J) = Z - D * (I >  = J) - D / 2
330    NEXT
340    NEXT
344    GOSUB 350: GOTO 400
350    FOR I3 = 1 TO NV%
360    FOR J3 = 1 TO NP%:T(J3) = S(J3,I3): NEXT
370    GOSUB 500:R(I3) = R
380    NEXT : RETURN
400    PRINT "RESPONSE/PARAMETERS"
405    FOR I = 1 TO NV%: PRINT R(I);"/",
410    FOR J = 1 TO NP%
420    PRINT S(J,I);",";: NEXT
430    PRINT : NEXT
480    PRINT "?": GET A$
490    GOTO 100
500 R = 0: REM  CALCULATE RESPONSE
510    FOR I5 = 1 TO M%
520 R = R + (Y(I5) -  FN Y(X(I5))) ^ 2
530    NEXT
540 R =  SQR (R / (M% - 1)): RETURN
600    REM    FIND NEW VERTEX(T)
610    FOR J6 = 1 TO NP%:SU = 0
615    IF F <  > 1 THEN  GOTO 660
620    FOR K6 = 1 TO NV%: REM   CALC CENTROID
630    IF K6 <  > JW% THEN SU = SU + S(J6,K6)
633    NEXT
640 C(J6) = SU / NP%
660 T(J6) = C(J6) * (1 + F) - F * S(J6,JW%)
670    NEXT
680    GOSUB 500: PRINT "/F=";F;" R=";R
690    RETURN
```

```
700   REM   EXCHANGE T FOR WORST
710   FOR I7 = 1 TO NP%
720 S(I7,JW%) = T(I7)
730   NEXT
740 R(JW%) = R
750   GOTO 1050
900   END : GOTO 100
1000 KI% = O: REM   ITERATION
1010   IF M% = O OR R(1) = O THEN   GOTO 100
1020   INPUT "MAX # ITER=";KX%
1030 EP = 1E - 6
1040   IF BR <  > O AND BR < EP THEN
      EP = EP / 10: GOTO 1040
1050 WR = R(1):BR = WR:JW% = 1:JB% = 1
1060   FOR I = 2 TO NV%
1070   IF R(I) >   = WR THEN WR = R(I):JW% = I
1080   IF R(I) < BR THEN BR = R(I):JB% = I
1090   NEXT
1150   IF KI% >   = KX% OR BR < EP THEN
      PRINT "END": GET A$: GOTO 100
1160   IF (WR - BR) / BR < EP THEN   PRINT : GOTO 400
1170   IF   PEEK ( - 16384) <  > 209 THEN   GOTO 1200
1180   GET A$
1190   GOTO 100
1200   PRINT :KI% = KI% + 1: PRINT "#";KI%;
1210   IF BR <  > PR THEN PR = BR:
      PRINT "!!!NEW BEST ";BR;" WORST ";WR
1220 F = 1: GOSUB 600: REM   NEW VERTEX
1230   IF R <  = BR THEN   GOTO 1400: REM   EXPAND VERTEX
1240   IF R <  = WR THEN   GOTO 700: REM   EXCH FOR WORST
1250 F =  - .5: GOSUB 600: REM   CONTRACT
1260   IF R <  = WR THEN   GOTO 700: REM   EXCH FOR WORST
1270   PRINT "CONTRACT";: REM   CONTRACT ALL VERTICES
1280   FOR I = 1 TO NP%
1290   FOR J = 1 TO NV%
1300   IF J <  > JB% THEN
      S(I,J) = (S(I,JB%) + S(I,J)) / 2
1310   NEXT J,I
1380   GOTO 1050
1400 RT = R: FOR I = 1 TO NP%:TT(I) = T(I): NEXT :
      REM   SAVE VERTEX
1410 F = 2: GOSUB 600: REM   EXPANDED VERTEX
1420   IF R <  = RT THEN   GOTO 700:
      REM   ACCEPT EXPANDED VERTEX
1430 R = RT: FOR I = 1 TO NP%:T(I) = TT(I): NEXT :
      REM   RESTORE
1440   GOTO 700: REM   EXCHANGE W/WORST
```

```
1    REM   PROGRAM RUNGE
2    REM   APPLESOFT VERSION
4    REM   TRANSLATED BY DJC
5    REM
10   FL% = O: REM   SET FL%=1 IF POINT BY POINT PLOTTING IS
       DESIRED, RATHER THAN CONNECT THE POINTS PLOTTING
40   FOR I = 1 TO 6:W(I) = 1: NEXT
100   HOME : REM   COMMAND CENTER
110   PRINT "T=";T,"H=";H: GOSUB 9400
120  C1 = CO *  EXP ( - K1 * T)
122   IF K1 = K2 OR T = 2 THEN
       C2 = K1 * CO * T *  EXP ( - K1 * T): GOTO 125
124  C2 = K1 * CO * ( EXP ( - K1 * T) -
       EXP ( - K2 * T)) / (K2 - K1)
125  C3 = CO - C1 - C2
126   PRINT "THEORETICAL",C1,C2,C3
130   PRINT "<1> NEW CALCULATION"
140   PRINT "<2> CONTINUE CALCULATION"
150   PRINT "<3> QUIT"
154   PRINT "<4> SET WEIGHTS"
160   GET A$:K% =  VAL (A$): IF K% = O THEN 160
170   ON K% GOSUB 1000,1100,900,200
180   GOTO 100
200   PRINT "INPUT WEIGHTS"
210   FOR I = 1 TO 6
220   PRINT "W("I")=";: INPUT "";W(I)
230   NEXT
240   RETURN
600  IX = 279 * (T - T1) / (T2 - T1)
610   FOR I = 1 TO NQ:Y = C(I) * W(I)
620  IY = 159 * Y * (Y >  = O) * (Y <  = 1)
625   IF J = 1 OR FL% = 1 THEN
       HPLOT IX,159 - IY: GOTO 635
630   HPLOT PX(I),159 - PY(I) TO IX,159 - IY
635  PX(I) = IX:PY(I) = IY
640   NEXT
650   RETURN
900   STOP : GOTO 100
1000 T = O:T1 = O
1010   GOSUB 9000
1030   GOSUB 9500
1040   FOR I = 1 TO NQ:CT(I) = C(I): NEXT
1100   INPUT "CALCULATE TO T=";T2
1110   INPUT "TIME INTERVAL ";TS
1120   INPUT "NUMBER OF STEPS PER INTERVAL ";NR
1130 NS =  INT ((T2 - T1) / TS + .499)
1134   HOME : HGR : VTAB 22
1140 H = TS / NR: PRINT "H=";H
1200   FOR J = 1 TO NS
```

```
1230   FOR L = 1 TO NR
1240 A = 0.5:B = 1: GOSUB 9100
1250 B = 2: GOSUB 9100
1260 A = 1: GOSUB 9100
1270 A = 0:B = 1: GOSUB 9100
1280   FOR I = 1 TO NQ - 1
1290 C(I) = C(I) + H * DS(I) / 6
1300 CT(I) = C(I):DS(I) = 0
1310   NEXT I
1320   NEXT L
1330 T = T1 + J * TS:C(NQ) = CO
1331   VTAB 23: PRINT "T=";T;"          "
1333   FOR I = 1 TO NQ - 1:C(NQ) = C(NQ) - C(I): NEXT
1340   GOSUB 600
1343   IF  PEEK ( - 16384) = 209 THEN
       GET A$:T1 = 1: TEXT : RETURN
1350   NEXT J
1360 T1 = T
1370   GET A$: RETURN
8000   FOR IS = 1 TO NQ - 1
8010 CT(IS) = C(IS) + H * DK(IS) * A
8020 DS(IS) = DS(IS) + DK(IS) * B
8030   NEXT IS
8040   RETURN
9C00   REM  CHANGE THIS PART TO CHANGE THE PROBLEM BEING
       SOLVED
9010 NQ = 3:CO = 1
9020 C(1) = 1:C(2) = 0:C(3) = 0
9090   RETURN
9100 DK(1) =   - K1 * CT(1)
9110 DK(2) =   + K1 * CT(1) - K2 * CT(2)
9190   GOTO 8000
9400   PRINT "K1=";K1,"K2=";K2
9410   PRINT "CONCENTRATION",C(1),C(2),C(3)
9420   RETURN
9500   INPUT "K1=";K1
9510   INPUT "K2=";K2
9520   RETURN
```

APPENDIX II: COMMODORE 64 PROGRAMS

```
80 REM        ******************
90 REM        *                *
100 REM       *   PROGRAM  FAC  *
105 REM       *                *
110 REM       *       FOR       *
115 REM       *                *
120 REM       *   COMMODORE 64  *
130 REM       *                *
140 REM       ******************
200 INPUT P,Q
210 N=P+Q:WL=-N*LOG(2)
220 M=N:GOSUB 1000:WL=WL+FL
240 M=Q:GOSUB 1000:WL=WL-FL
250 M=P:GOSUB 1000:WL=WL-FL
260 W=EXP(WL):PRINT"PROBABILITY=";W
270 END
1000 REM SUBROUTINE TO CALCULATE LOG FACTORIAL (FL) OF M
1005 IF M<0 THEN PRINT"ILLEGAL INPUT":GOTO 200
1010 IF M=0 THEN FL=0:RETURN:REM  ZERO FACTORIAL = 1
1020 IF M<NX THEN 1100
1030 FL=.5*LOG(2*PI)+(M+.5)*LOG(M)-M+1/12*M
1040 RETURN
1100 PR=1
1110 FOR I=1 TO M:PR=PR*I:NEXT
1120 FL=LOG(PR):RETURN
```

```
8 REM         ******************
9 REM         *                *
10 REM        *   PROGRAM  VDW  *
11 REM        *                *
12 REM        *       FOR       *
13 REM        *                *
14 REM        *   COMMODORE 64  *
15 REM        *                *
16 REM        ******************
20 R=.082057:A=1.39:B=.0391:G$="NITROGEN":F$="NO"
100 PRINT"⊐"
```

```
110 PRINT"GAS=";G$,"A=";A,"B=";B:PRINT:
    PRINT TAB(15)"**";F$;"**":PRINT
120 IF T<>0 THEN Z=P*V/(R*T):REM  COMPRESSIBILITY FACTOR
130 PRINT"P=";P,"T=";T:PRINT"V=";V,"Z=";Z:PRINT
140 PRINT"TYPE NAME OF VARIABLE TO BE CHANGED"
142 PRINT"(TYPE<C> FOR CELCIUS,<Q> TO QUIT)"
145 PRINT"  *ENTER 0 TO CALCULATE VALUE*":PRINT
150 GET A$:IF A$="" THEN 150
160 IF A$="G" THEN GOTO 200
162 IF A$="A" THEN GOTO 300
164 IF A$="B" THEN GOTO 400
166 IF A$="P" THEN GOTO 500
168 IF A$="V" THEN GOTO 600
170 IF A$="T" THEN GOTO 700
172 IF A$="C" THEN GOTO 750
174 IF A$="Q" THEN GOTO 900
190 GOTO 100
200 INPUT"NAME OF GAS,A,B";G$,A,B:GOTO 100
300 INPUT"A=";A:GOTO 100
400 INPUT"B=";B:GOTO 100
500 INPUT"P=";P:IF P<>0 THEN F$="NO":GOTO 100
510 P=R*T/(V-B)-A/(V*V)
520 F$="OK":GOTO 100
600 INPUT"V=";V:IF V<>0 THEN F$="NO":GOTO 100
610 V1=R*T/P:K=0
620 V=R*T/(P+A/(V1*V1))+B
630 IF ABS(V-V1)<1E-6 THEN F$="OK":GOTO 100
640 K=K+1:V1=V:IF K<100 THEN GOTO 620
650 F$="NOT CONVERGING":GOTO 100
700 INPUT"T=";T:IF T<>0 THEN F$="NO":GOTO 100
710 T=((P+A/(V*V))*(V-B))/R
720 F$="OK":GOTO 100
750 INPUT"DEGREES CELCIUS=";C
760 T=C+273.15:F$="NO"
770 GOTO 100
900 END
```

```
2 REM       ***********************
3 REM       *                     *
4 REM       *   PROGRAM NEWTON    *
5 REM       *                     *
6 REM       *        FOR          *
7 REM       *                     *
8 REM       *   COMMODORE 64      *
9 REM       *                     *
10 REM      ***********************
```

```
15 PRINT"⬛"
20 DEF FNY(X)=A+X*(B+X*(C+D*X)):REM FUNCTION
30 DEF FND(X)=B+X*(2*C+3*D*X):REM DERIVATIVE FUNCTION
40 T=1E-6:REM CONVERGENCE CRITERION. CHANGE TO SUIT
100 INPUT"CONSTANTS:A,B,C,D";A,B,C,D
110 INPUT"INITIAL X";X
200 REM NEWTON ITERATION
210 K=0
220 X1=X
230 X=X1-FNY(X1)/FND(X1)
240 K=K+1
250 IF ABS((X-X1)/(X+X1))<T THEN GOTO 300
260 IF K<100 THEN 220
270 PRINT"TRIED 100 ITERATIONS W/O FINISHING"
280 PRINT"LAST TWO VALUES: ";X,X1
290 PRINT"PERHAPS...";
300 PRINT"THE ROOT IS ";X
310 END
```

```
2 REM          ********************
3 REM          *                  *
4 REM          *  PROGRAM  ROOTS  *
5 REM          *                  *
6 REM          *       FOR        *
7 REM          *                  *
8 REM          *   COMMODORE 64   *
9 REM          *                  *
10 REM         ********************
11 PRINT"⬛"
12 T=1E-6
14 PRINT"ROOTS BY REGULA FALSI- TOL=";T
15 PRINT"FUNCTION DEFINED AT STATEMENT 20"
20 DEF FNY(X)=X↑3+913*X↑2-1023
22 INPUT"TYPE <M> FOR MANUAL SEARCH,<A> FOR AUTO";A$
24 IF A$="M" THEN GOTO 600
26 IF A$<>"A" THEN GOTO 22
30 PRINT"LOWER LIMIT FOR SEARCH";
32 INPUT X1:Y1=FNY(X1):X=X1
40 PRINT"UPPER LIMIT";:INPUT XB
50 PRINT"STEP";:INPUT XS
70 X=X+XS:IF X>XB+XS/2 THEN
   PRINT"NO ROOT IN THIS RANGE":GOTO 30
80 Y=FNY(X):IF SGN(Y)=SGN(Y1) THEN X1=X:Y1=Y:GOTO 70
90 IF SGN(Y)<>SGN(Y1) THEN X2=X:Y2=Y
100 PRINT X1;"<ROOT<";X2;:GOSUB 500:REM  CALC NEW X,Y
```

```
110 IF Y=0 THEN PRINT"ROOT=";Y:STOP:GOTO 10
120 IF SGN(Y)=SGN(Y2) THEN X2=X:Y2=Y
125 IF SGN(Y)<>SGN(Y2) THEN X1=X2:Y1=Y2:X2=X:Y2=Y
130 IT=0
140 GOSUB 500:IF ABS(X1-X)<T THEN GOTO 200
150 X1=X:Y1=Y:IT=IT+1:IF IT<10 THEN GOTO 140
160 PRINT"CHOOSE:<S>WITCH PIVOT,<R>ESTART,<C>ONTINUE";:
    INPUT A$
180 IF A$="C" THEN GOTO 130
182 IF A$="R" THEN GOTO 30
184 IF A$="S" THEN GOTO 160
190 X=X2:Y=Y2:X2=X1:Y2=Y1:X1=X:Y1=Y:GOTO 130
200 PRINT"THE ROOT IS ";X,"(TOL=";T;")":END
500 X=(X1*Y2-X2*Y1)/(Y2-Y1):Y=FNY(X):PRINT
510 PRINT"Y(";X;")=";Y:RETURN
600 INPUT"VALUE OF X";X
602 PRINT CHR$(145)"Y(";X;" )=";FNY(X);"    ";
610 PRINT TAB(25)"MORE?(Y/N)";:INPUT A$
620 IF A$="Y" THEN GOTO 600
630 GOTO 30
```

```
2 REM       ********************
3 REM       *                  *
4 REM       *  PROGRAM SYNDIV   *
5 REM       *                  *
6 REM       *       FOR         *
7 REM       *                  *
8 REM       *  COMMODORE 64     *
9 REM       *                  *
10 REM      ********************
11 REM
12 REM  REAL ROOTS OF A POLYNOMIAL BY SYNTHETIC DIVISION
15 T=1E-6:REM  TOLERENCE FOR CONVERGENCE TEST
18 PRINT"⊐"
20 INPUT"ORDER OF POLYNOMIAL";N
25 PRINT"ENTER COEFFICIENTS A(I)"
30 FOR I=0 TO N
40 PRINT I,:INPUT A(I)
45 NEXT I
50 B(N)=A(N):C(N)=B(N)
55 K=0:INPUT"INITIAL GUESS FOR R";R
60 FOR I=N-1 TO 0 STEP -1
70 B(I)=B(I+1)*R+A(I)
80 C(I)=C(I+1)*R+B(I)
90 NEXT I
```

```
95 IF C(1)=0 THEN DR=1:GOTO 110
100 DR=-B(0)/C(1)
105 IF ABS(DR)<T THEN GOTO 200
110 R=R+DR:K=K+1
115 IF K>100 THEN PRINT"ITER=";K:GOTO 250
120 PRINT R;:GOTO 60
200 PRINT:PRINT"THE ROOT IS";R
210 FOR I=1 TO N:A(I-1)=B(I):NEXT I
220 N=N-1
230 PRINT"COEFFICIENTS OF REDUCED POLYNOMIAL"
240 FOR I=0 TO N
242 PRINT"A(";I;" )=";A(I)
244 NEXT I
250 PRINT:INPUT"TYPE <C> TO CONTINUE";A$
260 IF A$="C" THEN GOTO 50
270 END
```

```
2 REM        ********************
3 REM        *                  *
4 REM        *   PROGRAM LINBAR  *
5 REM        *                  *
6 REM        *        FOR        *
7 REM        *                  *
8 REM        *   COMMODORE 64    *
9 REM        *                  *
10 REM       ********************
12 REM ROOTS OF POLYNOMIAL BY LIN-BAIRSTOW METHOD
20 T=1E-8:REM   CRITERION FOR CONVERGENCE
50 PRINT"⌂"
100 INPUT"N=";N
110 PRINT"ENTER COEFFICIENTS, A(0),...,A(";N;" )"
120 FOR I=0 TO N:PRINT I,:INPUT A(I):NEXT I
122 IF A(N)=0 THEN N=N-1:PRINT"ZERO ROOT":GOTO 122
124 IF N<3 THEN GOTO 280
130 B(N)=A(N):C(N)=A(N):K=0
140 K=K+1:IF K>20 THEN K=0:T=T*10:PRINT"CONV???";T;EP
150 B(N-1)=A(N-1)+U*B(N)
152 C(N-1)=B(N-1)+U*C(N)
154 IF N=2 THEN GOTO 210
160 FOR I=N-2 TO 0 STEP -1
170 B(I)=A(I)+U*B(I+1)+V*B(I+2)
180 C(I)=B(I)+U*C(I+1)+V*C(I+2)
200 NEXT I
210 F=C(2)*C(2)-C(1)*C(3)
215 IF F=0 THEN PRINT"#";:DU=DU+1:DV=DV+1:GOTO 235
220 DU=(B(0)*C(3)-B(1)*C(2))/F
```

```
230 DV=(C(1)*B(1)-C(2)*B(0))/F
235 U=U+DU:V=V+DV
240 EP=SQR(DU*DU+DV*DV)
245 IF EP>T THEN GOTO 140
250 D=U*U+4*V:IF D<0 THEN GOTO 300
255 IF D>=0 THEN GOTO 400
260 N=N-2
270 FOR I=0 TO N:A(I)=B(I+2):NEXT I
275 A(0)=A(0)+B(0):A(1)=A(1)+B(1)
280 IF N>2 THEN GOTO 130
285 IF N<2 THEN GOTO 500
290 IF N=2 THEN U=-A(1)/A(2):V=-A(0)/A(2):GOTO 250
300 REM **** COMPLEX ROOTS ****
310 RE=U/2:W=SQR(-D)/2
320 PRINT"ROOTS: REAL,";RE;"   IMAGINARY,";W
330 GOTO 260
400 REM **** REAL ROOTS ****
410 R1=U/2+SQR(D)/2:R2=U/2-SQR(D)/2
420 PRINTREAL ROOTS:";R1;R2
430 GOTO 260
500 IF N=1 THEN PRINT"LAST ROOT";-A(0)/A(1)
510 PRINT"TOLERENCE=";T,"END OF ROOTS"
520 END




2 REM       ********************
3 REM       *                  *
4 REM       *  PROGRAM LINREG   *
5 REM       *                  *
6 REM       *        FOR        *
7 REM       *                  *
8 REM       *   COMMODORE 64    *
9 REM       *                  *
10 REM      ********************
12 PRINT"⊐"
15 REM  LEAST SQUARES LINEAR REGRESSION
20 DIM DX(20),DY(20)
30 READ M
40 FOR I=1 TO M
45 READ X,Y
50 DX(I)=X:DY(I)=Y
60 SX=SX+X:SY=SY+Y
70 PX=PX+X*X:PY=PY+Y*Y
80 PC=PC+X*Y
90 NEXT
100 D=M*PX-SX*SX
110 A=(SY*PX-PC*SX)/D
```

```
120 B=(M*PC-SX*SY)/D
130 VX=(PX-SX*SX/M)/(M-1)
140 VY=(PY-SY*SY/M)/(M-1)
150 RR=B*B*VX/VY
160 R=SQR(RR)
170 E=SQR((I-RR)/(M-2))/R
180 RE=(M-1)*VY*(1-RR):REM   APPROX RESIDUAL
190 GB=ABS(E*B):REM   STANDARD DEVIATION OF SLOPE
200 GA=GB*SQR(RE/(M-1)):
    REM   STANDARD DEVIATION OF INTERCEPT
210 GP=SQR(RE/(M-1)):REM   STANDARD DEVIATION OF POINTS
220 PRINT"INTCPT=";A:PRINT"(STD DEV=";GA;")":PRINT
230 PRINT"SLOPE=";B:PRINT"(STD DEV=";GB;")":PRINT
240 PRINT"R=";R:PRINT"E=";E:PRINT"STD DEV PTS=";GP:PRINT
250 PRINT"SUM OF SQUARES=";RE:PRINT
260 PRINT"THE INDIVIDUAL RESIDUALS ARE:"
270 RA=0:FOR I=1 TO M
280 D=DY(I)-A-B*DX(I)
290 RA=RA+D*D:PRINT D,
300 NEXT
310 PRINT:PRINT"SUM OF SQUARES=";RA
320 DATA 8,1,1.01,2,2.02,3,3,4,4.01,5,5,6,6.02,7,7.01,
         8,8.01


2 REM       ****************************
3 REM       *                          *
4 REM       *    PROGRAM SIMLINEQ      *
5 REM       *                          *
6 REM       *          FOR             *
7 REM       *                          *
8 REM       *      COMMODORE 64        *
9 REM       *                          *
10 REM      ****************************
11 REM
12 REM   DRIVER PROGRAM FOR SLE
13 REM
50 DIM QA(9,10),BB(9),JC(9),IR(9),JO(9),VY(9)
200 READ N:REM   NUMBER OF EQUATIONS
210 FOR I=1 TO N
220 FOR J=1 TO N+1
230 READ QA(I,J):A(I,J)=QA(I,J)
240 NEXT J:NEXT I
280 FL%=0:GOSUB 10000
290 PRINT"SOLUTIONS:"
300 FOR I=1 TO N:PRINT BB(I);:NEXT I
310 PRINT
```

```
320 PRINT"INVERTED MATRIX"
330 FOR I=1 TO N
340 FOR J=1 TO N:PRINT QA(I,J);:NEXT J
350 PRINT:NEXT I
360 PRINT"DETERMINANT=";DT
400 PRINT"UNIT MATRIX CHECK"
410 FOR I=1 TO N
420 FOR J=1 TO N
430 U=0
440 FOR K=1 TO N
450 U=U+A(I,K)*QA(K,J):NEXT K
460 PRINT U;
470 NEXT J
480 PRINT
490 NEXT I
700 DATA 3,0,-7,4,1,1,9,-6,1,-3,8,5,6
800 DATA 3,2,-7,4,9,1,9,-6,1,-3,8,5,6
900 DATA 3,-3,8,5,6,2,-7,4,9,1,9,-6,1
950 GET A$:IF A$="" THEN 950
990 GOTO 200
10000 REM SIMULTANEOUS LINEAR EQUATIOS:REF 2, PP287-291
10060 DT=1:MZ%=N:IF FL%>=0 THEN MZ%=N+1
10070 EP=1E-12
10080 FOR K=1 TO N
10090 PV=0
10100 FOR I=1 TO N
10110 FOR J=1 TO N
10120 IF K=1 THEN GOTO 10180
10130 FOR IS=1 TO K-1
10140 FOR JS=1 TO K-1
10150 IF I=IR(IS) THEN GOTO 10200
10160 IF J=JC(JS) THEN GOTO 10200
10170 NEXT JS:NEXT IS
10180 IF ABS(QA(I,J))<=ABS(PV) THEN GOTO10200
10190 PV=QA(I,J):IR(K)=I:JC(K)=J
10200 NEXT J:NEXT I
10210 IF ABS(PV)<EP THEN
      DT=0:PRINT"DETERMINANT ZERO":RETURN
10220 DT=DT*PV
10230 FOR J=1 TO MZ%:QA(IR(K),J)=QA(IR(K),J)/PV:NEXT J
10240 QA(IR(K),JC(K))=1/PV
10250 FOR I=1 TO N
10260 QA=QA(I,JC(K))
10270 IF I=IR(K) THEN GOTO 10320
10280 QA(I,JC(K))=-QA/PV
10290 FOR J=1 TO MZ%
10300 IF J<>JC(K) THEN QA(I,J)=QA(I,J)-QA*QA(IR(K),J)
10310 NEXT J
10320 NEXT I,NEXT K
```

```
10330 FOR I=1 TO N:JO(IR(I))=JC(I)
10340 IF FL%=0 THEN BB(JC(I))=QA(IR(I),MZ%)
10350 NEXT I
10360 IN=0
10370 FOR I=1 TO N-1
10380 FOR J=I+1 TO N
10390 IF JO(J))>=JO(I) THEN GOTO 10410
10400 JT=JO(J):JO(J)=JO(I):JO(I)=JT:IN=IN+1
10410 NEXT J:NEXT I
10420 IF 2*INT(IN/2)<>IN THEN DT=-DT
10430 IF FL%>0 THEN RETURN
10440 FOR J=1 TO N
10450 FOR I=1 TO N
10460 VY(JC(I))=QA(IR(I),J)
10470 NEXT I
10480 FOR I=1 TO N
10490 QA(I,J)=VY(I):NEXT I
10500 NEXT J
10510 FOR I=1 TO N
10520 FOR J=1 TO N
10530 VY(IR(J))=QA(I,JC(J)):NEXT J
10540 FOR J=1 TO N
10550 QA(I,J)=VY(J):NEXT J
10560 NEXT I
10570 RETURN
```

```
2 REM        ***********************
3 REM        *                     *
4 REM        *   PROGRAM MULTIREG   *
5 REM        *                     *
6 REM        *         FOR         *
7 REM        *                     *
8 REM        *     COMMODORE 64    *
9 REM        *                     *
10 REM       ***********************
12 REM
20 DIM QA(4,5),BB(4),JC(4),IR(4),JO(4),VY(4)
30 DIM SX(4),SY(4),VA(4),DX(30),DY(30)
50 N=2:REM   NUMBER OF TERMS TO USE IN FNF
100 PRINT"⊐":REM   COMMAND CENTER
105 IF M>0 THEN GOSUB 2900:PRINT
110 PRINT"COMMANDS:<R> FOR DATA INPUT AND REG"
120 PRINT TAB(9)"<I> TO INTERPOLATE"
130 PRINT TAB(9)"<Q> TO QUIT"
150 GET A$:IF A$="" THEN 150
```

```
155 IF A$="R" THEN GOTO 2000
160 IF A$="I" THEN GOTO 3000
165 IF A$="Q" THEN GOTO 900
190 GOTO 100
900 END
2000 PRINT "⊃":READ M:PRINT" X"," Y",M;"POINTS":PRINT
2010 FOR I=1 TO M:READ X,Y
2012 DX(I)=X:DY(I)=Y
2014 PRINT X,Y
2020 SY=SY+Y:SX=SX+X:YY=YY+Y*Y
2030 FOR K=1 TO N
2035 Y1=-(K=1)*X-(K=2)*X↑2-(K=3)*X↑3
2040 SX(K)=SX(K)+Y1
2050 SY(K)=SY(K)+Y*Y1
2060 FOR L=K TO N
2064 Y2=-(L=1)*X-(L=2)*X↑2-(K=3)*X↑3
2070 QA(K,L)=QA(K,L)+Y1*Y2
2080 NEXT L:NEXT K:NEXT I
2100 FOR K=1 TO N
2105 FOR L=K TO N
2110 QA(K,L)=QA(K,L)-SX(K)*SX(L)/M
2120 QA(L,K)=QA(K,L)
2130 NEXT L
2140 QA(K,N+1)=SY(K)-SY*SX(K)/M
2150 NEXT K
2160 FL%=0:GOSUB 10000:A=SY/M
2170 FOR I=1 TO N:A=A-BB(I)*SX(I)/M:NEXT I
2172 SS=0:PRINT"DEV OF POINTS",
2174 FOR I=1 TO M:X=DX(I):GOSUB 9500:D=DY(I)-Y
2176 PRINT D,:SS=SS+D*D:NEXT I
2178 SS=SS/(M-N-1):PRINT
2180 FOR I=1 TO N:VA(I)=QA(I,I)*SS
2200 FOR J=1 TO N SA=SA+SX(I)*SX(J)*QA(I,J)/M
2210 NEXT J:NEXT I
2218 SA=SA*SS/M
2230 GOSUB 2900
2300 PRINT"HIT ANY KEY TO RETURN"
2310 GET A$:IF A$="" THEN 2310
2320 GOTO 100
2500 DATA 6,1,6,2,11.01,3,17.99,4,27.01,5,37.99,6,51.01
2900 PRINT"INTERCEPT";A,"(STD DEV";SQR(SA);")"
2910 FOR I=1 TO N:
     PRINT"B(";I;")=";BB(I);" (";SQR(VA(I));")"
2920 NEXT I:PRINT"STD OF PTS=";SQR(SS):RETURN
3000 REM   INTERPOLATION
3010 INPUT"VALUE OF X";X:GOSUB 9500
3020 PRINT"Y(";X;")=";Y
3030 PRINT"<R> TO RETURN, ELSE TO CONTINUE"
3040 GET A$:IF A$="" THEN 3040
```

```
3050 IF A$="R" THEN GOTO 100
3060 IF A$<>"R" THEN GOTO 3010
3900 GOTO 100
9500 Y=A:REM  SUBROUTINE FOR CALCULATING Y=F(X)
9510 FOR K=1 TO N
9512 Y1=-(K=1)*X-(K=2)*X↑2-(K=3)*X↑3:Y=Y+Y1*BB(K)
9515 NEXT K
9520 RETURN




2 REM         ********************
3 REM         *                  *
4 REM         *  PROGRAM POLYREG  *
5 REM         *                  *
6 REM         *       FOR         *
7 REM         *                  *
8 REM         *   COMMODORE 64    *
9 REM         *                  *
10 REM        ********************
11 REM
12 REM
30 DIM DX(50),DY(50),BY(12),SX(12),SY(12)
40 DIM QA(6,7),BB(6),JC(6),IR(6),JO(6),VY(6)
100 PRINT"]":REM  COMMAND CENTER
102 PRINT"NUMBER OF DATA POINTS",M:PRINT"ORDER",N:
    IF N=0 THEN GOTO 110
104 PRINT"INTERCEPT",AA;"(";SA;")"
106 FOR J=1 TO N:
    PRINT"B(";J;")=";BB(J);"(";S*SQR(ABS(QA(J,J)));")":
    NEXT J
110 PRINT:PRINT"COMMANDS:":PRINT"  <D> DATA INPUT"
111 PRINT"  <R> REGRESSION":
    PRINT"  <E> EVALUATE POLYNOMIAL, INT., DERIV."
112 PRINT"  <Q> QUIT"
114 GET A$:IF A$="" THEN 114
116 IF A$="D" THEN GOTO 2000
117 IF A$="R" THEN GOTO 4000
118 IF A$="E" THEN GOTO 9000
119 IF A$="Q" THEN GOTO 900
120 GOTO 114
900 END
990 STOP:RESUME 100
2000 REM  DATA INPUT
2010 READ M
2020 FOR I=1 TO M
2030 READ X,Y
2040 DX(I)=X:DY(I)=Y:NEXT I
```

```
2050 GOTO 100
2100 DATA 6,1,6,2,11.01,3,17.99,4,27.01,5,37.99,6,51.01
4000 REM   POLYNOMIAL REGRESSION.
     M POINTS STORED IN DX(M), DY(M)
4005 REM   REQUIRES DIM STMT FOR DX, DY, BY, SY
4100 PRINT"⬚"
4160 KK=6:IF M<8 THEN KK=M-2
4170 PRINT".... ORDER OF POLYNOMIAL N<=";KK;:INPUT K
4180 IF K<=0 THEN GOTO 100
4182 IF K>0 THEN N=K
4200 DN=M-N-1:IF DN<=0 THEN PRINT"?????":GOTO 4170
4205 PRINT"ORDER N=";N,"POINTS M=";M
4206 PRINT"DF=";DN,"DET=";
4210 SY=0:YY=0
4220 FOR I=1 TO N
4230 SX(I)=0:SX(N+I)=0:SY(I)=0:NEXT I
4240 FOR I=1 TO M:X=DX(I):Y=DY(I):SY=SY+Y:YY=YY+Y*Y:DU=1
4250 FOR J=1 TO N:DU=DU*X:SX(J)=SX(J)+DU
4260 SY(J)=SY(J)+Y*DU:NEXT J
4270 FOR J=N+1 TO 2*N:DU=DU*X
4280 SX(J)=SX(J)+DU
4290 NEXT J:NEXT I
4300 REM   COMPUTE COEFFICIENTS
4310 QM=1/M:BY=YY-SY*SY*QM
4320 FOR I=1 TO N:BY(I)=SY(I)-SY*SX(I)*QM
4330 QA(I,N+1)=BY(I)
4340 FOR J=1 TO N
4350 QA(I,J)=SX(I+J)-SX(I)*SX(J)*QM
4360 NEXT J:NEXT I
4370 FL%=1:GOSUB 10000:REM   SLE
4380 PRINT DT:IF DT=0 THEN STOP:GOTO 100
4390 DU=SY:TE=BY:SA=1
4400 FOR I=1 TO N:QX=SX(I)*QM
4410 DU=DU-BB(I)*SX(I)
4420 TE=TE-BY(I)*BB(I)
4425 FOR J=1 TO N:SA=SA+SX(J)*QX*QA(I,J):NEXT J
4430 NEXT I
4440 AA=DU*QM
4450 IF TE>=0 THEN S=SQR(TE/DN)
4452 IF TE<0 THEN S=-SQR(-TE/DN)
4455 SA=S*SQR(QM*SA)
4460 PRINT"A=";AA:PRINT"B(I)=";:
     FOR I=1 TO N:PRINT BB(I);:NEXT I:PRINT
4470 PRINT"S=";S;:IF S<0 THEN PRINT"?"
4472 IF S>=0 THEN PRINT"/"
4474 PRINT"  <A>  AGAIN":PRINT"  <R>  RETURN":
     PRINT"  <S>  STAT"
4476 GET B$:IF B$="" THEN 4476
4480 IF B$="S" THEN GOSUB 4900:GOTO 4474
4482 IF B$="R" THEN GOTO 100
```

```
4484 IF B$="A" THEN GOTO 4170
4486 GOTO 4476
4900 S=0:PRINT"ACTUAL S=";
4910 FOR J=1 TO M:X=DX(J)
4920 GOSUB 9400:Y=Y-DY(J):S=S+Y*Y:NEXT J
4940 S=SQR(S/DN):PRINT S:IF N<>1 THEN GOTO 4980
4950 SY=SQR((YY-QM*SY*SY)/(M-1))
4960 SX=SQR((SX(2)-QM*SX(1)*SX(1))/(M-1))
4970 R=SX*BB(1)/SY:PRINT" ","R=";R
4980 PRINT"STND DEVIATIONS :";:IF N<>1 THEN PRINT
4994 SA=S*SQR(QM*SA):PRINT"(A)";SA:PRINT"(B)";
4996 FOR I=1 TO N:PRINT S*SQR(QA(I,I));:NEXT I
4999 PRINT:RETURN
9000 PRINT"⬛":REM  POLYNOMIAL EVALUATION,
     DIFFERENTIATION, AND INTEGRATION
9010 PRINT:PRINT"COMMANDS:":PRINT" <R> RETURN":
     PRINT" <F> FUNCTION"
9012 PRINT" <D> DERIVATIVE":PRINT" <I> INTEGRAL":PRINT
9020 GET A$:IF A$="" THEN 9020
9022 IF A$="F" THEN GOTO 9100
9024 IF A$="D" THEN GOTO 9200
9026 IF A$="I" THEN GOTO 9300
9028 IF A$="R" THEN GOTO 100
9030 GOTO 9020
9100 INPUT"AT X=";X:PRINT CHR$(145);TAB(20);
9110 GOSUB 9400
9150 PRINT"F(";X;")=";Y
9160 GOTO 9030
9200 INPUT"AT X=";Z:PRINT CHR$(145);TAB(20);:F=0
9210 FOR I=1 TO N
9220 F=F+I*BB(I)*Z↑(I-1)
9230 NEXT I
9240 PRINT"DF(";Z;")=";F;
9250 GOTO 9030
9300 PRINT"INT FROM";:INPUT Z1:
     PRINT CHR$(145);TAB(20);"TO";:INPUT Z2
9310 PRINT"INT=";:F=AA*(Z2-Z1):FORI=1 TO N
9340 F=F+(BB(I)/(I+1))*(Z2↑(I+1)-Z1↑(I+1)):NEXT I:
     PRINT F;
9380 GOTO 9030
9400 Y=0:REM  SUNROUTINE TO EVALUATE POLYNOMIAL
9410 FOR K=N TO 1 STEP-1
9420 Y=Y*X+BB(K):NEXT K
9440 Y=Y*X+AA
9450 RETURN
10000 REM SIMULTANEOUS LINEAR EQUATIOS:REF 2, PP287-291
```

```
100 REM       ********************
101 REM       *                  *
102 REM       *   PROGRAM TRAP    *
103 REM       *                  *
104 REM       *        FOR        *
105 REM       *                  *
106 REM       *   COMMODORE 64    *
107 REM       *                  *
108 REM       ********************
300 PRINT"⊐"
400 A=0
410 READ X,Y
420 X1=X:Y1=Y
430 READ X,Y
440 A=A+(Y+Y1)*(X-X1)/2
450 PRINT X,Y,"AREA=";A
460 GOTO 420
490 DATA 0,4,1,6,2,8,5,14
```

```
2 REM        ********************
3 REM        *                  *
4 REM        *  PROGRAM ROMBERG  *
5 REM        *                  *
6 REM        *        FOR        *
7 REM        *                  *
8 REM        *   COMMODORE 64    *
9 REM        *                  *
10 REM       ********************
15 REM
20 DIM A(20,20)
30 DEF FNF(X)=X*EXP(-X*X)
80 T=1E-6:REM  TOLERANCE FOR ACCURACY OF INTERGRAL
1010 NC=6:N1=4:REM  NC IS # CYCLES,
                    N1 SET INITIAL INTERVAL
1020 PRINT"⊐":INPUT"X1,X2 ";X1,X2
1030 H=(X2-X1)/N1
1040 GOSUB 1190:A(0,0)=A:PRINT A
1050 FOR K=1 TO NC
1060 N1=N1*2:H=H/2
1070 GOSUB 1190:A(0,K)=A:PRINT A,
1080 FOR L=1 TO K
1090 A(L,K)=(4↑L*A(L-1,K)-A(L-1,K-1))/(4↑L-1)
1100 PRINT A(L,K),
1110 IF ABS((A(L,K)-A(L-1,K))/A)<T THEN 1160
1120 NEXT L
1130 PRINT
```

```
1140 NEXT K
1150 K=K-1:L=L-1
1160 PRINT
1165 PRINT"...FINI...AFTER ";N1;"INTERVALS:AREA=";A(L,K)
1170 END
1190 SU=(FNF(X2)+FNF(X1))/2
1200 FOR I=1 TO N1-1
1210 X=X2-I*H
1220 SU=SU+FNF(X)
1230 NEXT I
1240 A=SU*H:RETURN




2 REM       **********************
3 REM       *                    *
4 REM       *   PROGRAM LAGRANGE  *
5 REM       *                    *
6 REM       *        FOR         *
7 REM       *                    *
8 REM       *    COMMODORE 64     *
9 REM       *                    *
10 REM      **********************
12 REM
15 PRINT"J"
20 DIM DX(10),DY(10),P(10),Q(10)
200 READ L$,N:REM  LABEL AND NUMBER OF POINTS
210 FOR I=1 TO N
220 READ X,Y
230 DX(I)=X:DY(I)=Y:NEXT
300 REM   CALCULATE P FACTORS
310 FOR I=1 TO N
320 P(I)=1
330 FOR J=1 TO N
340 IF I=J THEN 360
350 P(I)=P(I)*(DX(I)-DX(J))
360 NEXT J
370 NEXT I
380 DATA HEAT CAPACITY OF BENZENE,4,200,83.7,240,104.1
390 DATA 260,116.1,278.69,128.7
400 PRINT"INTERPOLATION FOR ":PRINT L$
410 INPUT"VALUE OF X";X
420 FOR I=1 TO N:Q(I)=1
430 FOR J=1 TO N
440 IF I=J THEN 460
450 Q(I)=Q(I)*(X-DX(J))
460 NEXT J
```

```
470 NEXT I
480 Y=0:REM   SUMMATION TO GET Y
490 FOR I=1 TO N
500 Y=Y+DY(I)*Q(I)/P(I)
510 NEXT I
520 PRINT"Y(";X;")=";Y
530 GOTO 410




2 REM       ********************
3 REM       *                  *
4 REM       *   PROGRAM DIVDIF  *
5 REM       *                  *
6 REM       *        FOR        *
7 REM       *                  *
8 REM       *    COMMODORE 64   *
9 REM       *                  *
10 REM      ********************
11 REM
12 REM   NEWTON DIVIDED DIFFERENCE INTERP W/SIMP RULE
13 REM       INTEGRATION AND 4TH-ORDER DIFF
14 REM
20 DIM DX(50),DY(50),T(50,8)
99 GOTO 200
100 PRINT"□":PRINT W$,"PTS=";M:PRINT"DEGREE";ID;"/";ND
120 PRINT"<&>DATA INPUT <T>TABLE <Q>QUIT"
122 PRINT"<F>FUNCTION <D>DIFF <I>INTEGRATE"
130 GET A$:IF A$="" THEN 130
132 IF A$="&" THEN GOTO 200
133 IF A$="T" THEN GOTO 300
134 IF A$="Q" THEN GOTO 900
135 IF A$="F" THEN GOTO 400
136 IF A$="D" THEN GOTO 500
137 IF A$="I" THEN GOTO 1000
199 GOTO 100
200 ND=0:REM   DATA INPUT
210 READ W$,M
220 FOR I=1 TO M
230 READ X:Y=COS(X)
240 DX(I)=X:DY(I)=Y:NEXT I
260 GOTO 100
290 DATA COSINE TEST,15,-3.5,-3,-2.5,-2,-1.5,-1,-.5,0,
    .5,1,1.5,2,2.5,3,3.5
300 INPUT"DEGREE";ID: IF ID<=ND THEN GOTO 100
305 IF ID>ND THEN GOSUB 9000
310 PRINT"□":PRINT"DIFFERENCE TABLE":PRINT
```

```
320 FOR I=1 TO M-1
330 FOR J=1 TO I
340 IF J<=ND THEN PRINT T(I,J);
345 IF INT(J/3)*3=J THEN PRINT
350 NEXT J
360 PRINT:PRINT
365 IF INT(I/5)*5<>I THEN GOTO 370
366 PRINT"    STRIKE ANY KEY TO CONTINUE"
367 GET B$:IF B$="" THEN 367
370 NEXT I
380 GOTO 130
400 INPUT"VALUE OF X";X
410 GOSUB 9400
420 PRINT"EST Y=";Y,"EST ERROR";ABS(ER)
430 PRINT"ACTUAL ";COS(X),"ACT ERROR";ABS(Y-COS(X))
480 GOTO 130
500 INPUT"VALUE OF X";X1:REM DIFFERENTIAL EVALUATION
510 S=.01:REM  INCREMENT FOR DERIVATIVE
520 H=S:IF ABS(X1)>S THEN H=X1*S
530 X=X1-2*H:GOSUB 9400:DX=Y
540 X=X1-H:GOSUB 9400:DX=DX-8*Y
550 X=X1+H:GOSUB 9400:DX=DX+8*Y
560 X=X1+2*H:GOSUB 9400:DX=DX-Y
570 DX=DX/(12*H)
580 PRINT"DERIVATIVE",DX
590 PRINT"ACTUAL";-SIN(X1),"DIFF";ABS(DX+SIN(X1))
599 GOTO 130
900 END:GOTO 100
1000 INPUT"LOWER AND UPPER LIMITS";X1,X2
1005 IF X1>X2 THEN GOTO 1000
1010 INPUT"NUMBER OF INTERVALS";N
1020 IF N/2<>INT(N/2) THEN
     PRINT"NUMBER OF INTERVALS MUST BE ODD":GOTO 1010
1030 H=(X2-X1)/N:X=X1:GOSUB 9400
1032 A=Y:X=X2:GOSUB 9400:A=A+Y
1040 FOR K=1 TO N-1:X=X1+K*H:GOSUB 9400
1050 A=A+2*Y*(1-(K/2<>INT(K/2)))
1060 NEXT K
1070 A=A*H/3:PRINT
1080 PRINT"THE INTEGRAL IS";A;"(";N;" INTERVALS)"
1082 PRINT"ACTUAL INTEGRALS";SIN(X2)-SIN(X1)
1090 PRINT"ENTER <H> TO CHANGE INTERVAL"
1091 PRINT"       <L> TO CHANGE LIMITS"
1092 PRINT"       <R> TO RETURN"
1100 GET A$:IF A$="" THEN 1100
1110 IF A$="H" THEN GOTO 1010
1112 IF A$="L" THEN GOTO 1000
1114 IF A$="R" THEN GOTO 100
1120 GOTO 1100
```

```
9000 REM CALC OF TABLE FOR NEWTON DIVIDED DIFF
9010 IF ID>M OR ID>8 THEN W$="DEGREE TOO BIG !":GOTO 100
9020 ND=ID:REM INTERPOLATION ORDER,ID,MAX ND
9030 IF ND<1 THEN PRINT"ND=";ND:STOP:GOTO 100
9040 FOR I=1 TO M-1
9050 T(I,1)=(DY(I+1)-DY(I))/(DX(I+1)-DX(I)):NEXT I
9060 FOR J=2 TO ND
9070 FOR I=J TO M-1
9080 T(I,J)=(T(I,J-1)-T(I-1,J-1))/(DX(I+1)-DX(I+1-J))
9090 NEXT I:NEXT J
9100 W$="TABLE READY":RETURN
9400 REM INTERPOLATION BY NEWTONS DIVIDED DIFF
9410 IF W$<>"TABLE READY" THEN
     W$="TABLE NOT READY":GOTO 100
9420 IF ID>ND THEN PRINT"MAX DEGREE=";ND:GOTO 9410
9430 FOR I=1 TO M
9440 IF I=M OR X<=DX(I) THEN GOTO 9460
9450 NEXT I
9460 MX=I+ID/2
9470 IF MX<=ID THEN MX=ID+1
9480 IF MX>=M THEN MX=M
9490 Y=T(MX-1,ID):ER=T(MX,ID)-T(MX-1,ID)
9500 IF ID<=1 THEN GOTO 9540
9510 FOR I=1 TO ID-1:D=X-DX(MX-I)
9520 Y=Y*D+T(MX-I-1,ID-I):ER=ER*D
9530 NEXT I
9540 Y=Y*(X-DX(MX-ID))+DY(MX-ID)
9550 ER=ER*(X-DX(MX-ID))
9560 PRINT"/";:RETURN




2 REM       ********************
3 REM       *                  *
4 REM       *   PROGRAM SIMPLEX *
5 REM       *                  *
6 REM       *        FOR        *
7 REM       *                  *
8 REM       *    COMMODORE 64   *
9 REM       *                  *
10 REM      ********************
11 REM
20 DIM S(6,7),T(6),TT(6),C(6),X(30),Y(30)
30 NP=3:NV=NP+1:REM  SET NUMBER OF PARAMETERS=NP
40 DEF FNY(X)=T(1)+T(2)*EXP(T(3)*X)
50 DATA COOPER,8,1,2.8,2,3.74,3,5.01,4,6.74,5,9.06,6,
   12.2
```

```
51 DATA 7,16.43,8,22.14,END,0
100 PRINT"⬛":REM  * COMMAND CENTER *
110 PRINT"ITER=";KI;"/";KX:PRINT"R=";BR;"/";EP:
    PRINT"PTS";M,T$
120 PRINT"PARAMETERS:";:FOR I=1 TO NP:PRINT S(I,JB),
    NEXT
130 PRINT"  <I> DATA INPUT":PRINT"  <G> INPUT GUESS"
132 PRINT"  <P> PRINT RESULTS":PRINT"  <C> CALCULATE"
134 PRINT"  < > ...":PRINT"  <Q>QUIT"
140 PRINT"?";:GOSUB 190
150 IF A$="I" THEN GOTO 200
152 IF A$="G" THEN GOTO 300
153 IF A$="C" THEN GOTO 400
154 IF A$="P" THEN GOTO 1000
155 IF A$="Q" THEN GOTO 900
160 GOTO 100
190 GET A$:IF A$="" THEN GOTO 190
195 PRINT A$;":";:RETURN
200 READ TI$,M:IF TI$="END" THEN GOTO 100
210 FOR I=1 TO M:READ X,Y
220 X(I)=X:Y(I)=Y
230 NEXT I
240 GOTO 100
300 FOR I=1 TO NP:PRINT I;":";:INPUT"VALUE,INC";Z,D
310 FOR J=1 TO NV
320 S(I,J)=Z-D*(I=J)-D/2
330 NEXT J:NEXT I
340 GOSUB 350:GOTO 400
350 FOR I3=1 TO NV
360 FOR J3=1 TO NP:T(J3)=S(J3,I3):NEXT J3
370 GOSUB 500:R(I3)=R
380 NEXT I3:RETURN
400 PRINT"RESPPONSE/PARAMETERS"
405 FOR I=1 TO NV:PRINT R(I);"/";
410 FOR J=1 TO NP
420 PRINT S(J,I);",";:NEXT J
430 PRINT:NEXT I
480 PRINT"?":GOSUB 190
490 GOTO 100
500 R=0:REM  CALULATE RESPONSE
510 FOR I5=1 TO M
520 R=R+(Y(I5)-FNY(X(I5)))↑2
530 NEXT I5
540 R=SQR(R/(M-1)):RETURN
600 REM  FIND NEW VERTEX(T)
610 FOR J6=1 TO NP:SU=0
615 IF F<>1 THEN GOTO 660
620 FOR K6=1 TO NV:REM  CALC CENTROID
630 IF K6<>JW THEN SU=SU+S(J6,K6)
633 NEXT K6
```

```
640 C(J6)=SU/NP
660 T(J6)=C(J6)*(1+F)-F*S(J6,JW)
670 NEXT J6
680 GOSUB 500:PRINT"/F=";F;"R=";R;
690 RETURN
700 REM  EXCHANGE T FOR WORST
710 FOR I7=1 TO NP
720 S(I7,JW)=T(I7)
730 NEXT I7
740 R(JW)=R
750 GOTO 1050
900 END:GOTO 100
1000 KI=0:REM  ITEREATION
1010 IF M=0 OR R(1)=0 THEN GOTO 100
1020 INPUT"MAX # ITER";KX
1030 EP=1E-6
1040 IF BR<>0 AND BR<EP THEN EP=EP/10:GOTO 1040
1050 WR=R(1):BR=WR:JW=1:JB=1
1060 FOR I=2 TO NV
1070 IF R(I)>=WR THEN WR=R(I):JW=I
1080 IFR(I)<BR THEN BR=R(I):JB=I
1090 NEXT I
1150 IF KI>=KX OR BR<EP THEN
     PRINT"END":GOSUB 190:GOTO 100
1160 IF (WR-BR)/BR<EP THEN PRINT:GOTO 400
1170 GET A$:IF A$="Q" THEN GOTO 100
1200 PRINT:KI=KI+1:PRINT"#";KI;
1210 IF BR<>PR THEN PR=BR:PRINT"NEW BEST";BR;"WORST";WR
1220 F=1:GOSUB 600:REM  NEW VERTEX
1230 IF R<=BR THEN GOTO 1400:REM  EXPAND VERTEX
1240 IF R<=WR THEN GOTO 700: REM  EXCHANGE FOR WORST
1250 F=-.5:GOSUB 600:REM CONTRACT
1260 IF R<=WR THEN GOTO 700:REM  EXCHANGE FOR WORST
1270 PRINT"CONTRACT";:REM CONTRACT ALL VERTICES
1280 FOR I=1 TO NP
1290 FOR J=1 TO NV
1300 IF J<>JB THEN S(I,J)=(S(I,JB)+S(I,J))/2
1310 NEXT J:NEXT I
1380 GOTO 1050
1400 RT=R:FOR I=1 TO NP:TT(I)=T(I):NEXT I:
     REM  SAVE VERTEX
1410 F=2:GOSUB 600:REM  EXPAND VERTEX
1420 IF R<=RT THEN GOTO 700:REM ACCEPT EXPANDED VERTEX
1430 R=RT:FOR I=1 TO NP:T(I)=TT(I):NEXT I:REM  RESTORE
1440 GOTO 700:REM  EXCHANGE W/WORST
```

```
2 REM          ************************
3 REM          *                      *
4 REM          *    PROGRAM RUNGE     *
5 REM          *                      *
6 REM          *          FOR         *
7 REM          *                      *
8 REM          *     COMMODORE 64     *
9 REM          *                      *
10 REM         ************************
11 REM
12 REM     TEST FOR CONSECUTIVE FIRST-ORDER REACTIONS
40 FOR I=1 TO 6:W(I)=1:NEXT I
100 PRINT"[]":PRINT"T=";T,"H=";H:GOSUB 9400
110 C1=C0*EXP(-K*T)
115 C2=K1*C0*T*EXP(-K1*T)
120 IF K1<>K2 OR T<>0 THEN
    C2=K1*C0*(EXP(-K1*T)-EXP(-K2*T))/(K2-K1)
122 C3=C0-C1-C2
125 PRINT"THEORETICAL ";C1;C2;C3:PRINT
130 PRINT"<1> NEW CALCULATION"
140 PRINT"<2> CONTINUE CALCULATION"
150 PRINT"<3> QUIT"
155 PRINT"<4> SET WEIGHTS":PRINT
160 GOSUB 770:K=VAL(A$):IF K=0 THEN 160
170 ON K GOSUB 1000,1100,900,200
180 GOTO 100
200 PRINT"INPUT WEIGHTS"
210 FOR I=1 TO 6
220 INPUT"W=";W(I)
230 NEXT I
240 RETURN
600 X=INT((T-T1)*39/(T2-T1))
610 Y=24-INT(22*C(1)*W(1)):POKE1024+X+Y*40,81
620 Y=24-INT(22*C(2)*W(2)):POKE1024+X+Y*40,87
630 Y=24-INT(22*C(3)*W(3)):POKE1024+X+Y*40,86
650 RETURN
670 PRINT"T=";T:FOR I=1 TO NQ
680 PRINT C(I);:NEXT I:PRINT:RETURN
770 GET A$:IF A$="" THEN 770
775 RETURN
990 STOP:GOTO 100
1000 PRINT"[]":T=0:T1=0
1010 GOSUB 9000
1030 GOSUB 9500
1040 FOR I=1 TO NQ:CT(I)=C(I):NEXT I
1100 INPUT"CALCULATE TO T=";T2
1110 INPUT"TIME INTERVAL=";TS
1120 INPUT"NUMBER OF STEPS PER INTERVAL=";NR
1130 NS=INT((T2-T1)/TS+.499):PRINT"[]"
```

```
1131 PRINT"<1> PLOT RESULTS":PRINT"<2> LIST RESULTS":
     PRINT
1132 GET Z$:IF Z$="" THEN 1132
1133 IF Z$<>"1" AND Z$<>"2" THEN GOTO 1132
1134 PRINT"◘"
1140 H=TS/NR:PRINT"H=";H:IF Z$="1" THEN
     PRINT"T=";T1;TAB(19);" I";
1200 FOR J=1 TO NS
1230 FOR L=1 TO NR
1240 A=.5:B=1:GOSUB 9100
1250 B=2:GOSUB 9100
1260 A=1:GOSUB 9100
1270 A=0:B=1:GOSUB 9100
1280 FOR I=1 TO NQ-1
1290 C(I)=C(I)+H*DS(I)/6
1300 CT(I)=C(I):DS(I)=0
1310 NEXT I:NEXT L
1330 T=T1+J*TS:C(NQ)=C0
1332 IF J=NS AND Z$="1" THEN PRINT TAB(36);T
1335 FOR I=1 TO NQ-1:C(NQ)=C(NQ)-C(I):NEXT I
1340 IF Z$="1"THEN GOSUB 600
1342 IF Z$="2"THEN GOSUB 670
1345 GET A$:IF A$="Q" THEN T1=1:RETURN
1350 NEXT J
1360 T1=T
1370 GOSUB 770:RETURN
8000 FOR IS=1 TO NQ-1
8010 CT(IS)=C(IS)+H*DK(IS)*A
8020 DS(IS)=DS(IS)+DK(IS)*B
8030 NEXT IS
8040 RETURN
9000 REM  CHANGE THIS PART TO CHANGE
           THE PROBLEM BEING SOLVED
9010 NQ=3:C0=1
9020 C(1)=1:C(2)=0:C(3)=0
9090 RETURN
9100 DK(1)=-K1*CT(1)
9110 DK(2)=K1*CT(1)-K2*CT(2)
9190 GOTO 8000
9400 PRINT"K1=";K1,"K2=";K2
9410 PRINT"CONCENTRATION ";C(1);C(2);C(3)
9420 RETURN
9500 INPUT"K1=";K1
9510 INPUT"K2=";K2
9520 RETURN
```

INDEX

acetic acid, dissociation of,88
ADC,128
APPLEDOS, 6
arrays,26
    finding largest and smallest element of,36
Arrhenius equation,64
ASC functin,38
ASCII, 7
assembly language, 2
BASIC, 3
Beattie-Bridgeman equation,43
    work calculated using,107
benzene
    entropy and enthalpy of,124
    heat capacity of,97
Berthelot
    equation,164
    second virial coefficient,17
binary code, 2
binomial coefficient,24
Boyle temperature,44
byte, 7
cadmium, vapor pressure of,79
carbon dioxide
    heat capacity,88
    work of expansion,108
carbon monoxide, PVT properties,18
carbon tetrafluoride, second virial coefficient,159
carbonyl sulfide (OCS), vapor pressure ,50
CHR$ function,54
complex roots of equations,58
compressibility factor of methane,91,92,98
conductance, equivalent,87
confidence interval,66
CONT statement,42
convolution
    functions,131
    integral,129
    Savitzky-Golay filters,133
correlation factor (linear regression),65

180   5658 7

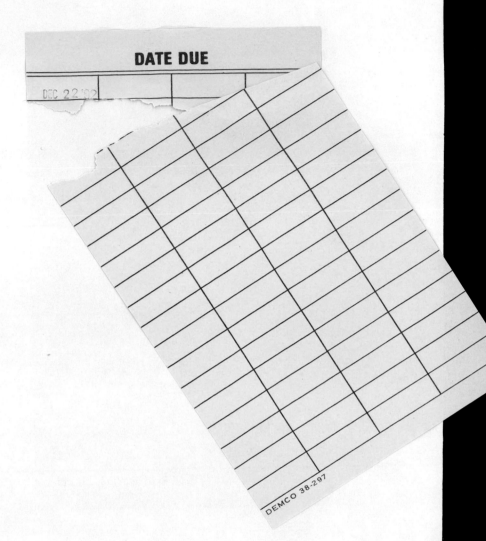

DATE DUE

DEC 22 '92			

DEMCO 38-297